Studies in the Comic Spirit in Modern Japanese Fiction

Harvard-Yenching Institute Monograph Series 41

Studies in the Comic Spirit in Modern Japanese Fiction

Joel R. Cohn

Published by the Harvard University Asia Center
and distributed by Harvard University Press
Cambridge (Massachusetts) and London
1998

Printed in the United States of America

The Harvard-Yenching Institute, founded in 1928 and headquartered at Harvard University, is a foundation dedicated to the advancement of higher education in the humanities and social sciences in East and Southeast Asia. The Institute supports advanced research at Harvard by faculty members of certain Asian universities and doctoral studies at Harvard and other universities by junior faculty at the same universities. It also supports East Asian studies at Harvard through contributions to the Harvard-Yenching Library and publication of the *Harvard Journal of Asiatic Studies* and books on premodern East Asian history and literature.

Cohn, Joel R. (Joel Ralph), 1949–
Studies in the comic spirit in modern Japanese fiction / Joel R. Cohn.
p. cm. -- (Harvard-Yenching Institute monograph series ; 41)
Includes bibliographical references and index.
ISBN 0-674-84711-3 (alk. paper)
1. Japanese fiction--Shōwa period, 1926–1989--History and criticism. 2. Comic, The, in literature. 3. Ibuse, Masuji,--1898– --Criticism and interpretation. 4. Dazai, Osamu,--1909–1948--Criticism and interpretation. 5. Inoue, Hisashi--Criticism and interpretation. I. Title. II. Series.
PL747.67.C64C65 1998
895.6'3440917--dc21 97-30523
CIP

♾ Printed on acid-free paper

07 06 05 04 03 02 01 00 99 98

Index by Mary Mortensen

TO THE TREES

Acknowledgments

This undertaking would not have been possible without the assistance and inspiration of numerous mentors, relatives, and friends. They know well who they are, and I am sure that they will understand if I omit what would be a very lengthy list of names. I would, however, like to express my particular gratitude to Professors Howard Hibbett, Itasaka Gen, Edwin Cranston, Asai Kiyoshi, and Kunimatsu Akira for their patient guidance over the years. Helpful comments were provided by Professors Haruko Iwasaki, Sumie Jones, Edward Fowler, John Stephan, and Dr. Etsuko Terasaki. My editors, Katherine Keenum and John Ziemer, labored valiantly to protect me, and my readers, from my worst impulses. The Edwin O. Reischauer Institute of Japanese Studies at Harvard University and the Japan Studies Endowment of the Center for Japanese Studies at the University of Hawai'i at Mānoa have very generously provided financial support for this research.

Contents

Preface

Like anyone who ends up spending far more time than he expected to on a project of this sort, I soon grew accustomed to having well-wishers, the idly curious, and those desperate for a topic for small talk ask me about my subject of study. Upon being told that it was "the comic spirit in modern Japanese fiction," almost all of my interrogators responded with one of two reactions. Those who instinctively associated the term "comic" with its best-known Japanese embodiment would exclaim: "Oh, *manga* (Japanese comic strips and cartoons)! Great!!" At this point it was my doleful obligation to inform them that, much as I enjoyed *manga* myself, and fascinated as I was with the Japanese public's apparently insatiable appetite for printed cartoons of all sorts, this was not what I was up to, although I do hope that some intrepid soul (or souls) will devote to this phenomenon the attention it clearly deserves. Those who grasped the implications of "modern Japanese fiction" almost invariably opted for the second response, which was generally some variation on the theme of "Is there really such a thing as comedy in Japanese literature? I've never seen any!" Here it was my far more congenial task to inform them that it does indeed exist, and I very much hoped to demonstrate this in no uncertain terms.

Suspicions about the non-existence, or at least invisibility, of a comic strain in modern Japanese fiction are not limited to readers with only a passing familiarity with the subject. A reviewer of an English translation of Maruya Saiichi's novel *Tatta hitori no hanran* (Singular Rebellion, 1972), who has himself lived in Japan and published a novel set there, finds himself making a startling discovery:

> Common sense suggests that the comedy of manners ought to flourish in Japan. What more fertile ground could there be for that gentle, slightly quaint literary genre than a country whose etiquette is ancient, embracing, lovely, and, at times, quite paralyzing? But, reasonable though such expectations may be, few novels that fulfill them have surfaced in the West. The modern Japanese novelists who have some following in our country—principally Yukio Mishima, Yasunari Kawabata, Tanizaki Junichiro, Kobo Abe, and Shusaku Endo—are capable of amusing us in diverse ways, but none could be thought of (even after allowing for the perishability of humor in translation) as a comic novelist.
>
> The arrival of Saiichi Maruya's "Singular Rebellion" . . . therefore comes as something of a surprise, and it urges us to ponder the degree to which an unwitting connivance of social and commercial forces may skew our vision at the outset by determining which works are translated. Could it be that the novel of delicacy, taciturnity, elusiveness, and languishing melancholy—traits we have come to think of as characteristically Japanese—is less characteristic than we thought?[1]

The reviewer's apparent equation of comedy with humor, faintly patronizing attitude toward comedy of manners (and, for that matter, toward Japanese manners), mysterious omission of Ōe Kenzaburō from his roster of novelists, and keen enthusiasm for an engaging yet somewhat contrived novel all raise questions of their own; but his speculations on the connection between "social and commercial forces" and the low profile of Japanese comic fiction are perceptive.[2]

Another reason advanced for the invisibility of Japanese comedy in the West is that its effects are simply not transferable across cultural boundaries: Umberto Eco hypothesizes that while the tragic impulse is universal, the comic "seems bound to its time, society, cultural anthropology. We understand the drama of the protagonist of *Rashomon*, but we don't understand when and why the Japanese laugh."[3] Assertions of this sort can easily turn into self-fulfilling prophecies. The "time, society, and cultural anthropology" of Aristophanes's Greece or Cervantes's Spain are, after all, hardly less remote than the high-tech, secular, and capitalist culture of urbanized contemporary Japan, yet many of us flatter ourselves that we have a reasonably clear notion of what made those long-departed Greeks and Spaniards laugh. Perhaps the barrier arises at least partly from a lack of will on the part of the observer to make the effort to understand why others laugh, or to see whether they laugh at all. Lee Siegel, in considering possible reasons for the equally striking obscurity, or at least disregard, of the rich comic tradition in India, conjectures that "perhaps this is because India, the land as well as its cultural heritage, is most often approached and perceived with solemnity, awe, and reverence—if not with disgust or fear—and such attitudes naturally preclude an interest in mirth and wit, in laughter and zaniness."[4] It should come as little surprise if Japan, in its various guises as the land of stoic samurai values, Zen, ethereal beauty, and single-minded drives for commercial and technological success, is perceived as equally inappropriate territory for comedy.

The purported invisibility of comedy in modern Japanese literature, for whatever reasons, is not simply a matter of a reductive Orientalist gaze: Japanese observers have also lamented that the comic component is missing, or at least "lost," in modern Japanese literature, and advanced any number of persuasive explanations for it.[5] Yet others see it clearly enough; as early as 1950, Isogai Hideo had announced that the comic spirit had "established" itself in modern Japanese fiction despite various social, historical, and cultural constraints and offered an incisive account of its development.[6] A number of Westerners, some of them not even specialists in such matters, have also found the comic spirit quite visible in Asia, at least in some of its classic literature. Frequently what they find is something that differs in some essential way from something in the West: James Feibleman sees the "calm amusement and resignation" that has "traditionally characterized the Chinese attitude toward existence" lying at "one end of the comic scale," with the precarious dramas of life and death that constitute the volatile "revolutionary comedy of Westerners" at the other.[7] Susanne Langer, in her illuminating discussion of "the comic rhythm," points to the prevalence in traditional Asian drama of "divine comedies" featuring a hero who struggles against natural or social obstacles "which his strength, wisdom, virtue, or other assets let him overcome." In fact, according to Langer, the comic rhythm constitutes "the basic feeling of dramatic art" in the "great cultures of Asia" (which she apparently takes to be India and China), unlike the West where "tragedy usurps its highest honors."[8]

The counterpoising of "comedy" and "tragedy" raises another issue that is crucial to this inquiry: how much validity is there to the application to Japanese literature of Western terms denoting concepts that have little or no indigenous meaning, or of which the Japanese themselves were unaware until fairly recently? According to at least one veteran American scholar of Japanese literature, the answer is, apparently, not much: the Japanese "could not cope with the dichotomy of comedy and tragedy; such considerations had no meaning in their lives."[9] What is meant here by an inability to "cope" is not clear, but even if the tragic-comic dichotomy had no meaning in their lives, various forms of something that we can fairly identify as "comedy" were very much present in many of those lives, as I hope to show in Chapter One. Moreover, the main point of this project is not so much to consider what these texts have meant to the Japanese as it is to consider how they relate to a pattern that exists, at least hypothetically, whether it has been recognized in Japan or not.

In a more general sense, though, when relying on a term like "comedy," with all its accretions of cultural and critical baggage going back to Aristotle and beyond, in the discussion of a body of Japanese texts, it is indeed necessary to be wary of the temptation to take elements of the Western tradition as normative simply because they are familiar[10] and to bear in mind the importance of, in the words of Masao Miyoshi, "interpreting Japanese institutions in their own terms rather than placing them in Western categories."[11] Most of the terms relating to the theory and practice of comedy used in this study are not Japan's own, and we do need to be judicious in applying them in ways that are not procrustean, irrelevant, or misleading; we should not set up false expectations. Nevertheless, if we were to conclude that it is impossible or pointless to use such terms despite our best efforts to apply them with due sensitivity to what they can and cannot do, where should we draw the line? How, and why, should we write about Japanese literature in English, or in any other language other than Japanese? The question is particularly pointed in the case of the phenomena under consideration here, for the terms most commonly employed in Japan to identify comic texts (notably *warai*, *kokkei*, and the imported *yūmoa*) are often overly simplistic, broad, or vague, perhaps even so misleading as to be counterproductive. Almost invariably they refer to a text's humorous quality, and nothing more.[12] They could be, and are, applied just as easily to a one-line joke as to a comic novel. So, at times, are "comic" and "comedy," but these terms, the latter in particular, also have a more or less firmly established literary sense: they can be, and long have been, used to refer to various characteristics above and beyond humor that distinguish certain types of drama and fictional narrative from others as well as from jokes and "funny stories."

The pitfalls risked by users and abusers of the notoriously slippery terminology of comedy do not arise only when it is transported across linguistic or cultural boundaries. Even within familiar native confines, its appearance can engender, or simply signify, confusion.[13] In any language, writing about comedy is a troublesome endeavor. Like time, music, and love, comedy is more readily and gratifyingly experienced than defined or analyzed. This has not stopped many intrepid and even sagacious intellects from training their powers upon it over the years, for to reject it outright as a subject of inquiry would be to deny the power of the human mind as well as the validity of inquiry itself. By taking the comic spirit in various works of modern Japanese fiction as the object of this inquiry, I have no interest in proposing that those modern Japanese texts I consider comic constitute a self-contained order reposing in splendid isolation behind walls of genre, language, culture, or "national character." "Japanese literature" is, like all literature, something more than exclusively Japanese, and we can certainly detect affinities in Japanese comic texts with patterns that appear in countless works from many other societies and ages—even if they differ from some of what Japanese writers and readers have generally associated with *kokkei* and other such terms. But at the same time we cannot ignore the fact that Japanese literature is the product of a particular set of historical, social, and cultural experiences, nor that it is written in a language which no other nation's writers employ. By focusing on the thematic, structural, and stylistic elements in the works of three writers, this study will attempt to see how modern comic Japanese fiction fits in the broader categories of comedy in general and modern Japanese fiction overall.

In the West, the comic mode has traditionally been more closely associated with drama than with fiction. Comic drama is conspicuous by its absence in the following pages, although the same is hardly the case on the stages of Japan, where playwrights such as Iizawa Tadasu, Inoue Hisashi, and Noda Hideki have contributed to the development and flourishing of a vibrant comic spirit. Extending the scope of this volume to include drama might have achieved greater completeness, but only at the cost of coherence. While there is some overlap of critical issues in comic drama and fiction, the physical components of drama offer comic resources (sight gags, physical grotesquerie, well-timed double takes, subtly ironic vocal inflections, the long and venerable tradition of rude noises) that fiction cannot emulate. Fiction, to succeed as comedy, must exploit some of its own distinctive resources: introspection, manipulation of narrative voice, the capacity to present scenes impossible to re-create on a stage. It is the mobilization of these resources for comic purposes that has interested me from the beginning of this study, and upon which I have chosen to concentrate.

Even a comprehensive study of modern Japanese comic fiction would require more time, space, and erudition than this author could devote to it; and in this volume I offer not an exhaustive treatment of the subject, but an introduction to what I take to be the major issues involved in dealing with the topic of comedy in the Japanese context, followed by examinations of the major comic works of three authors in the Shōwa period (1925–1989), which I believe to be the period in which comedy came into its own in Japanese fiction, and an attempt to draw such conclusions as they may suggest. While the emphasis will be on the comic aspects of the works under consideration, the stories and novels all have much to recommend them above and beyond their comic elements, and I trust that my discussions will reflect this.

This study presupposes a degree of familiarity with the general features and development of modern Japanese literature and often with the works discussed, many of which, unfortunately, cannot be found in English translation. Moreover, since the structure of comic fiction is one of the elements that distinguishes it from extended jokes, works should be read in their entirety, and preferably in their original language, for their comic nature to be fully apprehended. By way of partial compensation for those who have not read the originals or cannot read them, I have included more plot summary than would be necessary for better-known works before proceeding to more general analysis of the nature of their comedy. I have also offered translations of passages illustrative of various significant comic elements, not without a sense of trepidation at the comic delusions inherent in this procedure, and all too well aware that even the most vibrant, scintillating originals may be transformed into withered specimens indeed when rooted out of their native surroundings and transplanted into the chilly and alien soil of English academic discourse. Unless otherwise noted, the translations are mine.

I am also all too well aware that some of the content of this study, particularly that which relates to the still very active Inoue Hisashi, runs the risk of early obsolescence. This is an inescapable occupational hazard of writing about living, working authors; but I have no wish to renounce the opportunity of dealing with the concerns of our own age and of making the attempt to relate them to what has come before—and to what might follow. All these caveats notwithstanding, I offer this study in the hope that it will help in some small way to stimulate awareness of and interest in a body of literature that until now has been largely inaccessible to the English-language reading public. If future work in this field negates, supersedes, or refutes assertions made here, I will welcome this; if the present inquiry serves as a point of departure, it will have served its purpose.

Studies in the Comic Spirit in Modern Japanese Fiction

Chapter 1
Japanese Comedy

In what must be one of the longest-running comic chase scenes of all time, a pack of highly determined philosophers, critics, psychologists, and other ill-assorted seekers after truth has been rushing for well over two thousand years in hot pursuit of a band of clowns. Some of these clowns are clumsy, rag-tag buffoons, while others are sleek and nimble wits. Many are somewhere in between—or both. Only rarely have they had much difficulty in remaining a few steps ahead of their pursuers. Perhaps this is because their multiplicity of guises makes them elusive prey. More likely, it is because they are considerably more experienced than their adversaries in the offensive and defensive uses of banana peels. Despite their centuries of frustration, the learned pursuers (many of them descendants of that ancient and celebrated stock comic figure, the impractical pedant) show no signs of abandoning the chase.

Comedy is destined to remain an elusive subject because by its very nature it resists all attempts at confinement. Its quicksilver flow carries it through the territories of mental operations, of attitudes toward the nature of reality, and of modes of expression and performance, tying them together in complex ways but never remaining long in any particular place or relation. Additional difficulties arise when the discussion is extended beyond the Western cultural tradition, with its centuries-old accumulations of associations and assumptions. Is it possible to speak of "Japanese comedy" without violating the integrity of either term? Is there any point to it? The answers to these questions depend ultimately upon what one chooses to mean by "comedy," that word so stubbornly resistant to definition. But while a satisfactory definition may never be arrived at, it is at least possible to point to a set of criteria that will give us a good idea of when we are in the presence of comic literature and when we are not, and it is on this basis that we must proceed.

Since "comedy" is most frequently associated with humor, and with the laughter that humor inspires, the most widely recognized characteristic of comedy in literature is the presence of humor or mirth, not in the form of sporadic jokes or anecdotes but in sufficient quantity and intensity to color the entirety of a given text. This is not to say that anything that generates laughter can simply be treated as comic—tickling and nitrous oxide have as little to do with *Don Quixote* or Jippensha Ikku's rollicking picaresque *Tōkaidōchū hizakurige* (Shanks' Mare, 1802–1809) as onions and tear gas with the tragic qualities of *King Lear* or Chikamatsu Monzaemon's love-suicide drama *Sonezaki shinjū* (The Love Suicides at Sonezaki, 1703). The nature and causes of laughter have traditionally been the concern more of philosophers and psychologists than of literary critics, whose interest lies in its role in a larger scheme. In literature, comedy involves something more than humor, and, at least in the Western tradition, at the same time (as long as we are willing to accept the conventional formal classifications of works such as *The Winter's Tale* or, for that matter, *The Divine Comedy*) something quite else. In the Japanese tradition, literary comedy has been associated even more closely with humor; terms such as *kokkei, kaigyaku, oko, fūshi, warai,* and *kigeki* (roughly translatable as "humor," "wit," "nonsense," "satire," "laughter," and "comedy," each with many variations and shades of meaning), as well as more recent imports such as *yūmoa* and *parodei,* have all been applied to literary and other works in which humor is present as a predominant element, and to the extent that comic texts have been recognized as a distinct category, it is this presence that has been the determining factor, with little or no consideration given to their formal characteristics.[1]

It is in this respect that the lack of congruence between Japanese and Western schemes of categorization is most apparent. In the West, virtually all thinking on literary comedy, at least until the mid nineteenth century, has been shaped to a greater or lesser degree by the dichotomy between tragedy and comedy established in Greek drama, and in particular by the (highly imbalanced) discussions of the two modes in the fifth chapter of Aristotle's *Poetics.* Under this influence, it became customary to think of comedy in terms of what tragedy was not, or as tragedy's antithesis: a dramatic action in which affairs similar to those of everyday life are imitated by characters of an inferior sort, who are perceived as ludicrous because they display some type of defect or ugliness without experiencing, or inspiring, feelings of genuine suffering.

An influential addition to this model was provided by the Roman rhetorician Donatus: whereas tragic actions move from equilibrium to catastrophe, comic actions move from discord to a harmonious resolution. This formalistic view of comedy, which has been echoed in later treatises from Dante's *Letter to Can Grande della Scala* to Northrop Frye's *Anatomy of Criticism*, accounts for the "comedy" in the title of Dante's magnum opus and the inclusion of *The Winter's Tale* and *The Tempest* among Shakespeare's comedies despite their generally non-humorous qualities, a classification likely to appear problematic in places and ages where the classical standards are either nonexistent or ignored. It may readily be seen from the Dante and Shakespeare examples and from some outrageously funny contemporary works that end with the potential eradication of life on earth, such as Stanley Kubrick's *Doctor Strangelove* and Kurt Vonnegut's *Cat's Cradle*, that there need be no integral connection between comedy as generator of laughter and as narrative progress from discord or suffering to peace and harmony.

Another shortcoming of the happy-ending criterion is its lack of relevance to comic literature's analogues in other fields such as music and the plastic arts. Even if they rarely attain the degree of variety or complexity possible in literature, the spirit of parody, playfulness, and nonsense displayed in Mozart's *Musical Joke*, Saint-Saëns's *Carnival of the Animals*, Richard Strauss's *Till Eulenspiegel's Merry Pranks*, and P. D. Q. Bach's *Shepherd on the Rocks with a Twist*, or in numerous paintings by Hogarth, Grosz, Miró, and Red Grooms, as well as the frolicsome *chōjū giga* scrolls of the Heian period (794–1185) and the parodic *mitate-e* of the Edo period (1600–1868),[2] clearly shares something of the spirit of comic literature. What is shared is more than just the capacity to inspire a mirthful reaction in viewers or listeners; rather, a common outlook is at work, an outlook which straddles the boundaries between humor and comedy and between differing cultures as well as those between literature and the other arts.

A possible key to identifying the common factor in this outlook is provided by Aristotle's inclusion of the ludicrous as a basic element in his formula. According to Aristotle, what makes a dramatic character ludicrous is the existence of "defects or ugliness," which in turn implies the existence of a norm, an ideal against which imperfections may be compared and found wanting. Extending the scope of such comparisons beyond character traits, we can see in them a fundamental element of the comic outlook. In Arthur Koestler's admirable formulation, "The pattern underlying all varieties of humour is 'bisociative'—perceiving a situation or event in two habitually incompatible contexts."[3] In more traditional terms, comparisons of this sort form the basis of the concept of incongruity central to most theories of humor as psychological process. In many, though not all cases, the incongruity is not value-neutral: as Aristotle pointed out, comic characters are "inferior," typically embodying physical or character defects of some sort, and occupying a humbler social station than the protagonists of tragedy. The audience's invidious comparison of these inferior qualities with its own notions on standards or ideals of human appearance and behavior forms the basis of the other principal means of apprehending the comic, the superiority theory associated most notably with Hobbes and Freud.

Whether as jokes or as fictional or dramatic narratives of the kind we call literary, then, comic texts present their audiences with two terms— a norm or ideal and an imperfect reality, or an actuality and a defective perception— and expose the resulting paradox. One of the terms should not exist, but indisputably does; the other should, but for some reason does not. A joke need only expose the contradiction, something it may delay until the punch line, and the punch line need not resolve anything and, in fact, rarely does. In literary narratives, we can expect a structure that will include not only the exposition of a contradiction but its working out in some form of conflict (the agon), and a resolution in which one term of the contradiction asserts its dominance over the other. If an imperfect reality moves toward the ideal or if misperception is dispelled, a happy ending should be achieved, while a failure of the ideal to assert itself over an imperfect reality or a failure to dispel misperception results in the suffering typical of tragic action.

The movement toward a happy (even if not funny) end is simply one of the ways in which comedy as a literary mode differs from the joke. The literary narrative's greater length, more complex structure, multiple levels of meaning, and rich stock of evocative techniques devised by succeeding generations of authors make possible the creation of deep and sustained dualistic visions impossible within the narrow confines of the joke. Moreover, by expressing these incongruities through complex, contextualized characters rather than witticisms or anecdotes, literary comedy attains a psychological depth and power far beyond that of the joke.

Such, in somewhat simplified form, were the ideas that grew out of Greek drama to dominate Western thinking on comedy and eventually came to be applied to prose narratives as well as dramas. By the eighteenth century, however, works such as *Gulliver's Travels, Candide,* and *Tristram Shandy* were already demonstrating some of the limitations of this model; and by the mid twentieth century their remote progeny—Dada, surrealism, and then black comedy and the theater of the absurd—had rendered problematic some of the most basic assumptions about the nature of comedy. The conventional comic "happy ending" came to appear artificial, or at least gratuitous, after the ministrations of Didi and Gogo, Humbert Humbert, and Col. Jack D. Ripper, while belief in a coherent ideal order against which disorderly reality could be measured has withered under the relentless assaults of the absurdists, who offered instead a vision of human existence as a feeble and doomed attempt to impose a semblance of order on a world whose natural condition was one of unmitigated chaos. The long-held assumption that social life was the natural matrix of comedy was also shaken; as comedy's metaphysical bent became more pronounced, its characters were reduced from serving as the principal embodiments of comic contradictions to moving, speaking props pointing toward transcendent contradictions that threatened to engulf them all.

At the same time, the dichotomy between tragedy and comedy was proving increasingly untenable. If the range of comic incongruities is taken to include actions in which characters lacking in self-knowledge challenge existing natural or human law and consequently have their illusions or pretensions dispelled, it becomes possible to conclude that there is a fundamental similarity between comic and tragic actions, even to assent to Eugène Ionesco's assertion that "it all comes to the same thing anyway; comic and tragic are merely two aspects of the same situation, and I have now reached the stage when I find it hard to distinguish one from the other."[4] Nor was it easy to find much validity in the other distinctions between the two modes that dated back to the Greeks: the superior social status and personal attributes of tragic protagonists; the conviction that their suffering is genuine and compelling; the conviction that tragic contradictions, unlike comic contradictions, are inescapable; and the resolution of contradictions in a catastrophic rather than a festive ending. By the middle of the twentieth century, belief in the notion of superior and inferior orders of humanity was rapidly waning as economic, social, and political developments had deprived traditional elites of most of their claims to authority. Furthermore, two world wars and countless lesser conflicts not only dealt a severe blow to ideals such as "nobility" and "honor," but brought about destruction and suffering on a scale so massive as to test the mind's capacity for comprehension. Confronted with the horrors of mechanized genocide and the awesome destructive power of nuclear weapons, traditional forms of response no longer seemed adequate; the violation of the most fundamental assumptions about the existence of standards of human decency was so complete that the sense of horror could give way to a sense of the ultimate absurdity of it all. As the advent of black comedy has shown us, it is only a short step from a vision of extreme tragedy to one of extreme comedy, and the distinction rests as much in the eye of the beholder as it does in the scene beheld.[5]

If we now feel that it is impossible (or pointless) to suffer without seeing the absurdity of our situation (and thus laughing), and equally impossible to laugh without being aware of the ultimate unendurability of our situation (and thus suffering), what can we substitute for the traditional view of comedy as antithesis of tragedy? Is it at all meaningful to continue thinking of comedy as a distinct category? Apparently it is, for works recognized as comic continue to appear; and by so recognizing them, we implicitly continue to acknowledge the existence of some traits that even the darkest visions, even the most all-encompassing expressions of absurdity share with comic works of a more conventional nature. A sense of the ludicrous, somehow conducive to mirth, arising from the incongruity between what is and what we think should be, is still very much with us. We seem to require this sense, or at least find it inescapable, and so comedy not only survives, but flourishes, no matter how inauspicious or desperate the circumstances.

This very capacity for survival, in fact, has come to be regarded as one of the most important distinguishing characteristics of comedy. As formalistic criteria have become increasingly problematic, attention has been devoted to another, more fluid criterion, the idea that comedy is an expression of life as an indomitable force, a celebration of the vitality that allows us to triumph over all forms of restriction, adversity, and decay. Whereas in other modes life may be sacrificed for transcendent ideals and values, and the sacrifice endowed with an air of nobility, in comedy life itself is the supreme value, and its continuation and propagation, at any cost, constitute the motivating instincts of the comic spirit.

The concept of the comic as affirmation of the life force figures prominently in Henri Bergson's famous study *Le rire* (Laughter, 1900) in the form of *élan vital*, which he sees as artificially impinged upon by "mechanical" restraints in the fundamental ludicrous situation. The literary implications of this idea were powerfully developed by Susanne Langer, who characterized comedy as a festive celebration of the animal drives and vitality of mankind in the face of the world's adversities and surprises, and asserted that comic action consists of "the upset and recovery of the protagonist's equilibrium, his contest with the world and his triumph by wit, luck, personal power, or even humorous, or ironical, or philosophical acceptance of mischance."[6]

The supremacy of the life force in comedy and its capacity for constant self-renewal help to explain another element peculiar to the comic mode, the non-reality of comic suffering. No matter how savagely they are knocked about, comic characters seem to feel little pain, and their audience vicariously feels even less, for it is certain that every time they fall they will be back up again in an instant to resume their antics with energy undiminished. Even in the most savage Punch-and-Judy routines and grimmest black comedies, hapless creatures subjected to seemingly endless rounds of violence, humiliation, and disappointment somehow manage to keep muddling on. Thanks to their unwillingness to accept defeat (or rather their failure to acknowledge its existence) and the mindlessly mechanical repetitiveness with which they are victimized, their suffering resembles what we witness in *grand guignol* and television cartoons more than what we witness in tragedy.

Proponents of the idea of comedy as affirmation of life found support for their arguments in the work of the Cambridge school of anthropologists, who traced the origins of Greek comedy to protohistorical fertility rites associated with the agricultural cycle in which, to oversimplify again, a sterile old order, typically personified by a dying king, is replaced by an energetic new one to the accompaniment of much mirth, revelry, and a temporary release from normal social strictures. As writers on comedy such as Langer and William Wimsatt are careful to point out, though, it is futile simply to see latter-day comic drama as a reenactment of ancient myths and rituals; comedy is too universal and too protean a phenomenon to be accounted for in this way.

What ultimately matters most is not the issue of ancestry or prototypes, but rather the problem of identifying the elements that recur repeatedly in all sorts of literary expressions of the comic impulse in various times and places. These include an atmosphere of mirth; thematic emphasis on the incongruity between real and ideal or between perceptions and reality; an expression of such themes through integral narrative devices such as emplotment and characterization rather than merely through a string of jokes; a narrative structure that moves from distress to satisfaction or from discord to integration; an affirmation of the life force in the face of social, physical, or even metaphysical constraints; and a refusal to believe in the reality of suffering. None of these is limited to comic works alone, of course; and no comic work need contain all of them. But in most ages and cultures we find these elements occurring together in an infinite series of permutations and combinations that makes them seem more appealing, more artistically coherent, somehow more compelling than each would be in isolation. Whether through intrinsic properties or sheer force of habit, these permutations and combinations appear to be organic in a way that many others are not. The patterns are neither rigid nor invariable, and different people will apprehend them in somewhat different ways; but when some critical mass of these elements is apprehended in a work by any given reader, the result is a sense that one is in the presence of a text that is not just humorous but a comedy.

To be sure, the comic patterns in Japanese texts do not always correspond neatly to Aristotelian or other Western schemes, and there has been relatively little articulation of the concept of comedy as a distinct entity in Japanese critical writings. Among premodern works on the subject, the most prominent is *Waranbegusa* (Children's Leaves, 1651–1660), a treatise on Japan's preeminent genre of comic drama, *kyōgen*, by the actor Ōkura Toraaki. Although it is devoted largely to the training and performance practices of the players, *Waranbegusa* also contains some illuminating passages on the comic properties of the plays themselves. Toraaki attempts to elevate the status of *kyōgen* by disregarding its roots in popular entertainment, tracing its origins instead to traditional literary arts such as court poetry and romances. He also strongly emphasizes its identity as a complementary variant of the Nō drama that creates humorous effects by showing the common behavior and language of ordinary characters in everyday situations (unlike the ideal or elevated world of Nō) and sometimes even parodies the plots of Nō plays. Like Nō, however, *kyōgen* must be tasteful in its language and acting, not crude or offensive; and in its most elevated form, it transcends the limitations of humor and achieves a pathos that approaches the sublime.[7] Since *Waranbegusa* was a collection of instructions to his artistic successors in the

Ōkura troupe, not intended for public circulation, the direct influence of Toraaki's ideas cannot be said to have been wide; but surely it is noteworthy that the most famous discussion of a comic genre in traditional Japanese culture has relatively little to say about laughter and finds its ultimate vindication in the transcendence of humor rather than in its indulgence. We can readily see Toraaki's doctrines reflected in the performance practices of his own and the other surviving *kyōgen* troupes—in which the humorous elements are all too often so highly stylized as to be virtually inaccessible to contemporary viewers.

In the modern period, there has been increased but by no means copious attention to comedy in Japanese critical discourse, much of it posed in terms framed by various Western theorizers including Freud, Bergson, and Bakhtin. The first well-known example appeared, appropriately enough, in the critical manifesto generally celebrated as the inaugurator of the new era in Japanese fiction, Tsubouchi Shōyō's *Shōsetsu shinzui* (The Essence of the Novel, 1886). As might be expected in a pioneering effort of this sort, Tsubouchi's discussion does not always reveal a firm grasp of the alien material he had set out to introduce to the Japanese public, but it does contain some perceptive comments. His description of incongruity as the basis of the ludicrous and his recognition of the need to intersperse tragic and comic passages to create complex effects are sophisticated for their time, even if his definition of comic plots as those in which the protagonist "flourishes in the end" (*shin'yō naku sakayure*) in contrast to tragic plots in which the protagonist comes to a pathetic end (*hakanaki saigo o tsuguru yoshi*) is overly simplistic.[8]

Natsume Sōseki, who had made a far more intensive study of theoretical questions and had a deeper understanding than Shōyō, offered a considerably more advanced theory of comedy in the fourth chapter of his massive attempt to formulate a comprehensive theoretical framework for literature, *Bungaku ron* (On Literature, 1907). Like many other sections of the book, Sōseki's description of comedy suffers from a certain terminological opacity, but it also contains some acute insights. His description of the basic comic relationship as a form of association that reveals unexpected similarities of sound (*kuchiai* or "wordplay") or ideas (*tonsai*, which Sōseki associates with the English term "wit") is essentially in keeping with standard incongruity theories; but in his observation that in comic associations the differences must remain greater than the similarities, he offers a hint at resolving the problem, all too ignored in discussions of comedy even today, of distinguishing comic associations from other forms of similarity-based association such as metaphor and, as Sōseki himself points out, the *kakekotoba* or conventionalized double entendre of the Japanese poetic tradition. Sōseki also joins Shōyō in deploring the comic fiction of the Edo period, which he characterizes as petty-minded attempts at invidious ridicule lacking in intellectual or spiritual distinction—a position which, as we shall see below, did not prevent him from endowing some of his own early forays into comic fiction with distinctly Edoesque overtones.[9]

The ethnologist Yanagita Kunio, in a number of essays on humor, focused his attention less on its causes than on its outward manifestations and effects as well as its role in Japanese culture. For Yanagita, like most Japanese (and many non-Japanese) writers on the subject, comic texts are simply those containing passages that inspire laughter. His identification of brevity, ephemerality, and lack of structure as the primary traits of humor in his 1928 essay "Warai no bungaku no kigen" (The Origin of Humorous Literature) reflects his tendency to see comedy in terms of jokes rather than texts,[10] and indeed none of these characteristics are conducive to fictional elaboration. He was, however, concerned with the question of humor in literature and offered in this essay and elsewhere a number of explanations for literary comedy's failure to flourish in modern Japan. First, in an apparent reversal of Toraaki's theory but in conformity with prevailing doctrines on the nature of fiction, he drew a distinction between humorous writing and the "documentary" (realistic) literature (*kiroku bungei*) that had established a predominant position in the modern era. Second, he saw a tendency for humor in Japan to be concentrated in performance-based elements (the voices and gestures of performers) rather than texts, which explained its decline to its current low state as literacy became more widespread. Finally, he drew attention to a social feature with particularly important consequences in the Japanese case, the difference between humorists who direct laughter at themselves and those who direct it at others: "While laughter is a pleasurable sensation, the condition of being laughed at by others was essentially not a happy one, and so even now there are few who willingly consent to serve such a function, and even those who inadvertently perform such benevolent acts seem to hasten to return themselves to the fold of the laughers, or from the outset place the object of their laughter in the distance and attempt to laugh along with the crowd themselves."[11] Despite these unpropitious circumstances, Yanagita saw humorous literature as beneficial to society and called for its revival, possibly by adopting the *gesaku* techniques of shifting the object of laughter away from direct personal involvement and concentrating on descriptive technique (*byōsha no gijutsu*) and realistic use of language (*kotoba no shasei*).

Most later writers have tended to accept more or less uncritically Western theoretical formulations and concentrate their attention on the status of comic literature in Japan. Writing in 1930, still in the early stages of his rapid ascendance to the status of dean of mid-century Japanese critics, Kobayashi Hideo identified comedy with the mechanistic theory of Bergson and observed that because the Bergsonian comic act of exposing mechanical encrustations on the living is an act of intellect, it is a difficult pursuit in Japan, a "land of sentiment"; but he also finds promising indications that a recent proliferation of "nonsense" literature might signal the development of a brighter form of humor to replace the inhibitions of previous generations.[12]

In the postwar period, Nakamura Mitsuo quickly took advantage of the prevalent mood of soul-searching and reappraisal to assail the baleful effects of the *shishōsetsu*, the autobiographical-style realist fiction that was widely acknowledged to constitute the mainstream of prewar literature. Conspicuous among its traits, he asserted, was its lack of humor, which was one of the essential elements of great literature, present even in those works that are not formal comedies, in both the West and traditional Japan; and his "Warai no sōshitsu" (The Loss of Laughter, 1948) remains one of the most cogent and insightful studies of the difficulties facing would-be comic writers in modern Japan, despite autobiographical fiction's gradual fall from pre-eminence.[13] Throughout the postwar decades, other critics and scholars including Asō Isoji, Iizawa Tadasu, and Hamada Taizō have continued to contrast the wealth of comedy in traditional Japanese literature with its relative paucity in the modern era.[14] Some also engaged in theoretical formulations, most notably Yamaguchi Masao's exposition of the role of the Trickster figure; but the focus has largely remained on the element of humor that appears in various (otherwise unrelated) works and on its salutary social functions of maintaining the social order by ridiculing deviant behavior or improving it by ridiculing abusive or illegitimate authority, rather than considering comedy as a textual category with its own formal properties, including elements above and beyond humor.

Still, there are any number of Japanese texts, both traditional and modern, in which many or all of these elements can be found occurring together and which on this basis can be called not only humorous but comedies. However deeply grounded they may be in particular national or cultural attributes, on a deeper level these works show unmistakable connections with something that appears to be a more general human impulse—even if the reasons for Japanese classifications of certain texts as comic or humorous may not always be readily apparent to non-Japanese readers, as a glance at the tables of contents of some contemporary Japanese anthologies of comic literature will show.[15]

Most of the principal comic elements are already on display in the earliest written record of Japanese civilization, the *Kojiki* (Record of Ancient Matters, completed in 712). Although the motives for its composition are now classified as more historical than literary (even if such a distinction would not have meant much to its compilers), it contains much material from myth and legend, some of which attests to the existence of a vigorous sense of the comic among the early Japanese. In particular, the episode concerning Ame no Iwayado (the "heavenly rock-cave door") recounted in book I, chapter 17, of the *Kojiki* is often cited as the earliest known example of a Japanese comic narrative. The details are well known: the sun deity Amaterasu having shut herself up in a cave, the Plain of High Heaven and the Japanese islands are plunged into darkness. The distressed deities have one of their number, Omohikane, devise a plan, and after various ritual preparations, the deity Uzume appears before the cave door:

> She [Uzume] laid a sounding-board before the door of the heavenly rock cave, and drummed her feet on it until it resounded. As she became possessed, she pulled out the nipples of her breasts and pushed her skirt-string down to her private parts. Then the Plains of High Heaven shook, and the eight hundred myriad deities all laughed together.
>
> The Heaven Shining Deity [Amaterasu] was astonished. She opened the door of the heavenly rock cave a crack and said from inside it, "I though that when I secluded myself the Plain of Heaven would be dark, and the Reed-Plain Land [Japan] too: why then does Uzume make merry and why are the eight hundred myriad deities all laughing?" Then Uzume said, "We are laughing with joy because there is a deity more illustrious than you." Koyane and Futotama pushed the mirror toward the Heaven Shining Deity so that she would see it. At this, she was even more astonished, and little by little she ventured from the doorway to peer into it, whereupon the Hand Strength Deity, who had been standing concealed, grasped her hand and pulled her out. Then the deity Futotama drew a rope behind her and said, "Go

no further back than this!" And when the Heaven Shining Deity had come out, both the Plain of High Heaven and the Central Land of Reed Plains naturally became light again.[16]

The most frequently cited comic element here is the laughter inspired by Uzume's erotic dance. One of the most graphic examples of laughter in all of Japanese literature, it suggests the penchant of the early Japanese for a broad, earthy style of humor; but a contemporary audience may not necessarily find itself laughing (or recognizing this as comic) for the same reasons that the myriad deities did. For them, the bawdiness of the performance presumably provided quite sufficient grounds, but in the twentieth century, countless burlesque acts later, it does not. For a modern audience to find the scene funny, either it must envision the dance as being performed with appropriately humorous gestures, as it no doubt was (although the *Kojiki* is silent about the details), or else the circumstances under which the dance was performed must strike us as comic in some way. This is certainly the case: an erotic dance performed by a deity as part of a desperate ritual can now be found incongruous in a way that it presumably could not by Uzume's divine companions on the Plain of High Heaven.

To what extent this incongruity was felt by the creators of the myth is less clear. As commentators such as Yanagita and Matsumura Takeo have pointed out, because laughter was thought by the ancient Japanese, like members of other primitive societies, to be an effective way of propitiating or placating deities, it played an important role in magico-religious rites. In particular, the laughter engendered by the exposure of the female genitalia was thought to be effective in promoting or renewing the regenerative powers of life, just as the female organs themselves were thought to have the power to subdue malevolent spirits.[17] At any rate, the association of laughter with displays of vitality and (successful) efforts to restore light and life to a disturbed world is very much in keeping with the comic gestalt pattern.

But there is more to the comedy in this episode than the powerful but crude dance of Ame no Uzume. The deception of Amaterasu with the mirror involves a more sophisticated piece of comic business: not only is she drawn out by the most basic kind of comic misperception of reality, a failure of self-recognition in one of its simplest possible forms, but she, as the supreme deity, is turned into a comic butt with an incongruous double standard; for her determination to sulk in her cave is all too easily undermined by her naive curiosity and credulity, and she ends up being drawn out by an almost equally naïve scheme. Uzume, by contrast, plays the basic comic role of the life-affirming Trickster who prevails by virtue of adaptability and sheer energy, her relatively low social status notwithstanding, although she must serve as a laughingstock herself even as she plays her tricks on others.

The Ame no Iwayado story, then, mixes humor of the crudest, most basic sort with a number of more complex features that distinguish comic literature from humor per se. Similar combinations are found elsewhere in the *Kojiki*, such as the episode recounted in book II, in which the elder Ukashi becomes a victim of the trap that he himself had set to waylay Emperor Jimmu's men, and which concludes in a scene of triumphal merriment as the victim is taunted with the nonsense refrain *ee shi ya ko shi ya, aa shi ya ko shi ya.*[18]

Throughout its ensuing history, the comic literature of Japan has, like that of other cultures, remained in constant flux, oscillating repeatedly along a variety of axes. There is earthy physical comedy in Yamazaki Sōkan's *haikai* verse collection *Shinsen inu Tsukuba shū* (New Doggerel Tsukuba Anthology, ca. 1523–1532) and the picaresque fiction of Jippensha Ikku, and urbane comedy of manners in the *Momiji no ga* (Autumn Excursion) chapter of the *Tale of Genji* and the *kibyōshi* (yellow-cover chapbooks) of Santō Kyōden. There is good-natured mirth in the eighth-century *Man'yōshū* (Collection of Ten Thousand Leaves, ca. 759) and the *haikai* of the Teitoku school, and pointed satire in Ihara Saikaku's tales of the Floating World and the *kanbun* essays of Narushima Ryūhoku. There is witty wordplay of all sorts, from the elegant verse puns in the tenth-century *Kokinshū* (Collection of Ancient and Modern Poems) to the exuberant and elaborate concoctions of the Edo fiction writers, and sardonic probing of human foibles in the late-Heian *Konjaku monogatari* (Tales of Times Now Past, late twelfth c.) and the *kokkeibon* fictions of Shikitei Sanba. The expansiveness of an Ikku or an Inoue Hisashi is balanced by the concision of *senryū* verse and the comic vignettes of the *Tsurezuregusa* (Essay in Idleness, ca. 1330), while the no-holds-barred farces of Hiraga Gennai and Sakaguchi Ango are counterpoised by the subtle understatement of Ibuse Masuji. (Of course, some of these writers and works at times straddle both sides of a given dichotomy.) It is even possible to see in the movement from distress to supernal peace of the Nō dramas a Japanese analogue to the Western category of "divine comedy," and in the Zen *kōan*'s radical rejection of all mental categories and the language systems by which they are signified comedy in its purest, closest approach to the boundaries of the metaphysical, expressing by antirational means the ultimate absurdity of the human condition.

Perhaps the most conspicuous and enduring polarity of all, however, is that created by the existence of two distinct strains of comedy associated with two very different types of creators and audiences, the low or popular, whose texts are more often viewed as sources of amusement or of ethnographic or historical information than as artifacts with significant literary properties, and a culturally, socially, economically, and often politically privileged elite commanding the high ground of "art," marked by pronounced refinement of style and sensibility, as against the presumed crudity or vulgarity of popular forms. The ongoing dialectic between popular and elite cultures is hardly peculiar either to Japan or to comic literature; but an awareness of its role is essential to gaining an understanding of the development of Japanese comedy, because the elite culture has largely been hostile to comedy per se, and much of Japanese comedy has thus been shaped and colored by its popular-culture identity. While the distinction may have been a rather marginal one in the period of Japan's earliest written literature, when the governing and religious elites participated in the same folk-based culture as the rest of society, we find it established quite markedly by the Nara period (710–794), when a court-based elite culture, heavily influenced by the Chinese model, self-consciously set itself off from the culture of the peasants over whom it ruled. The change is clearly reflected in the later verses of the *Man'yōshū*.

As the court culture grew increasingly sophisticated, the contrast grew ever wider, establishing a pattern that would persist long after the aristocracy was replaced by the warrior class as the nation's principal political and cultural elite. Low or popular comic literature, which was originally grounded in the orally transmitted folk culture and primitive theater of peasant society, was characterized by energy and openness; and its breadth and adaptability have enabled it to reinvigorate itself continuously with material from new sources. In later ages it came to include the products of more literate non-elite groups (wandering Buddhist priests, low-ranking samurai, and merchants) and the wide variety of plebeian entertainments that developed with the growth of urban life. It tended to take as its subject matter scenes of a common, everyday nature, frequently involving the pursuit (or loss) of sexual, material, or bodily well-being. As the expression of an oppressed social group, or of disaffected drop-outs from the elite culture, it showed a marked lack of respect for authority, gleefully portraying the pretensions, vanities, and pratfalls of legendary and historical heroes, revered religious figures, and, when possible, temporal power-holders as well. When this last group was placed off limits, as in the Edo period, the non-elites could turn their gaze upon themselves and portray their own foibles with undiminished verve. While it often delights in exuberant displays of verbal dexterity for their own sake, low comedy may also be satirical and even subversive in its questioning of the legitimacy of authorities and, by extension, of the notion of legitimacy itself.

The comedy of the elite culture, as might be expected, is far more conservative: there is little glorification of the forces of vitality, and much emphasis on propriety and restraint, on the affirmation of values and styles which mark its members off from their social inferiors. The more importance a given order attaches to maintaining appearances in everything from speech and behavior to clothing and hair, and the more effort it devotes to making those appearances conform to ideals (such as the courtly or samurai codes) that serve to legitimize very real material and social privileges, the less interest it is likely to take in exploring the problems of daily life, the world of the body, and the naked expression of desire. Social life is portrayed as a comedy of manners, in which the style of the characters' actions and speech is examined more carefully than the contents. In such a state, the potentially disruptive spirit of comedy is most welcome when it can be directed at subjects abstract or remote enough to cause no discomfort to the existing order. Outlandish pretenders to high status are expelled by their betters, rather than pulled down from outside. In its most fully realized moments, such as the comic episodes in *Genji*, a supremely refined courtly code is established and maintained, and deviants are dismissed with a cool reserve more deadly than the jovial mockery of popular comedy; but since such subjects were generally considered to be beneath contempt in both courtly and samurai culture, the mere expression of interest in them was liable to be interpreted as a disqualifying signal, and so it was not ventured with great frequency. Elite comedy prizes refinement, complexity, and nuance in its handling of language just as much as in its handling of character; the elegant wordplay of the poems of the *Kokinshū* is as much an emblem of courtly sophistication as are the subtly nuanced formulas of seduction depicted in *Genji* and *Ise monogatari* (Tales of Ise, early Heian period).

Differences of form and genre are equally pronounced. While both types of comedy may adopt a satirical outlook (albeit, of course, with widely different aims and styles), or play on incongruities between sound and meaning of words, it is in popular comedy, where the broadly inclusive spirit prevails, that we find the greatest latitude for the kind of parody that is such a prominent part of the Japanese comic tradition. By appropriating the form and style of a well-known work while substituting less elevated characters and situations as subject matter, the parodist could mock the conventions of the original text, as in the case of *Nise monogatari* (Fake Tales, ca. 1630), a parody of *Ise monogatari,* or thrust characters into an incongruous environment that magnifies their shortcomings, as in the numerous Edo fictions which lampoon the inadequately sophisticated would-be gentleman of fashion, or take both tacks simultaneously, as in Saikaku's *Kōshoku ichidai otoko* (The Life of an Amorous Man, 1682). These techniques, however, are largely unavailable to the writer of elite-culture comedy: the styles and forms of the high tradition, which are among the most important of all the signs that set the sophisticated minority apart from, and above, the base masses, are virtually by definition immune from mockery. The use of parody to mock the mores and literary conventions of the lower orders is also highly circumscribed, since these are hardly considered worthy of attention to begin with. If the life of the lower orders is to be portrayed satirically at all, it is best done in a form sufficiently stylized and remote to appear relatively clean (and quaint), as in the elite culture's version of *kyōgen.*

An important characteristic of elite comedy, when it does appear, is that it frequently does so in its own distinct genres, rather than within the same genres as serious works. These comic genres typically develop as offshoots of "serious" genres; often their derivative, ludic status is explicitly signaled in their names, as in *kyōgen* ("wild words," the comic complement to the serious Nō drama), *haikai* (the "sportive" form of linked verse), and *gesaku* (the "playful" fictional works of the later Edo period). Many of these distinctly comic genres are appropriated into the elite tradition, often through the mediation of marginal figures such as wandering priests or low-ranking samurai, from popular culture, where comedy's dualistic vision, celebration of untrammeled life forces at the expense of artificial constraint, and subversive tendencies find a naturally conducive environment. Often these appropriations occur as reactions when the conventions of elite forms have reached a state of extreme rigidity, as their relatively loose conventions and parodic spirit offer a release from the rigors of an established aesthetic: elevated sensibilities and actions give way to the commonplace, and elegant but atrophied modes of expression are replaced by cruder, more vigorous forms. In due course, such a form may grow so far removed from its humble origins and so elaborate and stylized in the hands of the elite culture that its creative development approaches a rarefied dead end; the energies of popular culture, along with the more iconoclastically inclined demimonde elements on the underside of the elite, then set to work developing new anti-forms (such as kabuki, and the comic verse forms, *zappai* and *kyōka*). As the very existence of such elements suggests, there is never a simple black-and-white dichotomy between popular and elite, but rather a more or less spectral gradation, with a constant process of cross-fertilization being carried out in the forms of parody and cultural slumming.

Among the various comic genres that developed in premodern Japan, *gesaku* deserves some special notice both as a partial exception to the usual pattern of migration between subcultures, and as one of the supreme comic high points in Japanese cultural history. The term *gesaku* itself is less than satisfactory: as a general label for the popular fiction of the later Edo period, it covers a wide range of works in several categories ranging from the ponderously didactic historical romances of Takizawa Bakin to the insouciant burlesques of Santō Kyōden. Frequently, though, it is used more narrowly to refer to those categories (*sharebon, kibyōshi, kokkeibon*) that embody the spirit of "playfulness" (i.e., non-seriousness) evoked in the morpheme *ge*, which began to appear in the second half of the eighteenth century in Japan's urban centers, especially Edo. While each of these possessed its own more or less specific traits, collectively they constitute an outburst of boldly freewheeling parody, extravagant wordplay, and incisive satire that has had few if any equals in Japanese culture before or since. Moreover, *gesaku*, at least in its early days, shared with the contemporary comic verse form *kyōka* a distinctive position in Japanese literary history: because its initial creators and audience constituted an informal subculture in which highly educated but underemployed samurai from the lower echelons of the ruling class could mingle with sophisticated but socially lowly commoners from the urban merchant class, it possessed attributes of both high and low culture without belonging to either. It was never overtly appropriated by the upper echelon of the samurai class, even though it was practiced by some members of that elite.[19]

Although their position outside official culture seems to have partially shielded them at times, the censorious attentions of the shogunal authorities were an ever-present worry for writers for whom frivolity and irreverence were very much stocks in trade; and sometimes, especially when the shogunate was swept up in one of its periodic campaigns to restore purportedly traditional samurai morality and enforce the virtues of austerity on an unenthusiastic populace, these worries became realities. During one of the most ambitious of these campaigns, the Kansei Reforms of 1787–1793, the *gesaku* output of two of the leading writers of *kibyōshi* and *sharebon*, Hōseidō Kisanji and Koikawa Harumachi, came to an end; and Santō Kyōden's career in comic fiction was also effectively terminated in 1791, when he was condemned to spend fifty days in manacles following the proscription of *sharebon*.[20] Thereafter, creators of comic forms of *gesaku* were constrained to limit themselves to the most innocuous of themes and techniques; and samurai writers were largely forced to withdraw from the field entirely, leaving it in the hands of professionals from the commoner class, who soon found themselves ceaselessly crossing and recrossing the already well-trodden ground of pleasure-quarter shenanigans, country-bumpkin versus city-slicker buffoonery, and wordplay that owed as much to contrivance as to ingenuity.

As a combination of government hostility, irrelevance, and, presumably, sheer exhaustion led to the final decline and disappearance of *gesaku* in the years immediately following the Meiji Restoration of 1868, the dawn of the modern era paradoxically saw the high-low dichotomy that had become so firmly ingrained over a thousand years of aristocratic and samurai ascendancy reassert itself with a new vitality; and it continued to exert a powerful influence throughout the period of modernization. Drastic social and cultural transformations and the emergence of a new statist/capitalist order created, among many other things, a new elite that relied on new values and new kinds of credentials to legitimize its status. There was also a perceived need for new kinds of literature, since the serious traditional forms with their accumulated burdens of convention and associations did not adapt easily to dramatically changed conditions. As so often in the past, the new elite lacked the will or capacity to create new forms out of extant materials, but the time-honored technique of appropriation from below was now decidedly unattractive—not only were *gesaku* and most of the other popular forms of the Edo period already suffering from terminal atrophy, but all of them were irredeemably associated with the very backwardness from which the new elite was making such a determined effort to distance itself. Thus, the arrivistes of the Meiji period (1868–1912), like their predecessors of a thousand years before, found it most advantageous to turn outside, to the artifacts of a prestigious "advanced" culture, in this case not China but the West, where the predominant literary form, and the one most closely engaged with the social order, was the novel.

Aside from the prestige it derived from its place of origin, the novel offered several advantages over indigenous forms: it was incontrovertibly new and up-to-date, and exclusive rather than inclusive (since only the educated minority could be expected to appreciate it). It also possessed one other quality that no native popular form could hope to equal: it could be made, at least in the eyes of its advocates, absolutely and indubitably serious. This was of paramount importance. The explosive release of energy that marked so many aspects of the Meiji era might well have been expected to result in a great comic outpouring; but the Meiji elite, for all its newness, retained many of the Neo-Confucian values that had constituted the orthodoxy of its samurai predecessors, not the least of which were the disapproval of anything even remotely smacking of frivolity and the great value placed on the maintenance of an appearance appropriate to the dignity of one's status. Literature, as a public discourse, was no exception; in the official scheme of things, its principal function, exemplified by the Chinese classics, was to provide moral or spiritual edification, not formal or mimetic pleasure, let alone less elevated forms of diversion. It goes without saying that the Neo-Confucian orthodoxy was hardly conducive to the comic spirit in *gesaku* or any other form; even if enjoyed in private, guardians of public morality, whether official or self-appointed, could hardly see works displaying such a spirit in any terms other than as gross and frivolous anti-literature, produced by disreputable hacks. The raw energies of life were to be carefully controlled by social and moral constraints, and in these circumstances the comic dual vision was rendered impossible, or at least pointless. The same effect was produced by the Confucian emphasis on the virtue of sincerity (*sei* or *makoto*), which precluded indulgence in comic irony, exaggeration, or distortion.

While other Neo-Confucian values may have gradually lost currency under the Meiji modernization program, the emphasis on seriousness did not. If anything, the temper of the times only intensified it. Japan had a lofty national mission, an urgent task to perform, which called for all the strength its people had to offer; and the new elites, including the educated producers and consumers of literature, saw themselves as bearing the greatest responsibility. Any literature that was seen to take mere diversion as its end was relegated to artistic limbo, and even here the didactic strain of Edo popular literature (in the forms of historical and domestic drama and fiction) survived more successfully than the comic. In this respect, too, the imported genre of the novel, which was perceived as an inherently serious product of serious thinkers making significant contributions to the development of civilization, proved to be the most promising basis for the establishment of a new elite-culture literature.

The new literary program was set out most explicitly by Tsubouchi Shōyō, especially in his *Shōsetsu shinzui*, in which he stressed that fiction had a vital place in modern civilization, and could secure its claim to respectability by adhering to the principle of realism and at the same time avoiding all traces of vulgarity. In this respect, according to Shōyō, it could do no better than to make itself the diametric opposite of *gesaku*, which he assailed not only for its artificiality and didacticism, but also for the crudity and frivolity of its attempts at comedy. Despite his vision of the novel as a lofty artistic undertaking and his avowed disdain for the inadequacies and excesses of *gesaku* (which, as with many of his contemporaries, seems to have been more a matter of principle than of practice), Shōyō was by no means hostile to the spirit of comedy per se. In fact, he more or less explicitly accords comedy a place in his program for the Japanese art novel of the future, and his observation that the ludicrous (*kokkei, kaigyaku*) and satirical elements of comedy are subordinate to its general spirit of mirth (*kaikatsu*) offers a promising if vague strategy for overcoming the limitations of the *gesaku* approach.

Needless to say, Shōyō did not, for better or worse, exercise dictatorial powers over the development of Japanese fiction.[21] His discussion of comedy must have struck many of his first readers as alien, opaque, and abstract; what was remembered more clearly was his attack on the vulgarity and obscenity of such late-Edo-period *gesaku* productions as Ikku's *Hizakurige* and Baitei Kinga's *Shichihenjin* (Seven Odd Men, 1857–1863), along with his assertion that in a modern society writers were persons of consequence rather than déclassé entertainers. Thus, despite the survival into the Meiji period of such humorous popular forms as *gesaku* fiction (at least in the first decade or so) and *rakugo* (comic monologues) and even of a more erudite form of comedy in the *kanbun* satires by new-age dropouts such as the professional outsider Narushima Ryūhoku, comedy had an exceedingly difficult time establishing itself in the emerging novel-based genre of prose fiction known as *shōsetsu*.[22] Many of its early practitioners, including Futabatei Shimei and Ozaki Kōyō as well as Shōyō himself, had been steeped in the *gesaku* culture in their youth, and traces of its influence are clearly visible in their work. But the staples of *gesaku* comedy—the elaborate style with its dense matting of puns and allusions, the parody of familiar traditional themes and forms, the narratorial posture of disengaged frivolity informed by the pleasure-quarter sensibilities of *tsū* (connoisseurship) and *iki* (elegance)—were obsolete and irrelevant, and in these works we see the vestigial traces of an already moribund comic tradition rather than the genesis of a new one.

Without a doubt the most notable achievements in comic fiction during the Meiji period were the two early works of Natsume Sōseki, *Wagahai wa neko de aru* (I Am a Cat, 1905–1906) and *Botchan* (1906). As trenchant satirical portraits of some of the follies, vanities, and pretensions of intellectuals and bureaucrats struggling with the opportunities and confusions of their brave new world, both have aged gracefully and established themselves as fixtures in the modern Japanese canon. Sōseki's acute sensitivity to the ways in which the modern world impinged on traditional patterns is clearly reflected in the comic structures of both novels, in which elements of Edo sensibility (which he experienced firsthand in his youth and never lost the taste for) are transposed into a Meiji milieu and mixed with bourgeois comedy of family and class manners that may reflect his readings of such authors as Fielding and Meredith. From the perspective of the development of comic fiction, however, they might be referred to, like some of the fictions of Shōyō and Futabatei, in Fiedlerian terms as death-of-*gesaku gesaku* rather than as part of a transition to a new style.

Although it avoids the coarseness and artificiality assailed by Shōyō, *Neko* draws upon a number of familiar Edo conventions. Like Shikitei Sanba's *kokkeibon* classics *Ukiyoburo* (The Bath-House of the Floating World, 1809–1813) and *Ukiyodoko* (The Barber Shop of the Floating World, 1813–1814), it takes as its focal point a fixed, static space through which a variety of characters pass, and presents through the eyes of a detached observer the petty foibles of petty men and women, which, infinitely multiplied, constitute an entire world. Its verbal texture is thick with wordplay and witticisms, and its loquacity and looseness of form suggest both Edo fiction and the *rakugo* of which Sōseki was an aficionado. Its central characters, including a feline narrator and the rather unworldly intellectuals it observes, recall *gesaku*'s countless marginal and superfluous protagonists. The human protagonist Kushami sensei and his friends have, at least potentially, far more of an opportunity to take an active part in their society than their Edo predecessors did, but are largely content to remain whimsical bystanders (a stance markedly alien to the Meiji spirit) without apparent misgivings.

In the title character of *Botchan* we see a specimen of an unusual breed, a bold Japanese comic protagonist, even a comic hero, who responds to vanity and duplicity by challenging them with brashness and bravado rather than with evasive subterfuge. Again, Sōseki's satire of Meiji superficialities and excesses is sharp, and the dialogue repeatedly drops modish names like Madonna and Gorki; but as the tale of a dashing Edoite haplessly exiled among obtuse provincials, *Botchan* can also be read as a kind of Meiji *kokkeibon*, its protagonist a descendant of Kita and Yaji, the indefatigable Edo-bred picaros of *Hizakurige*. But this line is already near extinction: Botchan is a misfit not only in space but in time, trapped in a grotesque provincial outpost of the "modernization" apparatus and stubbornly clinging to his beloved Edo identity in a world where it is rapidly being relegated to the status of a mere curiosity. For all his pluck, even despite his final vindication, he lacks the strength and the guile required to impose his own will on the complex bureaucratic order that is developing with irresistible momentum all round him. The society of petty but shrewd provincial hypocrites with which he has tangled is only superficially bruised by the encounter. It will soon make a full and shameless recovery and will then resume its triumphant course, engulfing and ultimately eradicating the simple, honest Edo values. Botchan's nemesis Redshirt is sure to win his Madonna; he himself can only retreat to his native city and his sterile pairing with the aged family retainer Kiyo, the personification par excellence of old Edo, who wastes little time in proceeding to an impeccably Edokko grave in Kobinata.

Despite the success of both works, Sōseki soon left comic fiction behind to create novels of great psychological depth that, while not devoid of comic moments, grew increasingly more somber. Many of the themes he addresses in these novels—the strains of living in an age of wrenching change, uneasiness over the direction of Japanese society, the relationship between individuals, especially intellectuals, and that society, the relationship between individualism and egoism, even the love triangle—had been treated in a comic manner in *Botchan* and *Neko*. An outstanding scholar of English literature before he became a novelist, Sōseki was well aware of the importance of the comic spirit in British fiction; and as his critical writings show, he had devoted careful thought to the workings of comedy and its role in literature. It is difficult to believe that a writer of his talents would have been incapable of combining the comic spirit of his earlier works with the psychological depth and structural complexity of his middle and later works to create truly modern comic fiction of a high order. Why he did not is perhaps a question best left to qualified Sōseki psychoanalysts, but two points seem significant. As Jay Rubin has pointed out, the shift coincided with Sōseki's introduction in *Sanshirō* (1908) and *Sore kara* (And Then, 1909) of protagonists with a greater awareness of their own defects than those of *Neko* and *Botchan* had;[23] because their contradictions are spelled out, they allow less scope for pretense or ignorance susceptible to comic handling. One may also speculate that his turning away from comedy was not unrelated to his giving up his teaching post at Tokyo Imperial University to become the literary editor of the *Asahi shinbun*: if *Neko* and *Botchan* can be seen as twentieth-century analogues of *gesaku*, and the following *Kusamakura* (1906, trans. as *The Three-Cornered World*) as Sōseki's attempt at a *haikai* novel, the at least partially playful writings of a man enjoying a respite from the pressures of his serious official duties, his later novels were themselves serious work in his new position, and perhaps even justifications of his having renounced the ostensbily more prestigious status of university professor. When he sought relief from the strains of this work, it is understandable that he found it not in fiction, comic or otherwise, but in poetry or painting.

At about the same time that Sōseki was making this transition, there took place another event that was to have the gravest consequences for the development of comic fiction in Japan. This was the rise to mainstream status of the Japanese variant of Naturalism known as *Shizenshugi*, which marked the beginning of the long ascendancy of confessional or reflexive fiction called *shishōsetsu* or *watakushi-shōsetsu*. The Japanese Naturalists can be said to have followed the realist program set out by Shōyō twenty years earlier, albeit in a skewed way.[24] Their goal of eliminating from their work all traces of fabrication and excess in order to get at the naked "truth" was by no means a new one in Japan, but few previous writers had pursued it with such single-minded intensity. Even if the field within which they sought this truth was often restricted to themselves and their immediate surroundings rather than the broad social panorama, even if their work not infrequently lacked stylistic or formal elegance, and even if they often seemed intent on demonstrating their commitment to absolute honesty by luxuriating in revelations of humiliation and squalor, the Naturalists could not be accused of perpetuating the frivolities and vulgarities of Edo fiction.

The contributions made to modern Japanese literature by Japanese Naturalism and the damage it caused have been hotly debated since its advent, but with respect to comedy the picture is unambiguous. Because seriousness was paramount in the Naturalists' sense of artistic mission, their choice of materials, and their style, there was little or no place in their scheme of things for the dual vision or the urge to lovingly examine, explore, and play with the incongruities between appearance and reality upon which comedy thrives. Major comic techniques such as selective exaggeration, distortion, abstraction, and the use of fantasy were renounced as well.

Long after the Naturalists were eclipsed by various other movements, and even after movements themselves had ceased to be of much importance, their legacy—the *shishōsetsu*—retained its central status. Although it is generally considered to have reached its zenith in the Taishō period (1912–1926) in the hands of such practitioners as Shiga Naoya and Kasai Zenzō, autobiographical fiction continued to be a staple feature of the Japanese literary scene well into the postwar era, and has never entirely disappeared. Together with the complementary cult of seriousness, it continued to exert a chilling influence on comedy. If the duty of writers was to adhere unswervingly to reality, to that which they knew to be true and of which they could speak with absolute authority and sincerity, they were left with little choice but to focus almost exclusively upon themselves and dismiss the depiction of society at large and ordinary life, the most natural matrix of human comic foibles, as *tsūzoku shōsetsu* or "popular fiction." The foregrounding of the self and concomitant pushing of other characters into the background also deprived their work of the opportunity for the interplay of opposing characters upon which comedy so often depends. Shōyō's perception that the broad panorama of social life was the natural matrix of fiction and his awareness of comedy's place in fiction were both lost.

Moreover, as Nakamura Mitsuo has pointed out, a lack of distance between authors and their fictional alter egos, which was integral to the *shishōsetsu,* was hardly conducive to ironic distancing or a comic view of the self—and there was little else in view.[25] The situation is exacerbated by the self-image of many of the writers whose alter egos occupied center stage in these fictions: they saw themselves as a kind of self-selected counter-elite, distinguished by cultural aspirations and sensitivity rather than superior social status or wealth (although some *shishōsetsu* writers, especially those associated with the prominent Shirakaba School, did, in fact, possess these privileges too). Their quests were ultimately not for power or love but for truth and spiritual equilibrium; and the question that preoccupied them was the lofty one of how to live, not the more comic question of how to get by—which was probably of greater interest to the majority of their fellow citizens.

A final obstacle to comedy posed by the autobiographical approach stems from a more general feature of human nature. The *shishōsetsu* writers, in their dedication to realism and self-examination, may have been almost embarrassingly ready to lay bare the less savory corners of their souls or to flaunt their contempt for established mores before a shocked and titillated reading public. They may even have been willing to arrange their lives in a way that would fuel their art with optimal amounts of wretchedness and humiliation. As Yanagita pointed out, however, most human beings, and perhaps Japanese even more than most, are rarely inclined to acknowledge the contradiction between their higher aspirations and the less attractive realities, that is, to see themselves or present themselves to their audience, as ludicrous.[26] If comic treatment of characters depends upon the exposure of pretense or lack of self-knowledge, there was very little scope for it here; and so with a few conspicuous exceptions, comic protagonists are absent from the vast *shishōsetsu* corpus, even when their authors relax sufficiently to introduce an occasional comic minor figure or moment of mirth.

In principle, autobiographical fiction, even the *shishōsetsu* convention, should be full of comic possibilities. If, as many critics claim, twentieth-century literature in the West has been marked by the rise of a brand of black humor that can be characterized as "dark, meditative, self-doubting,"[27] or "a defensive humor of shock, a humor of lost norms, of disorientation, of lost confidence,"[28] the *shishōsetsu*, which tends to be so rich in qualities such as darkness, meditation, lost norms, and disorientation, would seem to offer fertile ground for humor as well, except that it lacks the focus on incongruities that is also requisite. One could even see in the *shishōsetsu* a kind of continuation of the *gesaku* tradition of retreat from a closed, dead-end (and deadened) public discourse into a private world, in this case not for a frustrated plebeian class but for intellectually inclined middle-class readers. Chafing under the constraints and impersonal routines of a modern mass society, they vicariously taste the forbidden fruits of freedom and unorthodox ideas through the struggles of a fictional hero and the (putatively indistinguishable) life of that hero's creator. But this escape, quite unlike the *gesaku* one, is by definition absolutely in earnest, even if the realities it entails are doomed not to measure up to the ideals it invokes—and so the *shishōsetsu,* in its less convincing moments, can occasionally read something like the adventures of Don Quixote as recounted by the Don himself rather than Cervantes.

As a practitioner of an elite art form cut off from the rich and promising resources that had been so valuable to the *gesakusha,* the *shōsetsu* writer with comic ambitions was faced with a major dilemma. Despite the gradual rise of various challenges to the hegemony of Naturalism and then of the *shishōsetsu* itself from the 1920s into the 1930s, the cult of seriousness retained much of its authority. To defy it was to risk exclusion from the ranks of authentic art writers in the eyes of many critics and readers, and few writers seemed inclined to object to the arrangement. Even the work of figures such as Kawabata Yasunari and Mishima Yukio, who had so little in common with Naturalist and *shishōsetsu* writers in other respects (and who, in Mishima's case, enjoyed a reputation for being funny and fun-loving in real life), maintains a level of seriousness that could not fail to gratify their most exacting predecessors.

The comic spirit being the incorrigibly transgressive force that it is, however, it did manage to rear its head from time to time in various forms. In the years after Sōseki's move away from comedy, fiction with notable comic touches was produced by Akutagawa Ryūnosuke and Tanizaki Jun'ichirō. Akutagawa's interest in the workings of the human mind included an acute sensitivity to the deceptions that human beings perpetrate on themselves and each other, revealed in works showing considerable comic versatility, including short, scintillating reworkings of historical material such as *Hana* (The Nose, 1916) and *Kiseru* (The Pipe, 1916) as well as longer aphoristic works such as *Shuju no kotoba* (Words of a Petty Man, 1923–1925). More ambitious, and arguably his comic masterpiece, is *Kappa* (1927), a darkly ironic novella-length fantasy that mixes utopian and dystopian elements to panoramically portray a grotesquely distorted society that is not so much an anti-Japan as a Japan stripped of its pretensions and evasions, against which the flaws of the originals are brought all the more sharply into focus.[29]

The even more versatile Tanizaki generally tended toward humor of a more attenuated sort; but as the ineluctable urgencies of the erotic (in both its libidinal and its romantic forms) were among his most persistent preoccupations, his numerous explorations of this terrain so rich in incongruity and delusion occasionally gave rise to fictions in which his highly developed sense of irony approached a condition of full-blown comic detachment. Among these are *Chijin no ai* (1924–1925, trans. as *Naomi*), a mordant meditation on the perils of eroticultural confusion in which a young man, trying to live out his yearning for an up-to-date Westernized existence, remodels an alluring but vapid café hostess into the centerpiece of his Hollywood dreams, only to suffer the consequences when she learns her lessons all too well and ends up shamelessly dominating and exploiting him. But despite the essential absurdity of the situation, the acuity of Tanizaki's satire, and a series of masterfully depicted social, cultural, and sexual pratfalls, the suffering and humiliation of the protagonist are portrayed so convincingly that the ultimate impact of the novel is something other than comic. Delusions and comic moments also abound in other Tanizaki works, including the two great novels of his last years, *Kagi* (The Key, 1956) and *Fūten rōjin nikki* (The Diary of a Mad Old Man, 1962–1963); but again the comic effect is substantially diluted, not only by the rich and powerful ambiguities that pervade both works, but by the author's inability to conceal his deep-seated conviction that sex is something, perhaps even the only thing, that must be taken seriously. For Tanizaki's characters, especially his men, the possibility of resisting the imperatives of the libido simply does not exist, even in those rare cases where the will to resist them does; and no matter how grotesque or deluded they may appear in following their urges, they are only doing what they have to do. In this sense, they are not suffering from the kind of curable folly or delusion that is subject to ridicule, and therefore they are not entirely comic. Perhaps the closest Tanizaki ever came to pure comedy was *Neko to Shōzō to futari no onna* (A Cat, a Man, and Two Women, 1936), in which a splendid comic theme, a kind of *ménage à quatre* in which the protagonist's love for his cat triumphs over the intrigues of his current and former wives, is given full play without the usual overlay of sexual urgency.

Whatever the merits of their comic turns, Akutagawa's and Tanizaki's artistic priorities clearly lay elsewhere; and these novels came no closer to inaugurating a sustained development of comic writing than had Sōseki's *Neko* and *Botchan*. It was only by coming directly to grips with the *shishōsetsu* phenomenon that a start was made toward creating a new kind of comic art fiction. The writer generally credited with first taking the self as his principal comic subject and voice is Uno Kōji, with the first successful work of this type being his 1919 story *Kura no naka* (Inside the Storehouse). Although the protagonist, Yamaji, is said to be modeled as much upon another (autobiographically oriented) writer, Uno's friend Chikamatsu Shūkō, as upon Uno himself, the story appears, at least at first, to be a conventional enough specimen of *shishōsetsu* technique: it takes the form of a rambling first-person confessional, with the words *watakushi wa* seeming to appear and mark "I" as the subject in just about every sentence.

Like many other *shishōsetsu* subjects, Yamaji is a feckless figure who stumbles from one disaster to another, generally without the benefit of much outside assistance. Unlike the conventional *shishōsetsu* protagonist, however, who is rarely capable of seeing beyond the pathetic side of his situation, Yamaji is able to see his setbacks as a cause for laughter rather than trauma and tears. Repeatedly he interrupts the flow of his narrative to comment on his own foolishness, or coyly to ask his audience to refrain, if at all possible, from bursting into laughter. He has the cunning required to engage in a series of tricky sexual duels, and the ingenuity to maintain contact with his beloved collection of kimonos and his custom-made futon, both of which have long been languishing in a pawnbroker's storehouse, but somehow this ingenuity is never quite enough to prevent all of his schemes from going awry. The end of the story finds him kimono-less, futon-less, loveless, and even audience-less—the final indignity for the *shishōsetsu* hero, who is willing to endure any amount of suffering or humiliation if only it can be transmuted into artistic success.

Like Botchan, Yamaji cuts a rather negative figure as a comic hero, but he does so within the ground rules of the *shishōsetsu* game.[30] Instead of a series of comic dichotomies between realistic and unrealistic perceptions expressed through conflicts between characters, we have in *Kura no naka* similar dichotomies expressed through Uno's ironic manipulation of a single narrator-protagonist figure. Aided by the gift of hindsight, we can read this story as an ironic rewriting of the *shishōsetsu* formula, in which the childish, self-indulgent side of the conventional *shishōsetsu* hero is played off against his more elevated role as artist and sufferer, sustained by a fine balance of humor and pathos—in which the *shishōsetsu* conventions themselves are as much at question as the author's self-image—a viewpoint, in other words, more Cervantesque than Quixotic.

In general, the Taishō period in which Uno was introducing a ludic note into autobiographical fiction was marked by a trend toward relaxation in many aspects of Japanese life, including sporadic challenges to the cult of seriousness in literature. The sense of public purpose and urgency that had energized the Meiji years was gradually dissipating, leaving in its wake a vacuum that may have bred a sense of malaise in some quarters but provided more favorable circumstances for the development of a comic outlook. Attempts to gain some relief from seriousness continued unabated into the early years of the Shōwa period (1926–1989), stimulated no doubt by the explosive growth of new forms of popular mass culture including motion pictures, radio, and mass-circulation magazines. The early Shōwa years also saw the rise of an entertainment-oriented urban subculture of *mobo* (modern boys) and *moga* (modern girls), the heyday of *ero-guro-nansensu* (erotic-grotesque-nonsense stories, cartoons, etc.), and even an attempt at founding a literary movement with aspirations to art status focusing on and appealing to this popular culture and including amusement among its avowed objectives. The new "movement," the Shinkō Geijutsu Ha or New Aesthetic School, turned out to be an organizational and aesthetic (but not commercial) failure; like some of the writers of Edo *gesaku*, its members strove to capture the latest urban manners and styles, but with little of their predecessors' sharp comic vision and stylistic ingenuity. Representative works by leading lights of the movement such as Ryūtanji Yū's *Apāto no onnatachi to boku to* (The Girls in the Apartment and I, 1928) and Asahara Rokurō's *Building to shōben* (Buildings and Urine, 1930) show much evidence of the difficulty they encountered in breaking away from the *shishōsetsu*, their commitment to "newness" (or at least novelty) notwithstanding. In the final analysis, their most memorable contribution to the development of twentieth-century Japanese comic fiction may have consisted in giving a boost to the career of the previously obscure Ibuse Masuji.

As the abortive Shinkō Geijutsu Ha project suggests, the appearance of cracks in the façade of seriousness in the late Taishō and early Shōwa years was accompanied by a gradual lessening of the tendency for writers to group themselves, or be grouped by critics, into conceptually oriented schools such as Naturalism, Idealism, Proletarianism, and Neo-Perceptionism. This, too, was to have a liberating effect on the comic spirit, and the period of the 1920s and 1930s saw considerable activity by several writers whose careers were to be noted for a substantial quantity of comic work, including Uchida Hyakken, Sasaki Kuni, Makino Shin'ichi, and Sakaguchi Ango, as well as Ibuse and Dazai Osamu. These promising developments were, however, soon to peter out in the face of ever-intensifying militarism, tension, and attempts by the government to control all aspects of life, which culminated in the outbreak of war in China and then in the Pacific. The sufferings endured by the Japanese population in the final stages of the war and the immediate postwar period were even less propitious for comedy, although Ibuse published his *Shūkin ryokō* (The Bill-Collecting Trip) in 1937, and two of Dazai's comic masterpieces, *Shinshaku shokokubanashi* (New Tales of the Provinces) and *Otogizōshi* (Fairy Tales) appeared in 1944 and 1945, respectively.

In the postwar period, a far freer cultural and intellectual atmosphere and the gradual erosion of traditional attitudes about the limits and functions of literature resulted in an increased volume of comic works in both popular and art fiction. Some of this was the work of writers resuming careers interrupted by the war, including Ibuse, Ango, Oda Sakunosuke, Ishikawa Jun, and Ozaki Kazuo. There has also been an increasing willingness to take up comic themes among writers who have made their debut since the war, among the most prominent of whom are Abe Kōbō, Ōe Kenzaburō, Kaikō Takeshi, Nosaka Akiyuki, Tanabe Seiko, Kurahashi Yumiko, Maruya Saiichi, Endō Shūsaku, Kita Morio, Tsutsui Yasutaka, and Inoue Hisashi.

The roles played by all of these writers in the development of Japanese comic fiction are worthy of scrutiny. This study, however, will be devoted to three figures who, in my opinion, have done the most to demonstrate that even in unfavorable circumstances the comic spirit can and does find expression in fiction of a high level on a sustained basis. None of them is exclusively a writer of comic fiction; rather than attempting to cover their entire careers, or even their total output of comic fiction, I will concentrate on those works that most fully embody the comic spirit, that is, those works in which comic dualities figure as an integral informing principle and not simply in the form of incidental humorous passages. It is my hope that this selection will serve to shed as much light as possible on the distinctive conditions shaping the development of comic literature in modern Japan, and the dilemmas facing its practitioners.

The first of the three is Ibuse Masuji (1898–1993). While it would be something of an exaggeration to claim that all of modern Japanese comic fiction has come out of Ibuse's salamander cave in the same way that, according to Dostoevski, Russian fiction emerged from Gogol's *Overcoat*, it is no exaggeration to assert that Ibuse did more than any other modern writer to bring comic fiction in from the margins of literary discourse in Japan, to open up new ground with a comic vision that was neither Edo nostalgia nor a *shishōsetsu* derivative, and to demonstrate, through his mastery of style and depth of insight, that comedy and high artistic achievement are fully compatible.

Ibuse's sometime protégé, Dazai Osamu (1909–1948), came to grips with the problem of comedy and the *shishōsetsu* legacy in a very different way. Like Uno, Dazai possesses the unusual talent of being acutely conscious of, and willing to lay bare, his own absurdities. He, too, makes himself the central focus of his comic gaze, but in a dazzling, seemingly endless variety of guises, settings, and voices. Sometimes he splits his comic persona into multiple characters and even overlays them with an Ibusean semi-fictive narrator, thus extending the potential of the *shishōsetsu* to, and sometimes beyond, its outermost limits. Although his comedy is often based on distinctively Japanese social, cultural, or linguistic features, Dazai never loses the conviction that these are ultimately a function of the human as well as the national condition, and for this reason he is the most accessible of all Japan's comic writers.

In the great comic cornucopia of Inoue Hisashi (1934–), we see the boldest exercise yet of comic imagination, and the most relentless assault on the notion of an essential connection between literature and seriousness. While it has little of Ibuse's subtle nuancing or of Dazai's emotional intensity, Inoue's comedy is immeasurably broader in scope. As if to make up for years of lost time through an explosive release of the pent-up comic energy, he joyfully deflates the vanities of Japan's "serious" writers and of authority in general, pulling out every comic stop within reach from crude slapstick, wistful self-mockery, and gesakuesque wordplay and parody to mordant satire, outrageous and grotesque fantasy, and topsy-turvy farce. Like a suddenly resurrected high priest of some long-lost fertility cult, he obliterates all restrictions and installs in their place an exuberant celebration of all the forces of life released from the confinement in which they had languished since the close of the Edo period. Yet even when the barrage of puns, sight gags, and phallic *tengu* masks is at its thickest, the reader remains in the presence of a tough, searching, and well-informed intellect posing numerous pointed questions about the nature of Japanese culture, and human nature itself.

Despite his reputation as a "magician of language," Inoue is intent on extending the domain of comic literature beyond the boundaries of "language" as words on a page or "text," assaulting it with nonsense, lampooning the conventions and physical limitations of the printed book format, and using language to evoke the extraliterary world of comic performance. His masterpiece *Kirikirijin* (The Kirikirians, 1973–1981), with its combination of earthy physicality, exuberant wordplay, devastating satire, grotesque and fantastic visions, and irrepressible will to parody, is both a summary and a celebration of much of what Japanese comic literature has been throughout its history. In particular, it is a celebration of the enduring vitality of the popular tradition from which the spirit of comedy draws so much of its inspiration. What role this spirit will play in a contemporary Japan where lines between elite and popular culture are rapidly blurring, if not becoming irrelevant, should be one of the more interesting—and significant—questions facing Japanese literature in the coming years.

Chapter 2
Ibuse Masuji
Out of the Cave

Among the best-known works of fiction to appear in Japan in the year 1929 were two major novels by established writers, Shimazaki Tōson's *Yoakemae* (Before the Dawn, serialized starting in April in *Chūō Kōron*) and Tanizaki Jun'ichirō's *Tade kuu mushi* (Some Prefer Nettles; published as a newspaper serial from December 1928 through June 1929 and in book form in November 1929). The Proletarian movement, then near its highest level of popularity and artistic achievement, was producing such representative works as Kobayashi Takiji's *Kani kōsen* (The Cannery Boat) and Tokunaga Sunao's *Taiyō no nai machi* (Street without Sunlight). From the third major stream of Japanese fiction at this time, a group of young non-Marxist writers committed to experimentation in language and narrative technique and generally known as the Shin Kankaku Ha or Neo-Perceptionist School, came the first serialized installments of Kawabata Yasunari's *Asakusa kurenai dan* (The Asakusa Crimson Gang); Yokomitsu Riichi was forging ahead with his long novel *Shanhai* (Shanghai).

Sharing the youthfulness and apolitical stance of the Neo-Perceptionists was a fourth category which has come to be associated variously with such labels as *Modanizumu*, Shinkō Geijutsu Ha (New Aesthetic School), and *ero-guro-nansensu*.[1] Neither as substantial nor as enduring as the others, it was nevertheless greeted with a flurry of enthusiasm by the reading public and is notable in the annals of modern Japanese literary history as the first movement whose works of fiction boasted a strong comic element. Led by, or at any rate most frequently identified with, such now-obscure figures as Ryūtanji Yū, Nakamura Masatsune, Yoshiyuki Eisuke, and Asahara Rokurō, its major offerings in 1929 included Asahara's *Jogun kōshin* (Women on Parade) and a number of stories by a then relatively obscure young writer named Ibuse Masuji.

Born in 1898, Ibuse had published a story entitled *Yūhei* (Confinement) as early as 1923, and several of his earliest works, such as the stories *Yofuke to ume no hana* (Plum Blossom by Night, 1925) and *Koi* (Carp, 1926), already showed the focus on quiet but telling moments, tone of ironic self-deprecation, and unprepossessing but finely wrought style which were to become his trademarks. These qualities attracted little attention in a literary arena dominated by autobiographical soul-searching, dramatic Proletarian appeals, and self-consciously avant-garde experiments. But as post–World War I Japan continued its unsteady advance toward the nebulous goal of "modernity," conditions were ripe for the appearance of a new kind of literature. As in the Edo period, physical and commercial expansion of the nation's metropolitan areas, especially Tokyo, was creating a new entertainment subculture, this time centered not on the merchant class but on white-collar workers and student types proud of their youthful energy and sophistication and fascinated with the variety of amusements which the new urban landscape had to offer. These people also constituted a new reading audience, courted vigorously by a publishing industry which, with its mass-circulation magazines and sets of cheap, uniform *enpon* (one-yen books), was joining the newspapers, radio, and motion pictures as an element of that sine qua non of cultural modernization, the "mass media."[2] By the late 1920s this readership had become a market force to be reckoned with, and the writers of *Modanizumu*, including Ibuse, were being pushed into the literary spotlight with the same breathless speed that marked the pace of modern urban life itself.

A taste for *ero-guro-nansensu* was one of the distinguishing features of the urban entertainment subculture that these writers took as their milieu. Like other manifestations of ero-guro-nansensu culture such as cartoons, ero-guro-nansensu fiction is little more than a historical curiosity today;[3] but its general characteristics, as displayed in the writings of such leading practitioners as Ryūtanji, Nakamura, and Asahara, are well known. Its setting is the city, preferably one of the more fashionable quarters of Tokyo. Its characters, both male and female, are impeccably youthful, modish, and unburdened by parents to obey or dependents to support. It celebrates the freedom of apartment life, or the then-novel delights of cafés, dance halls, and department stores. Its style tends toward the breezily informal. The seriousness of purpose so conspicuous in the previous generation, and in its literature, seems to have become lost on the way to the pleasure domes, but under the glittering surface runs a darker current of *carpe diem* hedonism. This current was symptomatic of the anxiety of an age in which luxury existed side by side with grinding poverty, and in which the newfound freedoms and prosperity rested on foundations whose fragility was all too readily apparent, and were, in fact, to vanish before very long.

None of these characteristics is generally associated with the literature of Ibuse Masuji, and it is hardly remembered now that he was once classified as a *nansensu* (if not *ero-guro*) writer. Even when the stories which won him this reputation are read today, many of them do not seem to fit the mold. *Kuchisuke no iru tanima* (Kuchisuke's Valley, 1929), for example, is set not in a Ginza café or a Jingūmae apartment, but in a remote mountain valley, presumably somewhere near the author's native place in a rural section of Hiroshima Prefecture. Of the story's three characters, only one is from the city. He is one of the early incarnations of what was to become a common figure in Ibuse's fiction, the self-effacing but keenly observant and dryly ironic narrator persona. In this instance he is an "ill-fortuned literary youth" (*fugū na bungaku seinen*),[4] living in Tokyo but with his roots deep in the country. The title character, an incorrigibly rustic old codger, could hardly offer more of a contrast to the young sophisticates of the urban subculture. Only the third character, his teen-aged granddaughter Taeto, possesses any ero-guro potential: she is both exotic (a Eurasian recently come to Japan from her birthplace, Hawaii) and erotic in an innocent, bucolic way. Even so, she is a far cry from the freewheeling *moga* (modern girl) type dear to the hearts of the *ero-guro-nansensu* writers. A chaste, devout Christian, she is sadly lacking in metropolitan polish: "I know. And we have often seen them. People seem to find it interesting that the modish girls in the dance halls of our bustling cities boast the same style as Taeto's. And these dance-hall girls even seem to take pride in the filthiness of their pale green jackets with the stand-up collars, and in the bagginess of their cut. But go, ladies and gentlemen, and make the round of the dance halls—you will probably encounter some girls wearing pale green jackets with stand-up collars, but you are not likely to see any as filthy or as baggy as Taeto's" (1: 46).

The story concerns the narrator's trip to the country (an undertaking generally greeted with about as much enthusiasm by the *moga* and their male counterparts, the *mobo* or "modern boys," as it had been by the readers and writers of Heian court romances ten centuries earlier) to defend the interests of the old man, who must relocate before his house vanishes under the waters of a soon-to-be-completed dam. As in many Ibuse stories, there is a highly Quixotic pattern here: the narrator has received a letter from Taeto appealing for help in getting the old man to move, but on his arrival he discovers that the old man is already reconciled to leaving. Thus the main conflict is dissipated almost as soon as it begins; and the rest of the story comprises a string of episodes involving the frustrated narrator's lusting after the girl, the move to a new house, and finally the disappearance of the old one, interspersed with vignettes of country life and illustrations of the old man's quirks. Beneath the looseness of structure and superficial lightness of tone, the inexorably rising waters behind the dam provide a somber crosscurrent. This is strongly underscored by the resonant final scene, in which all three characters watch a small bird circling repeatedly above the surface of the new reservoir and crying, apparently in search of its lost nest. Kuchisuke exclaims, "This here pond does such cruel things, for certain," sinks to the ground, and begins to sob (1: 59).

The language of *Kuchisuke no iru tanima* is notable for the title character's heavy use of a dialect like that of the author's native area. Characters in other early Ibuse stories such as *Shigure-tō jokei* (A View of Shigure Island, 1929) and *Tange-shi tei* (Life at Mr. Tange's, 1931) speak a similar dialect. Needless to say, this ponderous, somewhat antiquated, altogether unfashionable language sets the story even further apart from the usual milieu of the *nansensu* writers, with their predilection for racy contractions and up-to-date linguistic importations from the West. Kuchisuke also uses an occasional English word, but in his case these are remnants from his youth as a contract laborer in Hawaii rather than a display of cosmopolitan chic. The narrator, of course, shows off his Tokyo speech, but his relaxed pace, richness of implication, and careful choice of words clearly mark his voice as a distinctly Ibusean creation.

Some purportedly *nansensu* works by Ibuse from this period such as *Shigure-tō jokei* and *Josefu to joshi daigakusei* (Joseph and the College Girl, 1930) hold stronger claims to the distinction.[5] *Shigure-tō*, one of the first Ibuse stories to be published in a major periodical (*Bungei Shunjū*), contains several elements reminiscent of *Kuchisuke:* once again, a mild-mannered and urbanized but impecunious young narrator has exiled himself to a remote backwater where he finds himself in the company of an extremely crotchety middle-aged couple, whose coarse dialect is set off against his more polished speech. But this time the setting, a large abandoned steamship moored off a barren island, presumably somewhere in the Inland Sea, does have a distinctly nonsensical feel, as it is turned into a kind of fun-house mirror image of the urban scene. The characters call their home a *haisen apāto* (abandoned-ship apartment), evoking the new Western-style apartment buildings that were then being promoted in Tokyo as the last word in modern living.[6] The rusted surface of the ship's hull resembles *bunka irokabe* (Western-style wallpaper?); only one scaled-off iron plate reminds the observer that the ship is not really a modern concrete apartment building. The deck is a "rooftop garden" (*okujō teien*), and one of the third-class cabins is a "conference room" (*danwashitsu*) where the residents hold discussions while sitting on bales of straw.

It is not entirely clear how much of this is to be taken as a metropolitan sophisticate's self-satisfied look at the backwardness of country life, how much as a parody of metropolitan notions of fashion, and how much as simple "nonsense," playing with incongruities for the sheer fun of it. Ibuse avoids the temptation simply to portray the dialect speakers as comic butts by treating their quaint rustic accents or incongruously modern-sounding vocabulary as signs of backwardness or ignorance. The narrator uses these words as readily as the old couple, if not more so, and the story's principal comic incongruity is not the contrast between cosmopolitans and hicks but rather the disparity between the supposedly bright and happy "life of modern civilization and truth" the narrator imagines is going on back in the city and the succession of "utterly absurd events" (*nan to chōshō ni atai suru samazama na dekigoto bakari*)[7] that constitutes life for all the residents of the *haisen apāto*, narrator included. Isaku and Otatsu, his shipmates, pass their days in an interminable round of pointless quarrels, hurling the same insults at each other over and over until the function of language approaches a breakdown, and periodically stopping to engage in various activities uniformly pointless in purpose and method. The narrator's well-meaning attempts to mediate are doomed to failure, since his Tokyo accent and his scent of shaving cream and soap are enough to bring on an attack of hysteria in Otatsu.

The nonsensical goings-on notwithstanding, language is even closer to the center of the comedy in this story than it had been in *Kuchisuke*. It functions on several levels: the dialect and "standard" voices again express the contradictory worlds and worldviews of city and country people; but since the bonds which tied the narrator to Kuchisuke are absent here, and because his companions are even more eccentric, his carefully measured speech takes on a cooler, more ironic tone. Moreover, because the characters' attempts to describe their home in elegant or cosmopolitan-sounding terms are so hopelessly incompatible with reality, we are left suspecting that the life evoked by these terms is not actually being lived anywhere. The dry, almost statistical descriptions of the island and the ship, the deadpan recounting of outrageous words and actions, and the expression of seemingly innocuous ideas through odd vocabulary items, incongruous rhetorical flourishes, and fractured grammar, simultaneously casting a satiric light on the values held by the characters and their failure to live up to them, were refinements rarely found in the usual run of *ero-guro-nonsensu* fiction, and were also to be staple and effective comic techniques for Ibuse throughout his career.

The surface elements of *Josefu to joshi daigakusei*, published in the January 1930 issue of *Shinchō*, are closer to standard *ero-guro-nansensu* fare. This time the setting is Tokyo. The characters again form a triangle of narrator plus another male and female, with the female in this case, the college girl, belonging to the *ero-guro* category of free-spirited, flirtatious, new-era types. Under the guise of homework, she brings her uncle (the narrator) a series of "assignments" to be translated into English including such sentences as "I'm not good at listening, but when I hear your beautiful voice, I feel as if I'm living in a paradise of dreams" and "My only joy is the way you respond to my gay but lonely heart." When it finally dawns on him that she must be trysting with a foreigner and he confronts her with all the righteous indignation his humble circumstances allow, her reply is, "So you've finally figured it out" (*Yatto ki ga tsuita no ne*); and when he warns her of the risk of a calamitous pregnancy resulting from her liaison, she responds, "How vulgar of you, Uncle—I'm shocked! We don't even understand each others' languages."[8]

This comment can be taken as a summary of the entire story. Each of the characters has his or her own language; they do what their language does, and what they do in this story, very broadly, is miss connections. Joseph, the object of the girl's attentions, turns out to be a sixteen-year-old from Ireland, exiled for some apparently political reason, a would-be freedom fighter who can't shoot straight, speaks no Japanese, and shows little interest in (or even awareness of) the girl's advances. The narrator first dismisses him as foreign riffraff without even having met him, only to change his mind later and admire him for his naïve sincerity and commitment to a righteous revolutionary cause. The girl, unable to communicate with him directly, does not realize that he will soon leave to join his father in Shanghai. Mistaken assumptions, misperceptions, and cross-purposes continuously accumulate to create an overall effect that richly deserves the label "nonsense."

The failures of comprehension and communication in *Josefu to joshi daigakusei* are underscored by the narrator's use of another important Ibuse stylistic element, a ponderously artificial translationese heavily larded with archaisms, Sinicisms, and repetitive constructions rare in colloquial speech, as well as occasional English words. Traces of this style recall the schoolbook patterns used to translate European languages (and the Chinese classics) into Japanese. Here it serves not only to convey the alien feeling of the narrator's English conversations with Joseph, but to establish a sense of ironic distance between him and his flippant, weak-minded, but strong-willed niece, and also, no doubt, to juxtapose her vapidity with the equally strong delusions of the Proletarians, some of whose dogmatic catch-phrases he trots out in a wholly futile attempt to bolster his objections to her pursuits.[9] In this story, he is the oldest member of the triangle, but he is no more effectual than his previous incarnations had been. He relies heavily on a rather pompous, dignified style of speech in his struggle to conceal his all-too-obvious poverty and maintain an air of avuncular authority and moral superiority; for an author who was to delight throughout his career in portraying both old people and the prematurely old at heart, this voice would prove to be another favorite tool.[10]

Even more than in the setting and the characters, it is in its superficial frivolity of tone that *Josefu* most closely resembles other works of *ero-guro-nansensu*. Although a strong moral sense and uncomfortable forebodings lurk below the surface, the reader is free to interpret the story as a light-hearted sketch of youthful energy and new manners, taken to excess, in a clash with a singularly inept representative of authority. The same cannot be said for *Tange-shi tei*. The last of these four stories to be published and by far the best remembered now,[11] it marks a major shift in Ibuse's comic style despite the superficial retention of some *ero-guro-nansensu* trappings.

Like *Kuchisuke*, the story is set in a remote corner of the countryside. The characters, except for the narrator, are again headstrong, dialect-speaking eccentrics, and the title character is another crusty old man, but here the similarities end. Unlike the relatively innocuous and unassuming old people of the other stories, Mr. Tange is a fully realized comic character, vain and capricious, a petty tyrant over his tiny domain. The story revolves around his relationship with, or rather his abuse of, his aging manservant Eisuke; in the first scene he is found administering a bizarre punishment for such "offenses" as napping in the afternoon, planting gourd seeds without permission, and making the carp in the pond afraid of human footsteps (1: 124–126). The narrator, a visitor from Tokyo staying at the Tange household while excavating the nearby remains of an ancient kiln, learns that Eisuke was taken in by Mr. Tange years ago as a homeless, nameless waif and that, although he has now been married for twenty-four years, he has never lived with his wife. In fact, their only chance to meet occurs every two years or so when she comes to apologize after he has been scolded or taken sick. After a bit of reflection, Mr. Tange realizes that he has never actually done anything for his servant but give him a name; but his penitent mood is short-lived. Throughout the story, his main concern is to maintain the last remnants of his personal and family glory, which seem to have been none too bright even in their heyday.

The narrator's persona and point of view assert themselves more strongly in this story (although he still undergoes the humiliation of having the illiterate manservant tell him that the one ewer he has managed to unearth from the kiln site is "an ugly *sake* jar" [*bukotsu na tokkuri*, 1: 137]). His comments take on a more explicitly ironic tone: as he observes the grotesque "punishment" the master has devised for the cowering servant, he dryly notes that "even in backwaters like this, chastisement is administered very seriously indeed" (1: 123). At times he even makes bold to address his sarcasm directly to its object: when the suspicious Mr. Tange asks him about the contents of a letter to Eisuke from his wife (after having refused to read it to his servant in the first place), he coolly replies, "It said something about cruel punishments" (1: 132).

Compared to *Shigure-tō* or *Josefu*, there is relatively little *ero-guro-nansensu* flavor here—and, as we have seen, even those earlier stories were somewhat out of the *ero-guro-nansensu* mainstream. Still, the eccentric characters and apparent pointlessness of the action in all of these stories at least offer some basis for attaching the label to Ibuse's work in this period. Another reason had less to do with the nature of his writing. In the early years of Shōwa, terms such as *Modanizumu* and Shinkō Geijutsu Ha served critics as convenient labels for categorizing younger writers who were, on the one hand, outside of established groups and schools and who, on the other hand, refused to jump on the bandwagon of the Proletarians (whose writing they considered too polemical to qualify as genuine art). Publishers recognized the value of these labels. Shinchōsha, a leading promoter of the new non-Marxist writers, scored a major success with its twenty-four-volume *Shinkō Geijutsu Ha Sōsho* series, featuring authors such as Ryūtanji, Yoshiyuki, Abe Tomoji, and Ibuse; Kaizōsha soon responded with a *Shin'ei Bungaku Sōsho* series in sixteen volumes, which included some of the same authors, among them Ibuse.[12]

The writers themselves were not immune to this flocking instinct, despite their differences in background and style. Not only was it a conventional enough phenomenon in both Japanese society at large and in the literary world; it seemed to be a self-preservation tactic as well, as they found themselves struggling to avoid oblivion in the face of the Proletarian ascendancy. The early Shōwa years saw the formation of a number of groups and magazines dedicated to providing support and exposure for non-Marxist writers. Ibuse participated in the groups that put out the magazines *Bungei Toshi* in 1928 and 1929, along with such writers as Abe Tomoji, Funahashi Seiichi, and Kajii Motojirō, and *Sakuhin*, starting in May 1930, with, among others, Kobayashi Hideo, Kawakami Tetsutarō, and Nagai Tatsuo. The largest of these shifting combinations appeared in April 1930 with the assembly of a thirty-two-member Shinkō Geijutsu Ha Kurabu. Ryūtanji sought to establish himself as a spokesman for this group and the movement it purported to represent; another important organizer was Nakamura Murao, an anti-Proletarian theoretician and editor at Shinchōsha. Ibuse was one of the writers invited to attend the organizational meeting, and his recollection of the event, recorded thirty-three years later, makes clear both the group's main raison d'être and its lack of focus, as well as his own discomfort with it:

> I don't remember who first came up with the name Shinkō Geijutsu Ha. The first time I heard it was at a meeting of the editorial board of *Bungei Toshi*. We had invited four guests, Ryūtanji Yū, Kuno Toyohiko, Tsubota Jōji, and Nakamura Masatsune, all considered promising young writers at the time, and at this meeting I

heard Ryūtanji Yū and Kuno agree that they should work to establish the literature of the Shinkō Geijutsu Ha. Soon afterward a Shinkō Geijutsu Ha meeting was held at Ryūtanji's and Kuno's prompting. About forty people attended including myself, but I didn't know what the literature of the Shinkō Geijetsu Ha was supposed to be. Ryūtanji, who was the moderator of this meeting and also served as a kind of chairman, said that first of all we members had to cooperate with each other in finding the way to live our lives. He stressed that this was necessary in order for us to write the kind of fiction we all wanted to write. I think that is basically what happened; on the advice of Hori Tatsuo, I didn't attend any more of these meetings.[13]

With or without the participation of Hori and Ibuse, the Shinkō Geijutsu Ha was doomed to failure. Despite the perceived need for solidarity and mutual support, the diversity of the group's intended membership was an inherent weakness which could not be overcome; and attempts to create at least a semblance of unity by developing a coherent theoretical framework in the manner of other twentieth-century Japanese literary movements such as the Naturalists, Neo-Perceptionists, and Proletarians came to naught.[14] Even though many of its members did go on to illustrious careers,[15] the group never became a force to be reckoned with; in fact, the inaugural meeting described by Ibuse turned out to be its last.

At any rate, there are other, more substantial reasons for associating Ibuse with the members of this group. Like many of them, he turns away from the usual themes of most of his predecessors and contemporaries, be they the intense self-absorption and way-seeking of the urban intelligentsia (especially writers), the aesthetic and psychological concerns of writers such as Tanizaki and Kawabata, or the struggles of revolutionary activists and workers in the Proletarian vein. He creates a world that is explicitly escapist, at least on the surface, whether in the backwoods valleys of Kuchisuke and Mr. Tange, the floating apartment off Shigure Island, or the more familiar metropolitan landscape of *Josefu*. While many of his characters are old and countrified, in contrast to the usual cast of *ero-guro-nansensu* types, they share with the denizens of the urban entertainment subculture a lack of self-consciousness that sets them apart from characters in more conventional fiction. At the same time, the presence of the narrator as a kind of exile from the city provides an element of the urban identity expected by readers of the day.

Combining with this unorthodox subject matter to give Ibuse's stories the feeling of freshness characteristic of *Modanizumu* was his distinctive style.

Tongue-in-cheek rhetorical flourishes, sometimes gently and sometimes pointedly ironic, mix with rustic dialect and the relatively informal conversational tone frequently adopted by the narrative voices to create a somewhat different effect from the breezy style of writers such as Ryūtanji, but both styles represent a marked departure from the dignified and often oblique minimalism typified by Shiga Naoya, which was widely held to be the model of Japanese prose style at the time. *Modanizumu* may have derived some of its stylistic novelties from the experiments of the Neo-Perceptionists, but for the Modernists style was not only a means of achieving a particular artistic effect or of recording one's observations as accurately or strikingly as possible; it was also consciously exploited for its entertainment value, for the interest inherent in unconventional uses of words for their own sake. Ibuse, whose style was distinctive in other respects, certainly shared this trait.

The rejection of convention in both subject matter and style was accompanied by another departure with important implications for comedy: for the first time in modern Japanese fiction, there was a sustained effort to turn away from the predominant notion that an explicitly serious stance was essential to maintain an elevated status for writers and writing. To inject a strong element of mirth into a work was to invite accusations of regression to the inconsequentiality of *rakugo* or the frivolity of the (largely discredited) *gesaku* fiction of the Edo period, tantamount to an abandonment of the writer's mission; but the Modernists self-consciously rejected the idea that only an overt display of serious purpose legitimized artistic expression.

In fact, accusations of triviality could in many cases stick, for the absence of a serious stance in the work of most Modernist writers was indeed accompanied by a paucity of substance. Despite the aura of modernity created by their subject matter and their use of *shinkō* (new) in Shinkō Geijutsu Ha, their approach can be seen as more of a throwback to some of the *sharebon* writers of the Edo period than an extension of modern fiction. Their main objective was to capture the details of an exciting, unstable way of life while they were still fresh, and to do it in a way that relied more on novel subject matter and vocabulary than on innovative technique, psychological depth, or critical perspective. Once the freshness of their way of life disappeared, their only real claim to distinction vanished with it.

As a movement or market phenomenon, Modernism proved to have little more staying power than the Shinkō Geijutsu Ha did as an organization. Losing their mass readership and critical backing almost as quickly as they had acquired them, many of the Modernist writers soon found themselves relegated to a marginal status from which they were never to reemerge. Growing government control over literary expression, Japanese society's gradual shift to a war footing following the Manchurian Incident in 1931, and the Modernists' own failure to develop a coherent vision have each been adduced as the crucial factor in their demise. No doubt each played a part, but the shortcomings of the writers and the works themselves played a major role.

Ibuse was the most conspicuous exception to this tendency. Many of his stories from this period, including several once categorized as "nonsense" works, continue to be reprinted, read, and taken as objects of critical study; and the *nansensu* phase of his career is now almost entirely obscured. With the wisdom of hindsight, it is easy to detect in stories such as *Kuchisuke*, *Tange-shi tei*, or even *Josefu* flashes of the humaneness and acute powers of observation that were to characterize his entire oeuvre; but at the time these were easily overlooked amid the nonsensical goings-on on the surface, especially by readers who were predisposed by the author's reputation to consider him simply another member of the Shinkō Geijutsu Ha.

At the same time, Ibuse was also publishing works that, while they contain some of his typical comic elements, are devoid of overtly "grotesque" trappings and display the depth and quiet mastery of technique which were, in the long run, to provide the basis of his mature comic style. The earliest examples of this are two works that remain among his best known, *Sanshōuo* (Salamander, 1923) and *Koi*. These antedate the works from the *nansensu* period; but each was later republished in a reworked form, suggesting their particular importance to the young author; and it was the reworked versions which gained attention.[16]

As the titles indicate, both stories take animals as central figures; in the case of *Sanshōuo*, perhaps the most widely anthologized of all Ibuse's stories, they constitute the entire cast of characters. Though obviously allegorical, this tale of a salamander imprisoned in a tiny cave because his head has grown too large to fit through the opening is no Aesopian fable with a simple, easily identifiable "moral." Elusive and understated, it depicts, in highly ironic and apparently self-mocking terms, a soul trapped by its own shortcomings, and a series of responses to this hopeless condition which are simultaneously depressing and comical. The feeling of immobility and frustration that pervades many of Ibuse's early stories here takes the more compelling and ironic form of self-incarceration. The grim paradox of being restricted from all but the most trivial actions while one's mind remains aware of all the possibilities of freedom immediately suggests the often-portrayed predicament, or at least the self-image, of the modern intellectual in an authoritarian society. In *Sanshōuo*, though, the allegorical setting and all-animal cast impart a resonance that transcends any particular social context. At the same time, while the animals, especially the salamander, are not without their share of the quirks that mark so many of Ibuse's human characters, the absence of a specific context makes it difficult to dismiss them as a mere assortment of eccentrics.

An equally important source of the story's strength lies in its masterly tonal balance. Blatant bathos and histrionics alternate with passages of quiet, closely observed detail, while the desperation of the salamander's self-imposed predicament, the cruelty with which he imposes the same predicament on a frog who innocently wanders into his chamber, and the pettiness and self-deception of both animals create a mix of absurdity, irony, suffering, and despair most unconventional for its day (but anticipating the black humor of a later age).

The pattern is set in the first few lines. Starting with the declaration *Sanshōuo wa kanashinda* ("The salamander felt sad," 1: 3), Ibuse gives a brief account of the animal's gloomy chamber and the circumstances that led to its self-imprisonment. The salamander's next remark, *Nan taru shissaku de aru koto ka!* (loosely translatable as "What a foul-up!") is both the point of departure and also a kind of essence of Ibuse's distinctive comic voice, simultaneously a poignant, heartfelt lament and a pompous, pretentious expression of abiding misperception. While some of the poignancy was to disappear as Ibuse's style developed, the gentle expression of regret for the countless follies caused by human delusion, and only partially understood even after their disastrous consequences have unfolded, continues to reverberate through much of his later work.

At times the voice of the disembodied narrator intrudes to elucidate the salamander's failure to understand its situation: when, in the depths of despair over its inability to escape or even move about, it proclaims, "Iyoiyo derarenai to iu naraba, ore ni mo sōtō na kangae ga aru n da" (If I can't get out after all, well, I've got my own idea), the narrator immediately informs us that of course it had no such thing (1: 4). But the salamander's own declarations also repeatedly reveal the same failure. At one point it gazes down from its chamber at a school of tiny fish swimming in a pool:

> They seemed to enjoy swimming between the stalks of the water plants. They swarmed among the stalks, each trying not to be swept along by the river current. The school would lurch first right, then left, and if one of them should lurch to the left by mistake, the rest would all lurch to the left too, so as not to be left behind. If one of them was obstructed by one of the stalks and had to lurch to the right the rest would all follow his lead. Thus, it seemed to be extremely difficult for any one of them to run off freely from all the others. The salamander looked down on these little fish with a sneer. "What a totally unfree bunch they are!" (1: 5)

In the school of fish mindlessly executing leftward and rightward pirouettes with no other objective than conformity, we may see a characteristically oblique Ibusean swipe at those writers who had jumped on the Proletarian bandwagon more out of an instinctive fear of being left behind than from any deeply held conviction. But the irony is compounded by the salamander's comment on their lack of freedom (*Nan to iu, fujiyū senban na yatsura de arō!*), which quickly restores his own place as the comic focus.

As the salamander's desperation intensifies, so does the self-righteous warp in his viewpoint. Following an unsuccessful escape effort, he tearfully proclaims: "Oh Lord! Your ways are cruel. How oppressive of you to imprison me in this crypt forever, just because I neglected to leave it for a mere two years or so! I think I'm about to go insane!" (1: 7). The descent to a new level of delusion occurs when the salamander spitefully imprisons the frog, and the two of them pass their days trading taunts and intensifying their resolution to imprison themselves indefinitely.

Since the structure of *Sanshōuo* allows for no on-stage narrator whose self-deprecation and self-pity can be balanced against the comic traits of the other characters, the narrative voice has a more "objective" role than in other stories. Sometimes it adopts the familiar pompous tone to fine comic effect: "Ladies and gentlemen, you may never have seen a deranged salamander, but who could say that such a tendency was not present to a certain degree in the case of this salamander? One must acknowledge the fact that he had already been immersed in darkness so long that he was sick of it, and was no longer able to endure it. Does not even the leper beg ceaselessly for release from the chamber that encloses him? Does not even the most misanthropic of prisoners wish for that very same thing?" (1: 7). When the salamander, in the depths of self-pity, likens himself to a scrap of tin (*buriki no kirikuzu*), the narrator adds: "There must be no one who would enjoy trying to imagine himself in terms that are utterly absurd. Only those who have had their hearts torn by misfortune would consider thinking of themselves as a scrap of tin. Yes, these will certainly sink their hands deep into their pockets and lose themselves in idle thought, or wipe their sweaty hands on their vests; there are none as likely to indulge in cutting the pose of their choice, whatever it might be, as they" (1: 8).

But the narrative voice is not always so ironic, and absurdity is never permitted to overwhelm the sense of pathos. When the salamander becomes dizzy watching flower petals disappear in the center of a whirlpool, or when he shuts his eyes after watching two water bugs and the frog gamboling in the pool, afraid that the stimulation might prove too much for him, and leaves them shut because "the freedom, the possibility, of opening his eyelids and shutting them was all that was left to him" (1: 8), the horror of his fate is recalled sparely but forcefully.

A succession of finely observed, carefully placed details creates a contrapuntal effect against the absurdity and despair. As in other Ibuse works, the impersonal, inexorable flow of time and life evoked by these details also makes the ultimate insignificance of the things that engage the characters' attention all too evident. Particular care is devoted to the two varieties of moss that grow on the roof of the chamber: "The greenish scales of the liverwort spread out in a pattern like that of *jisho tori* [a type of children's amusement], while delicate blossoms bloomed on the ends of the thinnest red stems of the hair moss. The delicate blossoms turned into delicate berries which, in accord with the laws of seed dispersal among cryptogamic plants, soon began to scatter their pollen" (1: 4).

Sanshōuo's narration, continually filtering the events through a finely developed sensibility and expressing them in a style that subtly reflects that sensibility, evokes the strain of subjective lyricism associated with such classical forms as *zuihitsu* (prose miscellany) and *nikki* (poetic diary). *Zuihitsu* echoes are even stronger in *Koi*, a work that hovers on an ill-defined boundary between fiction and nonfiction in both subject matter and treatment.[17] As in many early Ibuse stories, the narrative voice belongs to a first-person, on-stage authorial alter ego, but this time he is the central figure rather than a passive observer, making this one of Ibuse's closer approaches to the *shishōsetsu* genre. The tone is gently lyrical as the narrator expresses his sense of loss and sadness at the death of his friend Aoki Nanpachi, filtered through contemplative recollection and embodied in the magnificent white carp that Aoki had given him as a token of their friendship. But even here, the motif of comic failure of self-knowledge glimmers through, this time embodied solely in the narrating "I." As he recalls, when he arranged to keep the fish in a pond in the garden of Aoki's lover's house, his excessive insistence on maintaining full rights of ownership even while he was giving up physical possession of it only served to upset his friend. Six years later, the same narrator who had busied himself with finding a new home for the fish, carefully removing parasites from its scales, and measuring its length, failed to notice that the man whose friendship made the fish so precious was dying: "I had often gone to visit his sickbed, but it never occurred to me in the least that he was seriously ill. In fact, I would get upset when he wouldn't accompany me on walks, and I smoked cigarettes at his bedside" (1: 14).

At this point, a subtle comic agon emerges as the narrator seeks to regain possession of the carp from Aoki's ex-lover as a way of both assuaging his guilt feelings toward Aoki and pressing his own claim to custodial rights to Aoki's memory. When he sends her a highly punctilious letter requesting permission to retrieve the fish from her pond, she consents but points out, in equally decorous terms, the impropriety of indulging in fishing while still in mourning.

When he finally enters her garden, Ibuse portrays the contrast between the intensity of his character's feelings and the meekness of his actions in language that points obliquely at his unawareness of, or his inability to admit to, the powerful feelings in his heart:

> Early Sunday morning, I took a box lunch, fishing pole, bait, and a basin and stole into the garden of the late Aoki Nanpachi's lover. I was feeling not a little excited. I should have brought her letter with me, just in case.
>
> The loquats, already a ripe yellow, stimulated my appetite. Moreover, I noticed that the foliage on the various plants around the pond had grown so dense that I could not be seen from the second-floor window or from the verandah, so I turned my pole upside down and knocked some loquats from the tree. It was almost evening before I managed to land the carp, and so I ended up eating without permission quite a number of loquats. (1: 15)

"Comedy" is almost too strong a word for this, even though the obtuseness depicted is essentially similar to that portrayed more broadly in other Ibuse stories. As in *Sanshōuo*, the comic element is fastidiously modulated and balanced, this time not with gloomy desperation but with elegiac lyricism. With its formal, precise sentences woven elliptically around a series of loosely connected incidents, *Koi* simultaneously captures the quiet intensity of a friendship, a poignant sense of loss, and the ironies of the narrator's behavior without straying into a sentimentality or sarcasm which would shatter the overall effect.

Much as *Sanshōuo* moves from an initial predicament growing out of the salamander's flawed character to a state of acceptance, or at least understanding, in a way that is frequently cited as characteristic of comedy, *Koi* progresses, however waywardly, from the note of distress sounded in the opening line ("For over ten years now I have been troubled by a carp," 1: 11) to a feeling of relief in the final scene, in which the narrator traces the outline of his noble carp on the frozen surface of its final home, the Waseda University pool, and concludes, "*Sukkari manzoku shita*" (I was completely satisfied). It is clear that the immediate motivation for this is his catching a view of the magnificent carp leading a school of lesser fish, reminding him that the spirit of his noble friend lives on; it is not so clear whether this suggests a coming to terms with inevitable death and evitable consequences of one's own folly, or is tinged with a continuation of that folly as he savors the carp's presence in the Waseda University pool, a great good place of male friendship that bonds him with Aoki's memory and excludes the troublesome female. If it is the former, we are dealing with comedy of a high order; if the latter, something more akin to an extended Bergsonian joke. In all likelihood, we are dealing with both, and indeed much of Ibuse's comedy ends up resting, with varying degrees of comfort, somewhere in the space between elevated human spirit and incorrigible human nature.

Sanshōuo and *Koi*, then, show that from the very outset of his career Ibuse was capable of integrating comic elements with the finely attenuated sense of pathos and stylistic subtleties that would eventually bring him acceptance as a "serious" writer. Under a surface frivolity, even his stories deemed *nansensu* contain some of these subtle qualities; and they were being noted and praised by critics such as Kobayashi Hideo[18] before the tide of Modernism and *ero-guro-nansensu* ebbed away. But comic elements are not the distinguishing characteristics of Ibuse's works from the 1920s that continue to be reprinted and read today. Instead, quiet lyricism and gentle irony overshadow the eccentric characters and their foibles in such stories as *Sanshōuo*, *Koi*, *Yofuke to ume no hana*, and *Yane no ue no Sawan* (Sawan on the Roof,

1929). Except for *Tange-shi tei*, the *nansensu*-period works in which the comic strain predominates have not fared so well; few are now read or discussed critically with any frequency, and most, including *Josefu* and *Shigure-tō*, were long out of print.[19]

While the early comic stories can still be read with enjoyment, it is apparent that Ibuse's control over his materials was not so sure in these stories as it was in the more lyrical works such as *Sanshōuo* and *Koi*, where the reality of suffering and death precludes a predominantly comic tone but the subsidiary comic touches effectively prevent a lapse into excesses of sentimentality or melancholy. In stories such as *Josefu* and *Shigure-tō*, where there is no such serious suffering, comedy, lyricism, and melancholy are combined less skillfully: the exaggerated characters and situations create comic expectations, but the lyricism and melancholy tone expressed through the narrative voice confuse the issue. Moreover, while comedy (as opposed to humor) generally requires a relatively clear structure and thematic focus, the quirks and foibles of the characters in these stories fail to add up to any perceptible themes. The vanity and petty tyranny of Mr. Tange expressed through his abuse of his servant, coupled with the relatively restrained self-mockery of the narrator, make *Tange-shi tei* something of an exception to this pattern, and undoubtedly do much to account for its relatively favorable reputation.

It was only after Ibuse introduced a more detached, objective narrative tone and a clearer thematic structure into his comic works that they could truly come into their own. Uncomfortable with the *nansensu* label and the Modernist movement even during their heyday,[20] he was already taking important steps in this process before he had completed the last of his nonsense stories by beginning to branch out into areas such as essays and historical fiction. In broad panoramas of war and natural disaster such as *Kawa* (The River, 1931–1932), *Sazanami gunki* (Waves, 1930–1938), and *Aogashima taigaiki* (An Account of Aogashima, 1934), there is little room for the wistfully sad, self-mocking alter-ego narrator of the nonsense stories; and the narrative voice is endowed with a new impersonality and objectivity.

As might be expected from the grim subject matter, there is little of the comic in any of these works; but by establishing in them his ability to create extended fictions that focused squarely on the external world rather than the personal preoccupations of the narrator, Ibuse laid the groundwork for a new phase in his comic writing as well. There were signs of this new style in the stories *Nyonin raihō* (A Female Visitor, 1933) and *Suri no Sanzaburō*

(Sanzaburō the Sneak Thief, 1933), and in 1935 he published the first portion of what was to become *Shūkin ryokō* (The Bill-Collecting Trip), a story which marked a turning point in his development as a comic writer.

Longer and more elaborate than any of his previous comic works, *Shūkin ryokō* retains familiar provincial settings and an unnamed, rather ineffectual participant-narrator, but there is much less emphasis on the emotional state of this figure. There is also a shift away from fantasy, lyricism, and the margins of Japanese life toward the observation of characters and situations which, for all their distortions, have the unmistakable feel of real life.

The story opens inauspiciously for a comedy, with the sudden death of a rooming-house operator, a friend of the narrator, shortly after his wife had run off with one of the student-boarders; he leaves behind a six-year-old son, Yūta, a mortgage on the building, and few visible assets. But Ibuse immediately establishes a comic mood with a fluid, slightly breathless cadence and a few deft strokes of detail portraying the deceased man's response to his wife's desertion: "From that time on, the proprietor became completely engrossed in *shōgi*, and when a game was going in his favor it became his habit to launch into a monologue on the certainty of his finding a beauty for his next wife. But just when he was on the point of beginning his search for a new wife, he suddenly caught pneumonia and keeled over" (2: 3).

The focus quickly moves from the dead man to the survivors, who, after a certain amount of indecorous haggling, agree to send the narrator, a typically Ibusean man of enforced leisure and righteous instincts, to collect what he can from the many boarders who left without paying their rent over the years, including the student. As he plans an itinerary through western Honshu and northern Kyushu, he is joined by one of the boarders, Komatsu-san, an "extremely beautiful but middle-aged single lady" (*taihen bijin de wa aru ga chūnen no dokushin fujin*, 2: 3). Hearing that the narrator plans to visit a delinquent ex-boarder in Iwakuni, she announces that she will come along and "squeeze some consolation money" (*isharyō o makiagete kuru*, 2: 9) from an evil ex-lover of hers living in the same town; if all goes well, she may even be able to clear the mortgage on the rooming house and provide some help for young Yūta. The narrator and an associate try to dissuade her, pointing out that their respective missions are totally unrelated and, besides, there are also debtors to be visited in Fukuoka, Onomichi, Okayama, Kobe, and Gifu, whereupon Komatsu-san primly springs another surprise: "Is that so? Well, if that's what you think, there's something I'd like to tell you, too. I also have old lovers in Fukuoka, and Onomichi, and Osaka and Okayama and Gifu, not just in Iwakuni. I'll take this opportunity to go and collect some consolation money from all of them" (2: 10). Thus one of those fortuitous improbabilities more common in comedy than in real life provides the impetus for the picaresque journey that occupies the bulk of the story, and also for one of its two main comic premises, the unlikely pair (or odd couple) who repeatedly bring each other's deceptions, idiosyncrasies, and misperceptions into sharp relief.

There is an obvious parallel here with Jippensha Ikku's Edo *gesaku* classic *Tōkaidōchū hizakurige*. Like Kitahachi and Yajirōbei, the traveling duo of that story, Komatsu-san and the narrator would each be of much less interest on his or her own; it is the juxtaposition of the two that makes the story succeed. But where Ikku's pair were friends and partners, albeit each with his own distinctive personality, the entirely different missions and styles (and sexes) of Ibuse's twosome, thrown together by coincidence and convenience, allow for a broader range of possibilities. In their separate fundraising campaigns, they are repeatedly brought together only to separate again, but their individual and shared adventures and misadventures develop an internal rhythm and soon come to overshadow the original purpose of the trip.

Most of the comedy in their relationship grows out of the contrasts in personality and style shown in his confrontations with the deadbeats and hers with the dubious ex-lovers, rather than from scenes of direct interaction between the two. Despite occasional moments of weakness and self-consciousness, this narrator, in contrast to those in *Shigure-tō* or *Josefu*, is no abject, apologetic figure. There is a note of assurance in his voice, and he is more willing than they to pass judgment on the other characters. Less of a passive observer, he takes on a more important role within the action of the story. He feels less need to remain within the good graces of others; when he returns to his inn dead drunk after a night on the town and inadvertently ends up in someone else's bed, he makes only the barest of apologies and amusedly dismisses the event as a "horrid gaffe" (*tonde mo nai fushimatsu*, 2: 34). His confidence and toughness are also apparent in his failure to be intimidated by the beautiful, strong-willed Komatsu-san. He enjoys challenging her with typically Ibusean understated insinuations and freely offers his suggestions, solicited or otherwise, on how she might best handle her highly delicate personal negotiations.

This more self-assured narrator probably reflects a new sense of confidence on the part of the author. Ibuse was no longer the obscure, struggling *fugū na bungaku seinen* of the *Koi* and *Sanshōuo* days; he had already outlasted the Proletarians and outgrown the Modernists, and as the literary sectarianism of the 1920s receded in the 1930s, he could feel vindicated in having taken his own approach. Another sign of this new self-assurance in *Shūkin ryokō* is Ibuse's insertion of a minor character named Tsuruya Yūzō, a delinquent exboarder dangling precariously between the conditions of would-be writer and has-been would-be writer. The son of a well-to-do family in the village of Kamo, Hiroshima Prefecture, Yūzō has returned home after a spell at Waseda University. He had managed to publish a few pieces in a coterie magazine but, according to Komatsu-san, he was too fat to cut a respectable literary figure, and his return to the country was a consequence of "having reached the end of his financial tether" (*kurashi no yukitsumatte*) in Tokyo (2: 59). This sardonic portrait of the artist as a young man, even with certain allowances for caricature, is far more precise, and far more detached, than anything that had come before; and this time it lacks the more sympathetic features invariably present in earlier incarnations of the Ibusean alter ego.

Like most Ibusean mouthpieces, the narrator of *Shūkin ryokō* has a strong sense of justice. He is collecting for a worthy cause and not for his own use. Surer of the righteousness of his mission than of the right way to go about it, he plans his strategies carefully, displays impeccable manners at all times, and insists on observing the full punctilio of introductory letters and sealed receipts that accompanies such transactions in Japan, despite the obvious indifference, boorishness, or outright hostility of the people whose money he is collecting. He feels a simple-minded, self-satisfied joy when he succeeds and struggles to suppress his disappointment when he fails.

Komatsu-san, one of Ibuse's relatively rare female protagonists, provokes her share of illuminating reactions from the narrator, but she is also notable as a figure in her own right rather than a mere object of the narrator's powers of observation; in fact, she succeeds in drawing the focus of the story away from him to an unprecedented degree. Initially she vaguely resembles a kind of adult descendant of Kuchisuke's granddaughter Taeto and the unnamed niece in *Josefu*, simultaneously ingenuous and seductive, vulnerable and scheming; but before long, through her own words and the restrained description by the narrator, she is revealed as a far more commanding figure.

Throughout the story, we see Komatsu-san in a dizzying succession of moods and actions, now soothing and polished, now alarmingly brash. Her manner is usually offhand, almost breezy; but when confronted by a stubborn adversary or a difficult situation, she calls on formidable reserves of toughness and cunning. We come to see fragments of her outrageous past, her beguiling and exasperating idiosyncrasies, and her keen instinct for protecting her own interests even while seemingly allowing herself to be victimized.

In contrast to the narrator's dutifulness (*giri*) and consistency, Komatsu-san's collection style is characterized by an appeal to human feelings (*ninjō*) and flexibility. Pledges of aid to Yūta notwithstanding, she is collecting money for herself, and her approach is by turns harsh and intimidating, casual and coquettish, or coolly businesslike, depending on her assessment of the prospective donor. She is convinced of her right to all the money she can extract from each man, explaining her dubious past away as a period when circumstances beyond her control turned her into a "bad girl" (*yamu o enai furyō shōjo*, 2: 23), but some of her negotiations lead to entirely unexpected outcomes. Her freewheeling approach provides a counterpoint to the narrator's rigidity at the same time that he quietly exposes the paradox between the ingenuous and the scheming elements in her personality.

Occasionally the two are played off against each other directly in comic scenes. Ibuse gets some mileage out of their repeated predicaments when other characters jump to the wrong conclusions about the pair of travelers or when Komatsu-san needs to conceal her companion's existence while playing or (overplaying) the role of the wronged woman with her ex-lovers. They also enjoy the opportunities that come their way to needle each other by gently playing on their weaknesses or vanities. After upsetting him by telling one of her ex-lovers that he is accompanying her as a traveling secretary, she compensates by allowing him to enter her as his secretary in the inn's guest resister. He soon finds more satisfying revenge when their taxi is stopped late at night by a hayseed policeman who is sure that Komatsu-san must be a geisha, even though she is "decked out like some fancy married lady" (*erō okusan-fū ni mekashikondoru na*) until the narrator quietly assures him that she is accompanying him on his journey as *his* secretary (2: 56).

While the relative ages of the narrator and Komatsu-san are not clear, there are strong echoes of the common Ibusean pattern of a repressed avuncular man played off against a spirited, usually younger woman. Frequently the erotic implications of these relationships are suppressed or evaded by the author; but Komatsu-san and the narrator are forced closer together than other pairs, and they gradually develop a kind of rapport which the others do not. He quickly develops a respect for her, and cannot help but feel somewhat attracted to her as well (like so many other men!) even if he cannot bring himself to admit it. The worldly Komatsu-san knows just what kind of effect she has on him and has little trouble waging a war of the sexes on two fronts. She also respects him; but in Ibuse's inhibited world even these feelings are usually left to drift below the surface, creating a tension which is only partially hinted at by the occasional exchanges of banter and needling.

As usual in Ibuse's fiction, the more intensely personal kind of truth emerges only inadvertently, and obliquely, and is then buried in a resumed flow of incident. One of the most telling moments comes shortly after Komatsu-san shakes off a hopelessly uncouth but very persistent suitor. When the narrator, having taken a perverse liking to the man, insists on telephoning him and advising him to give up the chase, she laughingly remarks, "You have pretty unusual tastes, don't you?" (*Anata mo zuibun monozuki na hito ne*). Embarrassed by her accuracy, and unable to admit that she has struck home, the narrator makes no reply. At the same time, he is too honest with himself to reject it or repress it completely, and his comment "this is indeed the case" (*masa ni sono tōri na no de aru*, 2: 51) marks this as one of those rare Ibusean moments when a fundamental truth is revealed. The emotional force is belied by his offhand tone, for her comment could apply as readily to the author as to the narrator, and has roots deep within his comic soul.

The *monozuki* predilection dates from Ibuse's earliest days as a writer, when he was an anxious outsider fixing his gaze on eccentric scenes on the margins of obscure country districts and the Tokyo metropolis. *Shūkin ryokō* is another expression of it; Komatsu-san herself, who has inadvertently penetrated so accurately the heart of the narrator, does not realize that in her own way she is as much an object of it as the other assorted characters, the customs, language, and landscapes encountered on the journey. Komatsu-san has created one of those occasions, rare but crucial in Ibuse's fiction, when two people can reveal that they see into each other's hearts for a fleeting instant. It is this, more than her beauty or her cool audacity, which makes the narrator feel attracted to her, respect her, and ultimately feel betrayed by her; but even this moment, for all its brevity, might not have been possible had it not been carefully camouflaged among numerous more comic incidents.

A final unmasking occurs in the town of Shin'ichi, after the narrator receives a letter sent by Komatsu-san from the home of an exceedingly wealthy citizen whom she had called upon as another source of consolation money: "I intend to stay on here awhile in the role of a housemaid. I will not see you again, because I'm afraid that my resolution would waver if I did. . . . I am ending my fundraising trip herewith. Please let me know how you are progressing from time to time. I may catch up with you and resume my own journey depending on my inclinations later, but as of now I expect that I will be able to live in peace here. . . . Please beware of food poisoning. Goodbye for now" (2: 65). Added to the letter is a postscript in a bold hand adding "Mr. Tsumura is currently a widower. He is a good person."

Even though his link with Komatsu-san was based entirely on coincidence and their feelings about each other have never been clearly stated, the narrator cannot help feeling a sense of betrayal. He sullenly hands over her luggage to the messenger who brought the letter and decides to leave the town promptly. Walking toward the station, he passes the Tsumura house, an imposing edifice with a row of earthen storehouses surrounded by a black earthen wall: "I stood in front of the gate and thought about shouting something in a loud voice, but since I wasn't qualified to do such a thing, I just passed on in silence. There was no reason to create bad blood between myself and her. And yet, I silently muttered to myself 'What an outrageous trick.' I wanted to move along quickly, but soon found myself coming to a halt and standing there again. And even as I thought to myself that it certainly wasn't true, I muttered the words 'What an outrageous trick,' over and over again" (2: 66).

On this note the story ends. To the extent that comedy involves the exposure of an incongruity between perceptions and realities, or between realities and ideals, this conclusion constitutes the main comic revelation of the nature of both characters: Komatsu-san, for all her bravura performances of the role of woman wronged, all her displays of righteousness and independence, and all her insistence that principles matter more than money, finally demonstrates that she, too, is all too human—*così fan tutte*. She enjoys the good fortune normally granted to comic characters who acknowledge the natural impulses of life and seems likely to enjoy also the happy ending most conventional in Western comedy and Japanese melodrama, a wedding.

Of course, in a truly conventional comedy, the revelation and wedding might have brought together the traveling Odd Couple in a final resolution of one of the narrative's central incongruities; but a more common Ibusean, or Japanese, comic fate falls to the narrator. Forced to see one more "reality" exposed as illusion and to face the true nature of his feelings toward Komatsu-san, he has wisdom to show for his reward rather than pleasure. For all his willingness to cling to the illusion that he has been betrayed, he also realizes that there was in fact nothing to betray, and is left to turn his frustration and disappointment in upon himself.

But the Odd Couple theme is only one of the main comic incongruities in *Shūkin ryokō*. Contrapuntally, there is a series of clashes between appearance and reality focusing on the delinquents visited by the narrator and the erstwhile lovers visited by Komatsu-san. Unlike the intensely personal theme of the pair, handled with reticence, these allow Ibuse ample scope to display his facility for caricature and satire. All of these characters are, or at least at one time were, well-off and well-respected figures in their own narrow provincial worlds, not petty impostors like Mr. Tange; and they do their best at bestriding these worlds in as colossal a fashion as their circumstances allow. This is obviously a precarious undertaking. Some, like Tsuruya Yūzō in his baggy morning coat and clogs at his grandfather's funeral, are merely innocuous walking incongruities; and Ibuse, himself the product of such a background, dwells on the details of their gardens and houses, their speech patterns, and their devious maneuverings with a mixture of fond indulgence and mordant sarcasm.

In other cases, especially those local magnates who abuse their power, the discrepancies between appearance and reality are dealt with more harshly. Komatsu-san's ex-lover in Iwakuni, for instance, is seen in his community as a "solemn and upright man of character" (*kingen jitchoku na jinkakusha*), a model citizen with a gracious wife from a highly respectable Tokyo family (2: 13). Unfazed by this reputation, Komatsu-san sets the record straight in no uncertain terms when she confronts him:

"Nozaki-san had told me that you and he were good friends, so I thought it would be all right to see you then. What's more, you came with a message for me from Nozaki-san, didn't you? You knew that Nozaki-san and I were engaged and that I was carrying his child, didn't you? And that after that I had a miscarriage . . ."

"The shame is more than I can bear. Disgraceful . . ."

"Even though I was your close friend's lover, and carrying his child, you acted like a brute. Nozaki-san had been your friend since you were children, hadn't he? So then, after Nozaki-san killed himself, and you said you'd take responsibility for the whole thing and proposed marriage to me, you turned around and proposed to a *gidayū* chanter, and went home to the country with her. That's what happened, isn't it?"

"Yes, it was completely inexcusable. You have me like a fish on a cutting board."

"I've held myself back from saying what I wanted to say for twenty years, but I finally decided to go ahead, so here I am. Perhaps I held back just a little too long . . ."

"It was all society's fault." (2: 19)

When the narrator, who happens to overhear this tirade, suggests that perhaps she was a bit too overbearing, she retorts that she was actually in a fright because the "model citizen" was holding her hand throughout the tirade! In Onomichi, she goes after an amateur blackmailer who had broken up one of her romances in Tokyo before returning home to succeed his father as proprietor of a small fishing fleet. After discussing the circumstances with the narrator, she decides to scale down her expectations from five hundred yen to fifty: "The better the man is, the more he's worth, is the idea. So for this one, fifty yen will probably be the best I can do" (2: 49). Komatsu-san's market-value approach mercilessly reveals one of *Shūkin ryokō*'s principal ironies: when respectable façades conceal unsavory pasts, the economic consequences are roughly the inverse of what common sense might suggest. Bad people should have to pay more, because their trespasses are worse, but they don't. It is the (relatively) good ones, who have a conscience that can be exploited, and more to lose from exposure, that have to pay the most. A similar contrast between reality and appearance is seen in a less intense form in the debtors visited by the narrator, all of whom are from propertied families; one of them, neatly enough, is the son of a moneylender.

Nevertheless, appearances and realities are not always so easy to sort out, as the narrator learns on a visit to the dental school dropout who ran off with the landlord's wife and who also owes the greatest amount of money. His family's home must have been an imposing compound at one time but is now a picture of ruin, with stunted barley and hemp seedlings growing where buildings used to stand. The narrator is greeted by a grumpy, suspicious middle-aged man speaking a rustic dialect, obviously the father, who sends him off to a nearby tin-roofed house in search of the son, only to reappear a few minutes later with the money and a crude invitation to the narrator to make himself scarce forthwith. But when the narrator returns to his inn, he discovers that the "madman in the haunted house" (*bakeyashiki no okichigai*, 2: 39) is another of Komatsu-san's ex-lovers, a gentle soul (according to her) whose only remaining joy in life comes from quietistic pastimes such as bonsai. He can also speak flawless standard Japanese. Struck by the miserable state into which he had fallen over the years since they had last met, she left him some "consolation money" instead of asking for any—money which soon ended up in the hands of the narrator.

It is tempting to believe that Komatsu-san is the one who has seen the man's true identity, and that the narrator only saw an act devised to ward off further persecution by an excessively cruel world. But it is more likely that both faces are genuine. Like the salamander or Isaku, he is too complex to be consistent, too human to be reduced to a formula. Neither Komatsu-san nor the narrator can see more than one of his facets, and their collision of misapprehensions creates one of the comic high points of the story.

Comedy functions on a number of other levels in *Shūkin ryokō*, some of which are familiar from earlier stories, while others take advantage of the new possibilities offered by a more elaborate structure. One of the familiar sources is the mosaic of social patterns and types. From the opening account of the lodging house and its proprietor through all the stages on the journey, it is filled with sharply etched vignettes of rickshaw pullers, chambermaids, a policeman, a taxi driver, and other everyday people, presented through oblique snatches of dialogue or sharply observed details of dress or mannerism.

There is a wide range of colorful secondary characters, both in Tokyo and on the road. The late landlord's son Yūta is simultaneously pathetic and faintly ridiculous. Overwhelmed by the tragedies that have overtaken him and by the unfamiliar adult world into which he has suddenly been thrust, the timid boy takes refuge (like his father) in his favorite amusements, so much so that the narrator can drive him to tears by failing to be properly impressed when he sets off some nice loud caps. It would have been easy to reduce him to a generic object of sentimentality and leave out unappealing little flaws, but, as in the case of Kuchisuke and the salamander, Ibuse's gentle but firm selection of detail prevents this.

A richer gallery of comic vignettes is found in the country. Many are little more than passing flashes of local color, played off against the travelers as specimens of a more easy-going way of life in the early stages of an irreversible decline, as when an oafish young man the narrator encounters in a fishing village, walking along barefoot in an army reservist's uniform, with Harold Lloyd glasses and a tiny mustache, responds to a civil request for directions with only a rude question of his own: "Whadda yah wanna go ovah to Okano's foah? Cause I think Okano's son is an arse" (2: 53).

Ibuse sardonically recounts the episode of a self-made fishing boat broker humiliated at a village meeting because he is unable to write out high-flown words he uses. The instinctive suspicion of outsiders, the obsession with maintaining appearances at all costs, the ostentatious recitation of big-city exploits more imaginary than real, and other conventional traits of the rural grand bourgeoisie are subjected to the same deadpan but deadly treatment.

The most developed of all these provincial figures is Dr. Minoya, the obstetrician introduced to Komatsu-san as a prospective marriage match by a wily ex-lover. Uninhibited lovers, who lend themselves readily enough to treatment as comic butts, tend to look particularly ridiculous from Ibuse's acerbic point of view; and Dr. Minoya, who seems to have become infatuated with Komatsu-san even before having laid eyes on her, is among the least inhibited, and most fatuous, of all. Before she meets him, Komatsu-san has already decided that he must be a dull, flaccid follower of the eminent rogue who had mistreated her, and an incompetent to boot—otherwise that gentleman would never introduce her to a member of his own circle. Her intuition, as usual, proves accurate; the doctor reveals himself to be a paragon of uncouthness who rouses her from her sleep for a meeting that he treats as an impromptu marriage interview, leaving him smitten and her contemptuous. Blind to Komatsu-san's cold-shoulder treatment, he attempts to join the traveling party and carefully follows their every move. When the travelers finally manage to elude him and the narrator telephones him to put a clean end to the affair, he finds himself talking to a geisha who tells him that the doctor is too busy to come to the phone, leaving him with one more illusion dispelled.

The surprise twists and turns that punctuate the plot, repeatedly upsetting the expectations of readers and characters alike and reminding them that no assumption is safe, constitute another comic dimension. Komatsu-san's revelations about the number and location of her former lovers, her sudden resolution to join the trip, the narrator's "horrid gaffe" and subsequent discovery that his host was Dr. Minoya, his inadvertent stumbling into a country funeral banquet, and the realization that one of the ex-boarders he has visited is the son of one of the ex-lovers visited by Komatsu-san are all lightning assaults on the expected flow of events, keeping the story from "developing" in a coherent way until it is suddenly ended by the ultimate reversal, Komatsu-san's disappearance into the household of one of her old tormentors. Creating a comic pattern of their own that punctuates the apparently steady progress of the journey, they serve to emphasize that the true "story" in *Shūkin ryokō* hinges on the interplay of the characters rather than on their actions. When Komatsu-san leaves, the story is over, even though the narrator will continue his own trip. The original goal of collecting money to redeem the boarding house and help Yūta, which the reader might have expected to be of some importance, is revealed in hindsight to have been a mere pretext for an account of Komatsu-san's rather different collection trip.

Shūkin ryokō also reflects changes in Ibuse's prose style that were already apparent in stories such as *Nyonin raihō* and *Suri no Sanzaburō* but reach a kind of culmination here. The conspicuously stiff, translation-like syntax is still occasionally used to comic effect, but most of the story is told in a looser, fast-paced style that creates an effect much closer to the rhythms and texture of ordinary spoken Japanese and is admirably suited to the increased length and picaresque mode of the story. At no time, though, do the dialogue or the narration become ordinary "talk"; they are sprinkled with offbeat Chinese and English terms, colorful localisms, and the pointed turns of phrase so characteristic of Ibuse's comic writing. While Ibuse had employed this more natural style in less comic works from early on (*Koi* being a good example), the ability to utilize its comic potential in *Shūkin ryokō* confirms his maturation as a comic writer.

The broadened scope of *Shūkin ryokō*, in both the number and variety of characters and the variety of situations and settings, enables Ibuse to exploit the comic possibilities of dialogue in a way impossible in the shorter works. This is most evident in the rapid-fire switches between formal and informal or polite and rough speech in the exchanges between the narrator and Komatsu-san, but it also shines through in the speech of the minor characters. Ibuse had an ear for the everyday speech of non-intellectuals uncommon in modern Japanese fiction and, even rarer, an ability to reproduce it in a manner both comic and telling. He was at his best when he manipulated the wide range of tonalities and politeness levels and the rich lode of vagueness available to Japanese speakers to illustrate the resourceful scheming and understated give-and-take of personalities that constitute the fabric of the story. Such passages, of course, are generally robbed of much of their effectiveness in translation, but a glimpse may be obtained in a scene from the memorial service for the landlord, where the businessman to whom he had mortgaged his building spars with Goban-san, the boarder who had taken on responsibility for disposing of the estate:

"But isn't it true, sir, that you are in fact as well as in name the co-signatory of this loan agreement? Judging from what we have been able to see since the bereavement, the man hasn't left a single relative, has he?"

"In other words, as long as your interest gets paid, it'll be all right, no?"

Goban-san seemed to have picked up his spirits, thinking that I must have come as an ally.

"We both live in the same neighborhood, so do you really have to be so merciless?"

Goban-san looked ready to drive Korando off, but his adversary also had no shortage of nerve:

"Merciless? I'm astounded. I only desire to consult with you, in order to determine who should assume responsibility. That is all."

"Anyway it'll be paid. I said I'll pay, and I mean I'll pay."

"Of course, as long as I can receive my payments I shall be satisfied, but . . ." (2: 6)

Ambiguity, always a promising source for comic dualities, is particularly effective in the rigidly conventionalized but eternally vague realm of Japanese social discourse. Sometimes it is tantalizingly impossible to judge whether or not the vagueness is intentional, as when the narrator returns to his inn in Iwakuni to be told by the proprietor, *Ima, oheya ni goraikyaku ga arimasu desu ga nō* (Um, there's a visitor in your room just now, so . . .) and is left to wonder whether this means that he has arrived just in time or that he is being warned not to interrupt Komatsu-san during one of her negotiations (2: 18). More often, it takes the form of calculated obfuscation in situations requiring delicate handling. When Dr. Minoya attempts to join the traveling party at Fukuoka, Komatsu-san tries to rebuff him with a smooth combination of acknowledgment of the payment, apology for having caused him to go to such trouble, and regards to be conveyed to her ex-lover, prefaced by an unobtrusive but pointed *De wa, kore de shitsurei itashimasu* (Well, then, that's all for now). The undaunted doctor also tries his hand at the game, countering with *Iya, kesshite sono ten wa goshinpai naku, dō itashimashite, daijōbu desu* (Oh, no, please do not worry about it at all, you're welcome, everything is fine) and proceeds to ask the narrator, *Zutto chokkō desu ka* (Going straight on?). The narrator, well aware that the doctor is actually trying to ferret out their destination, merely mumbles something to the effect of yes, they are (2: 44).

Repetition, another staple of comic language, is exploited by Ibuse to concisely establish traits of character revealed through pet expressions such as Komatsu-san's breezy but strong-willed *Oainikusama desu wa* (Well, isn't that just too bad), or to call further attention to those carefully chosen words, or the slightly pompous Sinicisms like *tonkō* (straightforward and unostentatious) and *jinkakusha* (personage of character), whose use (or misuse) quietly calls attention to the gap between the reputations of the local notables and their less than exemplary actions. Other expressions, most notably the *chikuten shita* (absconded) of the opening sentence, seem to be lovingly repeated for no other reason than the author's fascination with their sonic and imagistic qualities.

The repeated use of the term *hidoi koto* (outrageous) underlines the contrast between the narrator, with his superior powers of perception, and the ways of the world as embodied by Komatsu-san. She uses it in alluding to the mistreatment she has suffered at the hands of her men and also applies it to the narrator's taking her money from her impecunious ex-lover. The narrator, of course, agrees with all of this, and so his use of the same term in his final comment on Komatsu-san reveals his shocked discovery of the contradictions in her personality. Ultimately, this is not a world of "outrageous" scoundrels and their innocent prey. Everyone is outrageous in one way or another; the only differences are in the occasions they choose and the ways they hurt their victims. The narrator tries to be the least outrageous of all, and usually succeeds, but even he "lacks the qualification" to accuse others. His deep-seated inhibitions, rooted in powerful feelings of shame or inferiority which are never explicitly expressed, are crucial to the makeup of Ibuse's narrator persona and help give his fiction its characteristically reticent voice. Even the relatively self-confident narrator of *Shūkin ryokō* proves himself too much a captive of his inhibitions to wholeheartedly assume a stance of moral superiority that Komatsu-san's betrayal, of both her "principles" and of him, should have allowed. When he is walking off toward the train station in Shin'ichi, there is still something in him of the unrecognized, insecure *fugū na bungaku seinen* of fifteen years earlier.

Shūkin ryokō, then, was part of a transitional phase in which Ibuse moved toward the drier, more detached style, greater realism, and emphasis on storytelling that was to find full expression in his postwar fiction.[21] A slightly later work from this period, the long historical narrative *Jon Manjirō hyōryūki* (John Manjirō: A Castaway's Chronicle, 1937) was awarded the Naoki Prize, confirming his emergence as an important writer. Another major event was the appearance in 1939–1940 of *Tajinko mura* (Tajinko Village), a long story whose commercial success Ibuse was later to claim finally gave him a sense of confidence in his ability to make a living as a professional writer.[22]

Tajinko mura was the first of the series of longer works that Ibuse was to write over the next two decades portraying a community or a workplace through the eyes of a central figure whose occupation brings him into contact with various kinds of people. Written in the form of a diary in which a policeman stationed in a country village records the occurrences on his daily rounds, *Tajinko mura* reflects Ibuse's continued preoccupation with the details of village life and shares some of the gentle sense of humor and the affection that had colored his writings about country people since the days of *Kuchisuke* and *Tange-shi tei*. It contrasts strongly with his earlier works, though, in its narrative distance: the policeman-diarist is only slightly removed from the society he lives in. He is a participant first and an observer second; and if his powers of observation are superior to those of others, it is more the result of his privileged point of view than of a particularly acute consciousness.

Although it has its share of amusing moments, *Tajinko mura* is not a predominantly comic work; the lack of distance between observer and observed reduces the scope for ironic narratorial commentary, and the policeman's-diary format limited the possibilities for creating comically exaggerated characters. The same applies in greater or lesser degree to two of Ibuse's best-known postwar stories in this vein, *Honjitsu kyūshin* (No Consultations Today, 1949–1950) and *Ekimae ryokan* (The Inn by the Station, 1956–1957). Both show Ibuse's increased interest in exploiting the fictional effectiveness of a storytelling voice akin to the modern spoken language, in contrast to the artifice of the narrative voice of his early works. The former story is a third-person narrative of a day in the life of a warm-hearted doctor in a lower-class Tokyo neighborhood during the rough-and-tumble years shortly after the war, while the latter portrays, ostensibly in his own words, the world of the veteran head clerk of an old-fashioned inn in a busy downtown district of the city. The wry Ibusean comic spirit still sparkles from time to time in both stories; *Ekimae ryokan* in particular contains some fine touches. Many grow out of the ironic observations of the head clerk, a hard-bitten figure whose mildly cynical outlook suggests the changes which the war and immediate postwar years had wrought in both Japan and in Ibuse.

Ibuse comes to grips with these changes more directly in a number of shorter stories in the early postwar years, when like many other writers, he produced a sudden rush of new works. Many of these were set in the countryside and reflected his experiences during two-and-a-half years as an evacuee in his native village of Kamo. In *Oihagi no hanashi* (Talk about Highway Robbers, 1946), *In no shima* (The Isle of In, 1948), and *Shiraga* (White Hair, 1948), the countryside is no longer a quaint retreat from the complications of modern life; it has fallen prey to the same breakdown of order and common decency that beset the rest of Japan in these years. In this disillusioned world life is harder, the surprises nastier, and the note of mixed resignation and wonder on which so many prewar stories ended now gives way to one of depression tinged with sharp satire.

In no shima and *Shiraga*, like *Koi*, tread a delicate line between fiction and essay. The Ibusean alter-ego narrator reappears with a mask so thin that it threatens to disappear entirely. In the dark, attenuated comic moments in these stories, much of the mockery is directed at the narrator-victim, who stubbornly clings to his gentle illusions despite all the embarrassments and indignities that this entails. Yet even these moments are permeated with a sense of uneasiness, an awareness of the malevolent forces that the war (and its aftermath) have unleashed. Such malevolence presents a major dilemma for writers of comedy, for it lacks the elements of misperception and pretension that normally provide the material for the creation of incongruity, and the suffering it causes is often far too grave to be simply laughed away. As he so often does with harsher aspects of the human spirit, Ibuse prefers to point at it rather than directly address it in these stories, partially camouflaging it with the usual village antics.

The war itself was a different matter. Because the suffering and degradation it caused were of an order far beyond the trespasses of double-crossing lovers or the small-scale malevolences of village life, it would require a different approach, something far stronger and more direct, if it was to be addressed comically at all; and all the signs suggest that this was no easy task for a writer of Ibuse's temperament. It was only in 1950 with the story *Yōhai taichō* (Lieutenant Lookeast) that Ibuse fully came to terms with this dilemma, and the result was a work unique in his comic oeuvre, harsh and disturbing yet simultaneously understated and conciliatory. Set mostly in the fictional country village of Sasayama and the Malayan jungle, *Yōhai taichō* draws on the author's interlude as a rural evacuee as well as his wartime experiences in Malaya.[23] The story is told by a narrator who seems to be a resident of the village but takes no part in the action, which shifts from postwar Sasayama through a series of flashbacks to a troop train, Malaya, a troop ship, and then back to Sasayama. The title character, a former army lieutenant, returns home late in the war with a limp and a bizarre derangement: even after Japan's surrender, he persists in behaving as if the war were still in full swing and, in his periodic "seizures," barks out commands to helpless male villagers of military age and rants about martial virtues in worn-out army indoctrination catch phrases. He never divulges the origins of his physical and mental traumas, but the secret is finally revealed through a chance conversation between one of his former men and an ex-soldier from Sasayama on a repatriation train: both of the lieutenant's afflictions stem from a freak accident brought on by his obsession with upholding the sacred spirit of the glorious Imperial Army. One of his men, a private named Tomomura, was killed in the same accident while being punished by the lieutenant for making an ostensibly disrespectful remark about the "extravagance" (*zeitaku*) of the war effort.

The reader quickly recognizes in the ex-lieutenant not only the personification of mindless army discipline but a far broader embodiment of the fanatical militaristic spirit that had left Japan in such a disastrous state after a brief, vainglorious moment on the stage. In this figure, apparently based in part on an actual case,[24] Ibuse enjoys an ideal opportunity to explore the fundamental comic motifs of Bergsonian mechanical behavior and the untidy collision of personal delusion with impersonal reality. A memorable amalgam of pomposity, paranoia, sadism, and native cunning, the lieutenant earns his nickname Lookeast by regularly ordering his men to perform ceremonial salutes to the Emperor (*yōhai*) upon the least pretext, invariably followed by presumably inspirational "orientation" lectures on the nobility and sublimity of the Military Way: "If you can make a deep and thoughtful study of the Field Service Code, you too will suddenly come to understand the profundity of *yōhai*. And once you discover this wondrous profundity, there you will find unfolding before you a world of ecstasy" (4: 317).

After the accident, the lieutenant is reduced to mouthing a random assortment of commands, threats, and semicoherent fragments of militarist jargon. His men recognize his dementia immediately, just as they had recognized, and resented, his fanaticism. However, as Tōgō Katsumi pointed out in a perceptive discussion of this story,[25] the villagers in Sasayama accept his behavior and speeches as perfectly sensible, if not the epitome of patriotic virtue, as long as the war continues; only when "normal" (peaceful) conditions have been restored do they start treating him as a madman.

In this sense, the story constitutes an unusual variation on the basic comic premises. Where most comic narratives are based either on the transgression of (untenable) social norms by a character with heroic qualities or on the defense of legitimate norms by the expulsion or reconciliation of a transgressing comic butt, *Yōhai taichō* poses a question: what happens when norms are switched and a character who continues to uphold the old norms is suddenly turned into a transgressor? The village's prewar and wartime norms, compromised by their complicity with the militarism of the larger society, are shown as having been in clear need of transgression; but the only character to attempt it is the hapless Tomomura, who by paying for it with his life exhibits heroic but not comic qualities. Lieutenant Okazaki, in his wartime incarnation, had possessed some darkly comic traits, but this was by virtue of his acting out his community's illegitimate norms to an exaggerated degree rather than transgressing them; the lethal consequences of his actions resisted full-fledged comic treatment. The norms of the postwar order, with their professed commitment to peace and democracy, appear to be more legitimate, and by transgressing them in a relatively harmless way he is transformed into something closer to a conventional butt. And yet, on a deeper level the villagers' new norms are revealed by Ibuse to be a manifestation of something unchanging: their unquestioning conformity, their willing acquiescence to whatever is imposed on them by those in power—qualities more than a little reminiscent of the very militarism and authoritarianism that are now supposed to be so thoroughly discredited. The result is an ambivalent kind of satire in which both transgressor and transgressed are taken as objects and their flaws exposed.

Along with this ambivalence, one of the salient features of the satire in *Yōhai taichō* is a caustic tone, particularly in the portrayal of the military and of the insane brutality of war, which has little or no parallel in Ibuse's earlier language and characterization. Along with the narrator's depiction of the lieutenant's excesses, this is repeatedly expressed in the words of the soldiers themselves. Among the most hard-bitten of all are Yojū and Ueda, two returnees from Siberian prison camps who meet on the train. Yojū, on his return to Sasayama, dismisses not only the lieutenant's commands but all the military displays he had witnessed as "play-acting by a bunch of lunatics. A chorus of men in jackboots" (4: 324). Ueda, the veteran who reveals the lieutenant's secret, is startlingly outspoken and even cynical, completely devoid of the delusions shared by virtually all the other characters. After describing the accident to Yojū, his own sentiments are first couched in typically oblique Ibusean terms: "When you see the lieutenant, tell him this: his old orderly Ueda has told all there is to tell about his commander. Because of that, Ueda has completely ignored the scenery outside the window on the San'yō line for upwards of two full hours. As if he hadn't just come back to Japan for the first time in years. You tell him that for me" (4: 318). But when Yojū speculates that the "Soviet-style" indirection of his message may not be appreciated by the lieutenant, Ueda replies that unless his old commander is still deranged, he was probably one of the first to change his tune after the surrender, and adds that the accident in which Tomomura died and for which an innocent soldier was severely punished was all the lieutenant's responsibility, and that his former fear of his old commander has been replaced by a seething sense of loathing.

The villager who relates these episodes is the most transparent of all Ibuse's on-stage narrators, a passive observer who displays few personal qualities. Because he reveals no faults of his own to balance off against those of the other characters, there is a sharper focus on what he observes, intensifying the story's strongly satirical tone. As usual, the narrative voice provides a minimum of evaluative commentary; the gap between the narrator's observations and the characters' words and actions is telling enough. But after giving Ueda's account of the events leading up to Tomomura's death, even this noncommittal figure can no longer restrain himself from breaking out of his deadpan pose and appealing directly from the heart: "Just having said that war is an extravagant thing, he got himself slapped on the face and then found himself falling off the tailgate of the stalled truck right before he died. What's more, hitting his head on the concrete as he went down, he was drowned in a muddy stream which nobody even knew the name of. All in all, he was the victim of a truly nasty deal. It was as if he were showing us some kind of larger destiny compressed into the space of a single instant. 'Extravagant' is hardly the word for war" (4: 310–311).

Compared to the "it said something about cruel punishments" of *Tangeshi tei* or the "what an outrageous trick" of *Shūkin ryokō*, these are strong words: here we approach that extreme form of satire where comic indirection and duality give way to pure, unadulterated denunciation. Rarely is anguish expressed in such a direct fashion in Ibuse's fiction, and one can only guess at the depth of the sense of outrage underlying them. But, as Tōgō observes, the military is not the sole object of his satire; he is also contemptuous of those who, whether out of opportunism, habitual obedience to authority, or sheer simplemindedness, lost no time in jumping on the bandwagon of antimilitarism and democracy following Japan's defeat with the same enthusiasm and lack of understanding that they had devoted to the opposite cause a few short weeks or months earlier. The only character to confront the lieutenant directly, a young man in a surplus army uniform who comes to Sasayama to buy charcoal, can do no more than ineffectually hurl his newly learned pacifist slogans ("militarist specter," "imbecile aggressor," "fascist relic") while flapping his arms in the empty air as one of the villagers holds him back. Yojū, being a veteran and ex-POW rather than a black marketeer, may be more sincere when he assails the wrongs of the past; but there is also a hollow ring of dogmatic pomposity to his declarations (probably the result of his sojourn in Siberia), which in Ibuse's world invariably invites some skepticism on the part of the reader.

If the satire directed at the newly converted pacifists is somewhat less harsh than that directed at the militarists, it is because their delusions are less deadly. Their fickleness (or, more precisely, their willingness to defer to any authority, wherever it may lead) is portrayed as an innate element of human nature, or at least as much a part of their mentality as the petty vanities and other foibles that Ibuse had long delighted in portraying. Nevertheless, it is quietly but forcefully shown that it is precisely this quality, along with the community's proclivity for striving to maintain appearances and flattering those who succeed in putting up the grandest appearance, that is in no small way responsible for the creation of the monster lieutenant.

The most striking embodiment of these qualities is the lieutenant's own mother, a widow who somehow manages to accumulate a substantial sum of money while working as a chambermaid at an inn in a nearby town and then returns to Sasayama, where she erects a set of imposing concrete gateposts in front of her home. This gesture, with its overtones of the arches erected to honor chaste widows in Chinese tales of exemplary Confucian virtue, earns her the admiration of the entire community, including the mayor, as a "personage of character" and leads to the son of this "model family" being recommended for further schooling and eventually for army officer training. In the story's final scene, the mother, having succeeded in restraining her son after one of his outbursts, is observed quietly drawing water up from another token of her fixation with the material trappings of status, her chain well. Years ago, we are told, when this well had been the envy of the village and won her further flattery from the mayor and the school principal, she would draw more water than she needed, just in order to let the clank of the chain reverberate through the valley.

In this anticlimactic but quietly eloquent conclusion, we can sense something of the familiar gentle, even slightly bemused note of resignation upon which so many Ibuse stories end. Given the author's beliefs that basic human dignity must be respected regardless of individual shortcomings, in the end we have no choice but to accept the lieutenant for what he is. His flaws are far deeper and more dangerous than those of the villagers, but, just like them, he cannot be confronted or enlightened or expelled. We can only wait for the "fearsome skeleton" to disappear, and in the meantime cage it whenever its outbursts become too violent.

And yet, the unaccustomed harshness of tone and language of *Yōhai taichō* suggest that something is indeed different here. The deadly madness of Lieutenant Okazaki cannot be dismissed as simply as the follies of Ibusean villagers or the capricious punishments of Mister Tange. Even the outrages perpetrated on Komatsu-san by her lovers, cruel as they may have been, never broke down her resilience. In *Yōhai taichō* the sense of malaise that colors other postwar Ibuse stories is traced back to its cause, or as close as one can get to the cause, and the result is unsettling. If the lieutenant, and the whole cast of generals, politicians, and other leaders whom he represents, were entirely evil and fully responsible for the catastrophe, they could simply be exorcised and a healthy society restored. But in fact, their brutality was also a kind of insanity. Normally, the insane individual is a problematic figure in comic narratives: insanity is, after all, an affliction which the sufferer has no power to avoid or escape from, and the suffering it causes is rarely easy to laugh away. The suffering of insanity becomes less real, and thus laughable, only when its traits are transferred from an individual to a communal body, such as a village or an army.

When zany jesters, holy fools, and village idiots make their frequent appearances as individuals in the comic narratives of countless cultures, it is not so much as butts but as bearers of a higher truth that would be unpalatable if presented by other means, a truth which, more often than not, points to their "normal" host community as the order in which delusion and folly are rampant. Lieutenant Okazaki is depicted as seeming to possess some of these qualities of the holy fool: he is compared by the narrator to a woman possessed by a fox spirit, and regularly evades his pursuers in the village with a nimbleness that is described as uncanny or supernatural. But despite these appearances, in reality he is "not sublime at all, just sneaky" (4: 319). Unlike a genuine holy fool, he has no truths to offer. But his ravings and the reactions of the villagers do expose, however inadvertently, the flaws of the community that produced him. And if, as Ibuse seems to be suggesting, the delusions of Japanese militarism developed like some kind of malignant growth out of the countless milder delusions of the national village, the "normal" society that failed to recognize these delusions for what they were has its own collusions to answer for. In comedy, as in life, charlatans and lunatics can never have their way unless others allow themselves to become dupes. And when those who followed the military with blind obedience proceed to turn against it in an equally blind reaction, while others still long for bygone displays of pomp and circumstance, and the madmen are still very much on the loose, the danger is far from over. A disturbing conclusion, to be sure, but without its comic presentation things would be even worse: it could all too easily degenerate into a sermon or a harangue—exactly the kind of thing, as Ibuse suggests, that can be counted upon to get us into trouble in the first place. The only ray of hope lies in the possibility that someday all of these delusions, large and small, can be recognized and confronted, and it seems to be in this hope that *Yōhai taichō* was written.

In its sharpness of focus, emotional intensity, use of comic techniques to address issues of communal concern, and broadening of scope to encompass an entire society, *Yōhai taichō* occupies a distinctive position among Ibuse's comic works. Tōgō sees *Yōhai taichō* as a comic breakthrough for Ibuse, in which the embarrassed laughter that the author had previously directed at himself as a means of avoiding confrontation with the greed and folly around him is finally transformed into a direct satirical attack on highly deserving external targets.[26] And yet, there is little in Ibuse's later work that resembles or develops from it.[27] Perhaps Ibuse simply found the material too difficult to face. The direct expression of condemnation, ridicule, and malice conventionally attendant on the satirical perspective must also have posed problems: for all his sensitivity to injustice, and all the dark undertones in his work, condemnation has never been Ibuse's metier; and where others might have seen malevolence, he has found senselessness instead. And some instances of senselessness, and the sufferings consequent upon them, are so vast as to defy the imagination and resist any attempt at comic handling. In fact, the work for which Ibuse will no doubt be best remembered, the novel *Kuroi ame* (Black Rain, 1965–1966), deals with one of these: the atomic bombing of Hiroshima and the ongoing ordeals of its survivors. Others have found it possible to stop worrying long enough to love the bomb as a comic subject, but only a hypothetical bomb. Ibuse, for whom the bomb was not a nightmare fantasy but a historical and even empirical reality, was not one of them. Yet even in *Kuroi ame*, a number of familiar Ibusean comic motifs appear: a headstrong old man engaged in a Quixotic mission (in this case, trying to find a marriage partner for a niece widely suspected of having been exposed to a deadly dose of radiation in the blast), played off against an equally headstrong wife and a naïve young woman; the overbearing pomposity of authority figures, in this case career military men and bureaucrats, who cannot abandon their preoccupation with displays of their power even as the cataclysm has reduced all such displays to exercises in sheer absurdity; the intimate quotidian details, petty preoccupations, and posturings of village life; and the innate human dignity that somehow manages to survive and even to wrest some shreds of order and consolation from the most indescribable of horrors.

If *Yōhai taichō* marks a new phase in Ibuse's comic fiction, it is principally in the perfection of the more acerbic, hard-bitten style that he had already been developing for some years and the adoption of a broader range of narrative voices. *Ekimae ryokan* is one example of this. Another, and one that is arguably the peak achievement in Ibuse's postwar comic writing, is the novel *Chinpindō shujin* (The Master of Rarity House), which first appeared in 1959 in nine monthly installments in *Chūō Kōron*. Where *Yōhai taichō* harks back with a mixture of ridicule, bemusement, and sympathy to the easygoing village world of Ibuse's youth, *Chinpindō shujin*, like *Ekimae ryokan*, portrays the fast-paced, eternally scheming whirl of the city where he spent most of his adult life; and his tone shifts with his setting to a wryly amused detachment, almost Saikakuesque in its cool recounting of his characters' foibles and pratfalls.

The effect of this change in tone is reinforced by the adoption of a point of view that Ibuse had already used in other works, but was new in his comedy: the intimate person-to-person voice of the participant-narrator is replaced by a disembodied voice speaking from outside the action of the story and rarely sharing the emotions of the characters, unmistakably Ibusean but far freer and more pointed in its irony than its predecessors. It is also unusual in its heavy use of the formal *desu-masu* system of inflected endings throughout most of the narrative, simultaneously creating a feeling of orality and imparting a sense of distance between narrator and characters, as well as between author and reader. This feeling is reinforced by a continuous stream of narratorial embellishments (also present, less conspicuously, in *Shūkin ryokō*), such as "that was what she said" or "their conversation went like this," more characteristic of oral storytelling than of novelistic narrative technique.

The narrator's tone consistently suggests that he is telling this story simply because of his fascination with the world it evokes and the possibilities it offers for bravura stylistic displays; *Chinpindō shujin* is full of colorful turns of phrase drawing on postwar slang and the argot of antiques dealers and connoisseurs as well as the usual range of literary sources. Ibuse's eye for detail and his instinct for the mot juste are at their acutest, creating a vivid tableau of characters and manners. His depictions of antiques dealers, country people, restaurant staff and customers, and other incidental characters deftly balance comic exaggerations and distortions with realistic touches that point to the core of psychological truth underlying the extravagant exteriors.

The story line meanders like a picaresque journey through time, with the author stopping whenever the spirit moves him to indulge in a plenitude of digressions notable even by Ibusean standards, ranging from anecdotes about antique dealers and collectors, the histories, production techniques, and distinctive features of various pieces, explanations of antique-world terminology, and behind-the-scenes glimpses of the human and business facets of running a posh Japanese-style restaurant to disquisitions on the vagaries of country children's runny noses and a recipe for miso soup. Interwoven with these, and tying them together, is a series of key events in the sudden rise and equally precipitous downfall of the title character: a chance discovery that inspires his growing infatuation with antiques and the life of taste, his creation and management of an "ideal" restaurant, his expulsion from his own successful creation amid a flurry of intrigues and personality clashes, and his return to a life of freelance antique dealing.

Like the earlier *Tajinko mura, Honjitsu kyūshin,* and *Ekimae ryokan, Chinpindō shujin* is based on the author's observation of day-to-day affairs from the viewpoint of a particular occupation.[28] In this case, however, the occupation is more a way of life than a profession, and it only rarely affords any perspective on the broader world outside. Many of the characters are little more than caricatures whose interest lies mainly in their idiosyncratic preoccupations and whose only subtlety is expressed through their scheming. Even the title character is a vastly expanded version of this pattern, dominating the story more through the sheer magnitude of his manic energy, deviousness, and capacity for letting himself be carried away by self-gratifying fantasy than through qualitative differences from the others.

The story is animated by themes somewhat unusual for Ibuse but full of possibilities for comic exploitation. The dominant theme in the first part is the world of antiques and the hold it exerts over its devotees. Many of the story's most striking passages, especially in the early sections, deal with the manifold psychological facets of an ostensibly tasteful avocation exaggerated into a comic obsession. The mere description of a tempting-sounding piece is enough to send Chinpindō and his cronies into barely controlled paroxysms of craving, which they feel compelled to satisfy even if it means mortgaging their home, resorting to skulduggery, or, in dire cases, actually selling off other antiques to raise the necessary funds. Success only fans the flames: "Every time Chinpindō came up with a find, it would leave him feeling so happy and so agitated that he would go off and make the rounds of the antique shops in pursuit of his next find" (8: 139). When Chinpindō realizes his twenty-year-old dream of acquiring a certain statue of the Buddha which had once stood in the Sanjūsangendō in Kyoto, he takes it home, places it on an antique pedestal, and chants sutras before it daily in the hope of being granted further finds. In one of his more revealing turns of phrase, Ibuse has recourse to Buddhist terminology to assess the situation, attributing Chinpindō's excesses to his "deeply rooted delusions" (*mōshū*) and warning that they will be his "unending karma" (*tsukisenu gō*) (8: 153).

Along with the urge to possess them, the very mention of these objects can give rise to rich fantasies in which the enthusiast envisions the exquisite circumstances of their creation and use in bygone ages, momentarily slipping into a world of master craftsmen and aristocratic connoisseur-patrons far removed from the drabness of postwar Japan. Actual possession can bring on a state of rapture in which time seems to disappear altogether: having schemed his way into ownership of a Muromachi lantern, Chinpindō takes it home, places a candle in it, closes his shutters, and spends day after day silently gazing at the light it throws across his darkened room. The feel of a centuries-old Bizen-ware *sake* jar as he pours out a gentle stream of the heated liquid is as thrilling as the touch of any woman. Failing to obtain one of these objects, or having to sell it off, feels like abandonment by a woman to whom one has given one's heart (or at least one's libido), while making it one's own after a tortuous pursuit is like a reunion with a long-lost lover. It is as if Ibuse has finally discovered a way of depicting passion (and the extreme comic abnormalities it engenders) without running afoul of his inhibitions regarding love and sex. The parallel between antiques and women, drawn frequently throughout the story, is stated most eloquently early on by one of Chinpindō's friends, a college professor who had become absorbed in antiques in the aftermath of a failed love affair in his student days: "Antiques are like women. They're different from other businesses. If you don't feel that you've got something unusual, your eye for them will never develop. Antiques and women are both things that seem to have a value without having one. The value depends on the person who has them. Let's say you've fallen for some antique. It's because you've fallen for it that it has a value and that you develop. If you keep on bargaining, the seller will let you have it at some point. At some point, he'll give in" (8: 134).

The point of this bold hypothesis, of course, is not that women are objects, but rather that antiques can stimulate the same kinds of intense and peculiar reactions associated with erotic impulses. There is the incomparable thrill of first discovery, coupled with the burning desire to possess the discovered treasure. This is particularly the case for those diamonds in the rough that have eluded other collectors and miraculously turn up in obscure junk shops or remote mountain villages. When Chinpindō makes his first great discovery, the narrator comments: "Finds (*horidashimono*)—he was overcome by the allure of those magic moments when he discovered them and made them his own. It is an incurable affliction" (8: 119). Recognition, and acquisition, of such finds is both the goal and the proof of a highly cultivated taste. By discerning the hidden allure of a seemingly unprepossessing or undervalued piece, one makes it one's own in a way that could never happen with an article already desired by many—just as one can more easily cherish a woman whose attractions are known only to oneself than a well-publicized starlet whose charms are all too obvious.

The thematic link between antiques and women is established at the outset, when a tryst with Sanzō, an ex-geisha Chinpindō had first met during the war (also through antiques) leads to his first great "find," the Muromachi-period metal lantern that in turn inspires his decision to give up his job (and his evacuation home in Izu as well as the company of his wife), return to Tokyo, and immerse himself in full-time wheeling and dealing in antiques. His decision to establish and operate an "ideal *ryōtei*" as the ultimate means of indulging in, and cashing in on, his exquisite taste is also inspired by the exigencies of providing for Sanzō (and, incidentally, for his wife, who remains an insubstantial figure throughout the story). Likewise it is Sanzō who makes the scheme possible by vouching for him to Kutani, a wealthy shipowner who provides the building and the capital, after his associates in the antiques world had all assured Kutani that backing Chinpindō would be a highly dubious venture. However, after she turns down his proposal to make her his live-in head waitress, he begins to neglect her; and his final expulsion from the restaurant coincides with the shifting of her affections to Kutani.

A more sinister aspect of the connection between women and antiques is represented by Chinpindō's relationship with Ranran-jo, a fortyish woman who "passes as a tea master but actually conducts an antiques business without keeping a shop" (8: 164), hired at Kutani's behest to design the conversion of his former mansion into a *ryōtei*. Grasping and sly, she soon emerges as a dangerous rival for Kutani's favor, and with it control of the restaurant. She gradually probes Chinpindō's weak spots "like an eel feeling its way through the openings in a basket with its tail" (8: 173), and succeeds in gaining the upper hand through a series of subtle and devious maneuvers. She takes maximum advantage of his every stumble or indiscretion and, using the staff as her spies and allies, creates several of them herself by dangling temptations before him in the knowledge that he will fall victim to his own enthusiasms or be carried away by fantasies so potent that he is blinded to all possible risks. His purchase of a costly but fake statuette purveyed by Ranran-jo, his clumsy attempt to seduce a waitress who also turns out to be an object of Ranran-jo's affections, and even his penchant for embarking on food- and antique-gathering expeditions are quickly turned against him by his shrewder adversary. Although she is not without her own weaknesses, he is either blind to them or unable to exploit them. After artfully wriggling out of the one corner into which he manages to push her, she proceeds to execute her final and most elaborate stratagem, culminating in her complete ascendance and the final expulsion of the unsuspecting Chinpindō from his own domain.

In this woman-antiques parallel lies one of the principal ironies of the story: the same instincts and finely developed sensibilities upon which Chinpindō relies in dealing with antiques fail him completely in his dealings with women. As a result, the dream world of taste and prosperity that he had labored so hard to create slips out of his grasp. The worldly and shrewd Kutani, who understands Chinpindō's lack of a "developed eye" for women, and wins Sanzō for himself while keeping the wily Ranran-jo under control, has no eye at all for antiques, and accumulates them only to protect the fruits of his wartime profiteering. It is no coincidence that in the last section of the story, in which Chinpindō recovers from his debacle and regains his equilibrium in the antiques world, there are no longer any women in his life.

On a more fundamental level, *Chinpindō shujin* embodies a familiar comic theme, the inescapable and inextricable connection between the sacred and the profane, whether it be in the human mind or a Buddhist statue. The ideal of pure appreciation of beautiful objects almost invariably turns out to be tainted with baser impulses, and the passions they generate easily turn into greed or jealousy. This dark undercurrent may even lead to mutilation of the antiques, as when a *go* board of Chinpindō's is expropriated by one of his friends who planes off the top surface and uses it as a pedestal for a Buddhist statue during a round of "friendly" thefts. Chinpindō takes a perverse pleasure in stirring up his friends with hints about tantalizing pieces that may or may not be available somewhere and watching them squirm with envy; but he is always careful not to divulge too much information for fear that his listeners might attempt to steal a march on him, as he would certainly do in their place. When his friends are too poor to pose such a threat, he is quick to remind them of the fact. If a piece turns out to be a fake, it may become the object of intricate scheming as an owner or succession of owners tries to fob it off at the best possible price, even if this involves deceiving friends or benefactors. On the other hand, sellers who fail to appreciate the full value of one of their wares can expect that even their closest associates will hasten to relieve them of it as quickly and cheaply as possible.

The contrast between serenely beautiful, silently enduring objects and the sordid goings-on among the people through whose hands they travel is reminiscent of Kawabata Yasunari's handling of tea ceremony objects in *Senbazuru* (Thousand Cranes, 1952). But Ibuse has little of Kawabata's studied reverence toward art objects; he substitutes for it a livelier and warmer admiration, along with a worldly awareness that these are not always aesthetic abstractions passed from one owner to the next in an atmosphere resonant with deep emotional overtones. They can also become objects of nasty struggles, not only because of their irresistible appeal but also because, as Ibuse repeatedly reminds us, "Antiques are like women, but they also involve something else. They also involve money" (8: 190). As the antithesis of the otherworldly state that antiques are supposed to represent, the profit motive makes them subject to the same slings and arrows, the same spiritual and physical defilement that men and women inflict upon one another. While Kawabata's objects remain transcendentally aloof from the unsavory goings-on among their owners, Ibuse's often join his characters in becoming comic victims of forces they have no way of controlling or understanding.

The sacred-profane dichotomy is also evident in Ibuse's acknowledgment of the existence of fakes. Like certain comic characters, many objects are not necessarily what they appear to be, either through deliberate deception or innocent misapprehension; and in their ability to inspire the most elevated sentiments or the basest, they also bear a certain resemblance to human beings. A skillful forgery, or even a modern-day implement that happens to look like an antique, may provoke the same kind of thrills and passions as a genuine article. Even the most experienced connoisseurs are sometimes hard put to distinguish what is genuine and what is not, especially when their sense of judgment is clouded by lust for money or for a unique "find," or by the desire to outdo a rival; and the ensuing misperceptions and deceptions can give rise to all manner of comic situations, as in a scene where Chinpindō tries to sell a piece to a dealer who rejects it as a fake, then changes his mind and tries to buy it, only to have Chinpindō decide that it really is a fake after all and refuse to sell it (8: 170–71).

In the second half of the novel, which details Chinpindō's career as a restaurateur, the sacred-profane dichotomy takes on a new form, as his efforts to create a monument to taste, pleasure, and prosperity are gradually undercut by petty rivalries and jealousies. Avidly he seeks out and acquires the rarest, most pleasing delicacies, to be served in pottery and lacquerware made to the most exacting specifications by the finest craftsmen. No distance or expense is too great to ensure that his customers, and he himself, will be provided with a supremely pleasurable experience. When Chinpindō sets out for some obscure mountain district in search of the ultimate bean paste or to order a set of teacups, it is as much an adventure in connoisseurship as a business trip, and often a pretext for some private dealings on the side.

But like all comic idylls grounded in misperceptions, this one all too soon begins to disintegrate. Chinpindō must devote more and more time to vying with Ranran-jo for Kutani's favor and less to being an art businessman. Ill-advised cravings, whether for the wrong antique or the wrong woman, repeatedly get the better of him, until the downward spiral of machinations and counter-machinations is finally brought to a conclusion by a neat coup in which Ranran-jo and Kutani force the entire staff to abandon him. The discovery that Sanzō has become Kutani's mistress is the crowning indignity.

Thus the great fantasy that had sprung from nowhere to drive Chinpindō through a year of frenzy returns to nowhere. He emerges none the more enlightened from his experience (a half-hearted attempt at reflection quickly comes to naught); but by re-immersing himself in antiques dealing, he finds a safer means to reconcile his transcendent yearnings with his earthier impulses. The story ends on a characteristically Ibusean oblique note, faintly redolent of optimism even in the aftermath of catastrophe:

> The heat this summer has been extraordinary. Yet yesterday, just like the day before, Chinpindō was out making the rounds of the antique shops to see if there might not be a find to be had somewhere. As usual, he was wearing a beret to conceal his receding hairline, and he had a feeling that his appearance from behind looked windblown even when there was no wind blowing. The other day, having read Marukyū's letter and surmising from it that Imari ware should be appraised at its true worth in a year or so, he drank too much by way of anticipatory celebration, and upset his stomach. Lately he has been feeling a bit worn out owing to a case of diarrhea. (8: 249)

In true comic hero fashion, Chinpindō bows out with a show of resilience: despite the enormity of his setback, his original motivating fixation, the "incurable affliction," is as virulent as ever. His propensity for self-gratifying fantasy remains impervious to the blows of harsh experience, just as his comic vitality remains undiminished. An appropriate ending for a story based on a classic comic motif, the undertaking by a character of grandiose but skewed vision that soars boldly upward only to collapse resoundingly under the weight of reality when the character's delusions reveal themselves as a fatal structural flaw.

Chinpindō's creation of an "ideal *ryōtei*" echoes some of the earlier misguided or impractical projects of Ibuse's characters—the narrator's attempted "rescue" of Kuchisuke, the college girl's romance with the would-be revolutionary, the odd couple's bill-collecting trip—but this is the most ambitious of all, comic delusion writ large, and the one that comes closest to realization. Moreover, its perpetrator enjoys a range of action and breadth of comic manipulation unequaled in Ibuse's writing. His flaws—the inability to keep each of the main pursuits in his life (antiques, women, and money) from compromising the others, and his impractical devotion to taste in an all-too-practical world of power struggles and subterfuge—are also depicted on a grander scale than anything that came before or after in Ibuse's comic fiction.

The motif is somewhat obscured by being embedded in a loose narrative structure. Considerable space is devoted to an elaborate, leisurely introduction of Chinpindō and his cronies and their fixation on antiques before his scheme comes into view at all; and once it gets off the ground, another long section dwells on the mechanics of establishing and running the *ryōtei*. Only thereafter do the main intrigues begin, and these are interspersed with further digressions on details of antiques, food, and whatever else catches the author's interest. But this looseness, which is quite typical of Ibuse, particularly in his longer works, has its own function: it points to a larger and untidier pattern. If Chinpindō is the main character and his whim-whams the comic center of the piece, he is still just one element in a larger tableau. Unlike some Ibuse works in which one or two comic characters are played off against a more or less normal society, virtually all the characters in *Chinpindō shujin* have their own eccentricities, delusions, or pretensions. The continuous whirl of rogues and oddballs constitutes the larger comic vision of the story, a spectacle that the disembodied narrator views with a jaded sangfroid which occasionally borders on cruelty. When Chinpindō appears at one point to have outmaneuvered Ranran-jo and she calls "Truce!" (*tanma*), his innate optimism glows warmly for a moment and his wrath is transformed into a tearful spirit of reconciliation, but the narrator comments:

> It was all so, so naive. Could it not be that tears sometimes deceive the one who is shedding them? Chinpindō thought that these were tears of deep emotion. As a result, he relaxed and made up with Ranran-jo, but he had failed to realize that after every "Truce!" there follows a "Truce is over!" Dealing with someone like Ranran-jo in matters where personal interests are at stake, it is just a question of how much is conceded under what circumstances, and what kind of trick will be used to wind the matter up. . . . One can't let oneself get optimistic and believe that the ground dries up when the storm passes. (8: 224)

Throughout the story, all manner of mischief, skulduggery, and occasional outright viciousness are taken in stride. Unlike characters in earlier

Ibuse works, who rarely hurt each other intentionally unless their own interests are involved, the characters of *Chinpindō shujin* take a perverse pleasure in making life miserable for each other. Yet the condemnation of gratuitous malevolence that one would normally expect from the observer-narrator is replaced by the detached bemusement common among seasoned comic observers of the human pageant. There is no good or bad, no right or wrong, only a world of predators and prey, constantly devouring and in turn being devoured like so many fish in a cartoon ocean.

Chinpindō shujin, which was written some thirty-five years after Ibuse's emergence on the literary scene, represents his comic writing at its richest and most polished; but looking back over his career, one may find glimpses of his characteristic comic spirit, however subtle, in the conception or language of virtually any of his works. Categorizing individual works as purely "comic" or "non-comic" would be a futile exercise, for from the early stages of his career they have ranged in spectral gradations from the broadly-comic-with-darker-overtones (*Josefu, Shūkin ryokō, Yōhai taichō, Chinpindō shujin*) gently shading off through not-quite-so-comic (*Sanshōuo, Tajinko mura, Ekimae ryokan*) to the somber-but-with-comic-touches (*Kuroi ame*).

A number of Japanese critics have pointed out that Ibuse's work underwent fundamental changes over the decades. Kamei Katsuichirō, Kobayashi Hideo, and Tōgō Katsumi, for example, have noted a transition from strong emotional involvement with his characters (especially those who double as narrators) and lyricism (sometimes accompanied by sentimentality and overripe language) in the early works to a more trenchant style in which greater stress is placed on realistic description and on the flow of the narrative itself, beginning in the 1930s and reaching its full development in the early postwar years, nurtured by the author's growing self-confidence and the spiritual buffeting he received during the years of war and privation.[29] This thesis is as valid for Ibuse's more strongly comic fiction as it is for his work as a whole, although the long-standing critical lack of interest in some of his early *nansensu*-oriented stories such as *Josefu* and *Tange-shi tei* has led to an inordinate emphasis on the lyrical character of his early work. Tōgō's assertion that *Yōhai taichō* represents a major transition toward a more pointed satirical stance is also questionable, since the sharp confrontation of large-scale social and political forces that marks this story is not repeated in later works; if anything *Yōhai taichō* now appears to be more of an exception than a turning point.

Another important change, which has received less attention but has important implications for the development of Japanese comic fiction, involves his choices of character and milieu. Many of Ibuse's early comic works are poised on the nether edges of society: remote mountain villages, a boat anchored off an uninhabited island, or even a silent and desolate cave. The characters are as marginal as the settings they inhabit. Most are eccentrics, whether quietly or flamboyantly; few have any recognizable role to play in society. Even in the case of stories set in "modern" cities, the characters are marginal—including the narrator figure, whose sophistication is masked by his continual proclamations of poverty, humility, and general uselessness. In other words, because they never looked too familiar for comfort to their readers, they were relatively easy to perceive as comic objects of the simplest type, the butts of jokes.

By the time of *Shūkin ryokō,* though, the dropouts and the beneficiaries of enforced leisure start giving way to figures with more or less identifiable social roles. The delusions, pretensions, and idiosyncrasies remain; but now they appear among doctors, businessmen, soldiers, and the like, in situations which, no matter how odd, are far more plausible, no longer so easily dismissed as quaint representations of a backward rural world. The village of *Yōhai taichō* is a nation in microcosm, while the Tokyo of *Honjitsu kyūshin, Ekimae ryokan,* and *Chinpindō shujin* is a metamorphosis of the country village, its inhabitants suffering from all the familiar delusions in more polished forms.

A minority faction of critics represented by Isogai Hideo and Nakamura Mitsuo has called attention to elements of continuity or consistency in Ibuse's writing. Nakamura's "Ibuse Masuji ron" (On Ibuse Masuji) of 1957, for example, emphasized Ibuse's long-standing resistance to change in his *sakufū* or "way of writing," although he has elsewhere noted Ibuse's shift in comic focus away from himself (as represented by the narrator-participant) toward the rigid "dogmatism" (*kannensei*) which, in the form of Proletarianism and the precepts of the Neo-Perceptionist school, had been such a source of frustration to him during his early years in the literary wilderness.[30] From the perspective of Ibuse's significance as a writer of comic fiction, these elements of consistency have been at least as important as the changes.

Ibuse's use of language is one example of this. Language is one of the most powerful of all the instruments used to create comic effects in literature: the words selected and the ways that they are arranged have a crucial bearing on the way a given author exposes dichotomies between appearance and reality, or reality and ideal. Throughout the history of Japanese literature, the most common comic use of language has surely been wordplay, the bringing together of seemingly unrelated objects or concepts through ostensibly coincidental similarities in the words used to signify them. Ibuse, although he is not immune to the temptation to engage in the occasional pun, has largely turned his back on this venerable tradition and relied on other linguistic devices. Two of the most prominent are Sinicized vocabulary and dialectal speech. Critics who emphasize the changes in Ibuse's writing point to his decreasing reliance on these obtrusive expressions; but even in his relatively late works they remain a distinctive feature of his style, a kind of alternative idiom which highlights the distance between the perceptions or pretenses of the speakers and the phenomena they are purporting to describe. While not itself strictly a form of wordplay, dialect shares with wordplay a potential to devalue either its speakers (as comic deviants from an accepted "standard") or the objects referred to (by separating them from the privileged matrix of standard speech), or simply to create a value-free feeling of incongruity. Ibuse used dialect for all these purposes, but only rarely did he use it just to mock provincial characters as provincials; even in his early "nonsense" works, it far more commonly serves to amplify some discrepancy with reality (delusion) inherent in their character and not particularly related to their provincial status. The Sinicisms, with their implicit suggestion of erudition or superior sensibility, serve to undercut the authority of users (narrator and characters alike) by calling attention to their pretenses when they use them in incongruous or inappropriate situations; at other times, they function as decorous circumlocutions on the part of speakers assuming the classic comic posture of the *eiron* (a character who creates an incongruity by revealing less than he or she knows). In fact, much of Ibuse's comic language derives its effectiveness from the judicious use of understatement, the description of scenes or actions in a deadpan style that accentuates their oddness. Other favorite techniques are juxtaposition of styles in different voices (typically the narrator's versus those of the characters) and the mixing of styles and tones within the speech of a single character, showing the character's internal contradictions.

The role of the narrator is integral to Ibusean comedy, because the narrator is the principal medium through which comic dual visions are expressed. Sometimes the narrator's commentary provides a relatively objective point of reference that shows the other characters' delusions; in other cases, when the narrator functions as participant as well as observer, his own pretensions or misperceptions are revealed. Typically, his role resembles that of Lambert Strether in Henry James's *The Ambassadors* as described by E. M. Forster: an "observer who tries to influence the action, and through his failure to do so gains extra opportunities for observation."[31] While Ibuse generally shied away from an exclusive focus on his participant-narrators by carefully balancing them against a variety of other characters, the Ibusean participant-narrator is typically something of a privileged figure. Normally, he is the only one in the story capable of seeing the contradictions within both the other characters and himself, and unlike the others, he retains some measure of control over the exposure of his own misperceptions or pretensions rather than having them exposed inadvertently. As Nakamura has observed, there is a general trend away from focus on the narrator, culminating in postwar works in which the narrator no longer participates in the action (*Yōhai taichō*) and sometimes disappears entirely into a disembodied third-person voice (*Chinpindō shujin*). But even here the narrator keeps many of his familiar functions; although his own flaws are no longer balanced against the defects of other characters, his remains the only voice in the story endowed with a powerful ironic consciousness.

Ibuse's indirection as a storyteller is another element integral to his comic style that changed relatively little over the years. Almost invariably, he prefers to express dualities in oblique terms or to camouflage them in a welter of detail rather than to point straight at them. When the manservant Eisuke calls the narrator-archeologist's find a *bukotsu na tokkuri* in *Tange-shi tei*, for instance, we are left to sense the humiliating gap between the narrator's status in his own eyes and Eisuke's, as well as the gap between his aspirations and the paucity of his achievement, even though he makes no comment to either Eisuke or the reader. Rather than letting comic situations develop fully, Ibuse would often cut them off after having shown the direction in which they are headed. Thus we see the indirect confrontation carried on through letters by the narrator and Aoki's ex-mistress in *Koi*, the repeated turning away from scenes of mounting erotic tension in *Kuchisuke*, the abruptly cut off moments of self-realization in *Shūkin ryokō*, and the almost formulaic lyrical passages with which so many Ibuse works are concluded, a hand pointing at a moon which it will never portray.

The absence of malice, the downplaying of the superiority element, is another consistent element in Ibuse's comedy. The participant-narrator, even while he points out the delusions of his characters, is all too conscious of his own propensity for similar delusions, and refuses to place himself above them. Ibuse has no interest in engaging in merciless ridicule or even the kind of contemptuous sneering that occasionally surfaces in the fiction of an Akutagawa or a Kafū. Fools and impostors are rarely labeled as such either by the narrator or by each other. Even in the later fiction, without the tempering influence of the participant-narrator, the most harshly treated characters (Lieutenant Okazaki, Chinpindō, Ranran-jo) are never stripped of their dignity.

Ibuse's reluctance to place himself above his characters is also one of the reasons that his laughter, like his entire range of emotions, is muted. The lack of distance precludes the kind of broad laughter in which parts of the mind and heart are temporarily disengaged and sympathy suspended. Ibusean comic moments are attenuated and subtle rather than belly laughs. His laughter is dry and quiet, sometimes shading off imperceptibly to a wry irony that merely tickles the reader and disappears before it is ever perceived as comic. There is little room for slapstick, bodily functions, and other comic effects of the broader sort; nor are there many instances of bantering or comic contestations in which characters embodying antithetical principles directly confront each other and attempt to expose each other's flaws.

The use of comedy as a means of disengagement, an attempt by an insecure author simultaneously to expose his embarrassment or shame and conceal them beneath a ripple of (self-directed) laughter, is frequently noted in critical writing on Ibuse. Less frequently discussed is concealment of another sort, Ibuse's reticence with respect to two of the most obvious and durable of all comic themes, sex and evil (or intentional duplicity as opposed to delusion). Ibuse was fully conscious of the endless cycle of conflict and truce between the imperatives of dignified social behavior and the unruly demands of the libido; they figure prominently in works from the *nansensu* phase through *Shūkin ryokō* and on to *Chinpindō shujin*. However, the actual details, rich in comic potential as they may be, are treated with the same reticence as the more delicate emotions. Either they are buried in the remote past or shoved offstage and recounted obliquely (Komatsu-san's youthful indiscretions), or they are dismissed as momentary phenomena of no great emotional or psychological import (Chinpindō's). Love, the supreme testament to the human capacity for self-deception, is even rarer. When it does appear, it takes the form either of parody (like Dr. Minoya's infatuation) or the mannered, unconsummated sparring of *Shigure-tō* and *Nyonin raihō*.

The reasons for this aversion may be sought in that fundamental sense of decorum and moderation that marked Ibuse's work even when it was being labeled *ero-guro-nansensu*. An author who refuses to deprive his characters of their basic dignity will seldom feel comfortable venturing into the inherently undignified realm of sex. This tendency is particularly evident in the early works. *Shūkin ryokō* and *Chinpindō shujin* are more open in their acknowledgment of sexual activity; but here, too, the particulars are largely omitted, this time with the deadpan pose of a jaded observer who takes all such peccadilloes for granted. Thus we have a transition from youthful bashfulness to cool maturity—but the experiences which should have brought the transition about are left out completely!

Evil, in the form of the deliberate, gratuitous harming of others for one's own interests, is a difficult proposition in comedy: it lacks the necessary element of duality and tends to cause suffering too serious to deny. The closest equivalent that comic treatment can address is pretense which causes remediable suffering, but even this is relatively rare in Ibuse's universe; as with sex, he is fully aware of its pervasiveness, but shrinks from confronting it directly. He prefers to portray duality through the inadvertent, relatively benign form of folly or, when he does portray pretentious, deceptive characters such as Mr. Tange or Lieutenant Okazaki, view them as suffering from delusions of their own.

While a concern with "justice" (*seigi*) is frequently identified as one of Ibuse's more prominent attributes, his focus is on the victims; the victimizers (with a few notable exceptions such as *Sanshōuo*, *Tange-shi tei*, and *Shiraga*) are rarely present at all. There is little attempt to seek redress for wrongs, for evil is an inescapable element of human fate, and, like most of them, hard to remedy. In this sense it comes to resemble the less deliberate misapprehensions: it, too, is a form of unenlightened behavior to which we must somehow reconcile ourselves in order to keep living in an imperfect world. Like sex, though, it involves feelings too strong to be accommodated comfortably in Ibuse's gentle comic spirit, and what it suggests about humanity is so terrible that words can only convey it in the most indirect way. This awareness inspires the powerful undercurrent of melancholy against which the surface brightness is played in most of Ibuse's comic fiction, endowing it with much of its substance and bittersweet tone.

Just as Ibuse consistently preferred to base his comic fiction on explorations of the unfortunate discrepancy between perception and reality rather than the intentional deceptions involved in sex and evil, there was a considerable consistency in his choice of misapprehensions. The "dogmatism" cited by Nakamura is one of them; but on the whole we are presented with relatively few of the more common embodiments of dogmatism (writers, military men, politicians, pedants), and in most cases there is little hint of an abstract ideology. More common are misguided or Quixotic undertakings and a highly personalized type of vanity, which typically takes the form of a fixation on maintaining some kind of appearance that is either impossible to maintain, or, if it is possible, does not create the impressive effect that the character attributes to it. In keeping with Ibuse's aversion to grand gestures, most of these attempts are petty; the inveterate trickster is alien to his world, and even the comic dupe is relatively rare. Most attempts to bamboozle others are quickly revealed to be little more than self-deceptions, often rooted in a character's propensity to be carried away by self-gratifying fantasy visions of himself (or herself) as admired, important, or enjoying a life of freedom and pleasure. In many cases, especially older people (but not the narrators), there is also a strong element of Bergsonian stubbornness reinforcing these tendencies.

The situation of the earliest and most highly caricatured of all Ibuse's comic protagonists, the salamander, can be seen as a prototype for ensuing versions of the basic Ibusean comic predicament: trapped as a result of his own short-sightedness, he insists on maintaining (to himself, when there is no other audience) the illusion that he is free to leave the cave. By exercising his power over the hapless frog, he attempts to salvage a last tenuous prop for his amour-propre, but this also proves to be misdirected. Ultimately he is as much a prisoner of his own misconceptions as of his physical surroundings.

Other early works present variations on the same theme without the overtly allegorical trappings and with the added dimension of the narrator-persona. In *Kuchisuke*, a story whose comedy derives more from quirks and nonsense than from its theme, the title figure is relatively unpretentious, although exceedingly stubborn, and the narrator provides much of the affectation as he struggles to maintain the dignity that he assumes the others see in him while secretly losing himself in dreamy erotic preoccupations. The old man's unwillingness to abandon his long-cherished image of the narrator leads to a similar mistaken assumption on the part of his niece, and her letter summoning the narrator for "legal" assistance gives rise to further mistaken assumptions, including his campaign to "save" someone who no longer needs saving. In the more broadly comic *Shigure-tō*, each of the characters—the jealous and paranoid old man; the hysterical and contentious old woman; and the narrator, with his alternating overconfidence and embarrassment—is intent on living out his or her own vision, but here even more than in *Kuchisuke* the nonsense (along with the passages of local color and lyricism) overshadows the more thematic comic elements, and the comic focus is too diffuse to be fully effective.

The characters in *Josefu to joshi daigakusei* lack the rustic qualities that make so many other early Ibuse characters appear perverse and ludicrous, but the narrator again struggles to maintain a dignified front in the face of poverty, loneliness, and lack of self-assurance. While the title characters are not so concerned with appearances, the college girl, lost in self-indulgent fantasies based on poorly digested notions of romance and the exotic, can find no better object than an underaged captive of equally illusory visions of himself as patriotic hero. The pervasiveness of misperception is neatly epitomized at the end of the story when the narrator discovers that what Joseph had taken to be a "Mona Lisa" print is in fact a faded portrait of Saigō Takamori.

Tange-shi tei, which shares many of the country-*nansensu* qualities of other stories from this period, also establishes the figure of the old man obsessed with the trappings of his (not very considerable) status, while his mistreatment of his manservant is one of the early expressions of Ibuse's strong concern with justice. The vanities of the provincial gentry, and the rude realities underlying them, are given a more elaborate—and wholeheartedly comic—treatment in *Shūkin ryokō*; but unlike their more naïve predecessors, these characters' delusions are sometimes combined with a grittier element of overt duplicity. The narrator, as usual, provides a kind of counterpoint with his more self-consciously ironic efforts to present himself as a person of substance, and a new variation is added by Komatsu-san's memorable performance as the wronged woman who "couldn't help being a bad girl." As mentioned previously, *Yōhai taichō*, with its shift from relatively innocent quirks to murderous delusions, is something of an exception to the general Ibusean comic pattern; but here, too, in the portrayal of the importance of formalities in army and village life, the fixation with appearances is shown to be both a symptom and a cause of graver things.

Chinpindō shujin does not pose such basic questions, and its characters are more prone to self-indulgence and intrigue than to obsession with appearances; but this work, unlike most Ibuse creations, contains no sympathetic character (ordinarily the narrator, or perhaps a young woman) played off against the schemers. Chinpindō himself is a specimen of a type that has traditionally been a staple of comic writing but is rare in modern Japanese fiction (at least until the advent of Mishima), a creature of pure ego who is sure of what he wants and pursues it wholeheartedly, oblivious to what those around him will think or to any possible deeper implications of his desires and actions. He also shares the lack of self-awareness common to Ibuse's characters; in his case it takes the form of an inability to control ill-advised impulses rooted in those baser desires that coexist with his aesthetic refinement. His attempt to establish himself as a man of taste and a successful businessman in modern Japan's most chaotic hour proves just as futile as the narrator's attempt to "protect" Kuchisuke, or Shigematsu's attempt in *Kuroi ame* to prove that his niece is not a victim of radiation sickness.

In most comic narratives, when dualities or misperceptions are exposed, the misperceiving character is made aware of the delusion, or, if he or she remains incorrigible, the community (erstwhile dupes who have become aware) can move to expel the disrupting figure. Either of these developments will produce the "happy ending" long associated with comedy, in which the removal of delusion signals the restoration of truth and harmony, and creates a feeling of satisfaction in the audience. Ibuse's stories, though, rarely end on such a conclusive or auspicious note. Most of Ibuse's endings have a slightly unsettling, tentative feel, often gently lyrical, as in *Shigure-tō* or *Tange-shi tei*, where the characters' delusions are grounded in a larger time-space continuum, showing their essential insignificance in the greater scheme of things. Others are less gentle: Chinpindō may realize that Ranran-jo was able to use his own weaknesses to outmaneuver him, but his governing delusions are shown to survive more or less intact. The narrator of *Shūkin ryokō* is shocked by Komatsu-san's decision to stay on with one of the men from her past, but it seems unlikely to change him—or her—in any fundamental way; the pretensions and vanities of the provincials whom they have visited, of course, are in no danger of changing either.

In other words, in Ibuse's unmasking of comic contradictions, the characters' delusions are exposed to readers, but usually not to the other characters or to themselves; in most cases they and their delusions simply go on caroming off each other in a closed, static world. There is very little growth or enlightenment. Delusion, Ibuse seems to be telling us, is an incurable affliction (*nan to mo itashiyō mo nai yamitsuki*), and there is nothing for its victims to do but muddle along with it as best they (we) can. The most that can be hoped for are small, contingent revelations like those experienced by the salamander at the end of *Sanshōuo* (at least before Ibuse excised the last several lines of the story in the 1985 edition of his collected works) or the narrator at the end of *Shūkin ryokō*, rather than becoming aware of the bigger revelations that will make them wiser beings.

In this respect, there is an ironic, inadvertent accuracy to the *nansensu* label of Ibuse's early years. To the extent that it deals in incongruities, in things that do not make sense, all comedy can be said to deal in nonsense. But normally it strives to find some sense, create some kind of order out of the contradictory elements of life's whirl. Ibuse, on the other hand, left things unresolved and unresolvable, and so nonsense can be said to be at the heart of his comic vision. This, to be sure, is a different matter from the "nonsense" of conventional *ero-guro-nansensu* writings, much of which was pointless; Ibuse portrays pointlessness, but the portrayal itself has a point.

Reminiscing in 1952 on the circumstances surrounding the creation of *Sanshōuo*, Ibuse remarked, "I wanted to write about mankind's path from despair to enlightenment, but of course when it came to writing about becoming enlightened I didn't have the personal experience to back it up. I couldn't help making it sound trite, so I gave up."[32] In a sense, this comment may be applied to much of what followed. The reader, although denied the gratification of seeing enlightenment, or even the dispelling of misperception, the triumph of justice, or any such resolution within the scope of the narrative, is made aware of the truth about the characters' delusions, and through it of a larger truth: if incurable delusion is the inevitable, "normal" state of affairs, then we, like the characters, will have to devise a way to live with it as best we can. If we stumble into caves from which there is no way out, at least we can forgive each other for the things our delusions and despair make us do while we are trapped inside.

Ibuse himself was resigned to living and writing without the "personal experience" of enlightenment, and even to living and writing in the ordinary, unenlightened world without making the attempt to break out. But unlike Sōsuke in Sōseki's *Mon* (The Gate, 1910), doomed to be left standing outside the gate forever yet never to be content without passing through it, Ibuse made his peace with this state of affairs. This is clear from the affectionate attention that he lavished throughout his career on the ways of common people (their "commonness" being as much a matter of spiritual as of social status) and the details of everyday life, and also from the general absence in his work of overt concern with more rarefied themes that have constituted the mainstay of so much modern Japanese writing, such as the search for a personal way, a higher truth, or an authentic self-identity by an individual of extraordinary sensitivity or talent, often in conflict with a restrictive family structure or social system. Such quests are impossible in Ibuse's comedies, whose inhabitants are, like most comic figures, virtually all members in good standing of the ordinary camp. Aside from their struggles with one another, each is engaged principally in an intense struggle with that impersonal, implacable force, reality. Here again we find Ibuse closer in spirit to Saikaku or the Edo *gesaku* writers for whom observation of human foibles is paramount, the very locus of their amorphous "attitude toward life" or "philosophy," than he was to the many writers of modern Japan who instinctively treat such details as points of departure or obstacles to be transcended.

Ibuse's vision of a Japan of village roots and easygoing ways is, to be sure, essentially of prewar vintage. After several decades of high economic growth, high technology, and postindustrial postmodernity, even his postwar cityscapes may appear as quaint as Kuchisuke's valley must have appeared to the Tokyo dwellers of 1929. Ibuse never showed much interest in extending his version into the realm of that contemporary Japanese everyman par excellence, the *sararīman*, even though it would no doubt have provided a singularly rich lode of the pretensions and delusions upon which he focused so frequently. Perhaps he saw it as devoid of the residual innocence that always lurked at the bottom of his characters' hearts. Perhaps the regimented structure of the modern bureaucratic organization did not leave enough room for the expression of individuality—a fatal disqualification for an author who always collected and cherished unorthodox characters the way Chinpindō and his friends seek out out-of-the-ordinary antiques.

Ibuse's unwillingness to confront certain unpleasant or difficult themes head-on and his lack of a conventional "critical spirit" have periodically been cited by hostile critics.[33] In the context of modern Japanese literature, Ibuse's writing must be regarded as out of the mainstream; and in a tradition where seriousness of tone tends to be equated with serious ideas, it is easy to point to the comic elements in his work as an attempt to avoid coming to grips with important issues by laughing them away.

But the qualities that distinguish Ibuse from his contemporaries—and to a certain extent from other comic writers—were also the qualities instrumental to his success in the first sustained effort to introduce a comic perspective and technique to modern Japanese literature. He has, of course, received ample defense from less rigid critics, and his special place in the history of modern Japanese comic fiction now seems secure. As early as 1949 Itō Sei was acknowledging that the credit for bringing the comic outlook to modern Japanese literature belongs to Ibuse.[34] This assessment was soon echoed by Isogai Hideo in his 1950 essay "Ibuse Masuji: Kindai bungaku ni okeru warai no teichaku" (Ibuse Masuji: The Establishment of Laughter in Modern Literature), which remains among the most penetrating analyses of both the comic elements in Ibuse's fiction and of his groundbreaking role as a comic writer.[35]

Nakamura Mitsuo has turned the tables on the "critical spirit" argument by suggesting that while Ibuse is now classed with Kawabata as one of the least "thought-oriented" (*shisōka rashii*) of modern Japanese writers, future readers may see both of them as "one pole of modern literary thought" (*gendai no bungaku shisō no ikkyokuten*).[36] He prudently declines to elaborate on the nature of this "thought," but the perception is a keen one. Like Kawabata, Ibuse can be intensely lyrical and equally intensely harsh, not infrequently within the scope of a single piece (or a single page). Both writers are prone to veer away at crucial moments, leaving behind only some sharply etched but finally elusive image to cover their trail. Kaikō Takeshi's comment that what is written in Ibuse's work matters less than what is not written[37] could apply almost equally well to Kawabata. Both writers also shared a distrust in the dogmas and rules by which human beings attempt to impose order on their world, focusing on the countless ways in which artificial formulas slowly disintegrate under the inexorable pressure of reality. Perhaps this is what Nakamura had in mind; at any rate, the contrast between this approach and the attempt to establish or discover such formulas, which most Japanese critics associate with the term *shisō*, could not be more clearly drawn.

In Kawabata's case the mistrust of formulas is closely related to the theme of time, in particular the ephemerality that dooms all attempts at salvaging some imperishable absolute from the flux, and his awareness of this doom charges his work with a mood of poignant resignation. Ibuse, also resigned to the harshness of fate, to the inevitability of cruelty and loss, looked instead to human nature itself as the source of our failed hopes and mistaken assumptions. But he was able to detect within the human heart a glimmer of brightness amid the gloom. This glimmer is the human capacity to accept and forgive the failings of others, so that one's own failings may also be accepted. Given the frailty of the heart, the glimmer is sometimes a dim one, and sometimes it is threatened with being engulfed completely. But it can never be snuffed out as long as life continues, and it is in this tenuous play of dark and light that Ibuse develops his comic vision. If he offers only a glimmer instead of enlightenment, this is not a sign of insufficient "thought"—rather, it signifies "thought" which has gone beyond the realm of concepts or values, and gazed directly into the human spirit that gives birth to them. This is the achievement of a comic master of high order.

Chapter 3
Dazai Osamu
Laughing at the End

The long personal and literary association between Ibuse Masuji and Dazai Osamu is regularly treated as an important feature in accounts of both writers' careers. According to Ibuse, their first meeting took place shortly after Dazai had come to Tokyo to begin his university studies in 1930, and was preceded—in the rapidly developing Grand Dazaistic style—by a letter in which Dazai threatened to kill himself if refused an interview with his literary hero.[1] They soon established one of those mentor-disciple bonds celebrated in modern Japanese literature (and in Japanese society in general), which was to continue in one form or another up to Dazai's death in 1948. Much attention has been devoted to its salient points, both high and low, including Ibuse's patient nurturing of his wildly erratic protégé through suicide attempts, drug addiction, and lesser catastrophes; his role in Dazai's marriage to Ishihara Michiko, Dazai's promotion of the publication of what became the 1948 *Ibuse Masuji senshū* (Selected Works of Ibuse Masuji) while Ibuse was still living as an evacuee in his native village in Hiroshima; and the enigmatic last line of a letter written by Dazai shortly before his death in which he branded Ibuse an "evil man" (*Ibuse-san wa akunin desu*).[2]

Of greater interest in a consideration of Dazai as a comic writer, however, is the prehistory of this association. By Dazai's own account, he first became aware of Ibuse some seven years before their initial meeting when, at the age of fourteen, he came upon *Sanshōuo* in an obscure literary magazine:

> I, who was then a first-year middle school student in Aomori in the far north, was so excited on reading it that I could barely sit still. . . . I didn't read it as a chil-

dren's tale. By then, I secretly considered myself quite a sophisticated reader of fiction, and in *Sanshōuo* I felt with excitement that I had discovered a hidden, anonymous genius.

From then on, when my brothers brought back various literary magazines from Tokyo on their summer vacations, I would search through them for stories by Ibuse, and each time I read one I would actually shout with delight.[3]

The admiration that Dazai developed for Ibuse's writing seems to have been both wholehearted and permanent; five years later, when he was one of a student group publishing a literary magazine at the Hirosaki Higher School, he asked Ibuse to contribute a piece and even attempted, without success, to call on him during a visit to Tokyo.[4]

It was unusual enough that a teenager growing up in a remote provincial town in the 1920s had access to this kind of reading matter; even more intriguing is his "discovery" of a writer still lost in almost total obscurity. The basis for this precocious shock of recognition may be discerned from the direction Dazai took in his own career as a writer. There is much in Ibuse—his penchant for understatement, his painstaking observation with its concomitant deflection of focus away from himself, his habitual reticence in baring his deepest feelings—which is alien to Dazai. But there is also something which, as Dazai must have realized, was hardly to be found in the work of anyone else writing in Japan at that time: an acute linguistic sensitivity carefully made to serve an outlook that was tinged with a deep melancholy yet unmistakably comic.[5]

Dazai seems to have envisaged himself as a comedian, or at least a clown, some time before he developed literary aspirations.[6] There is little reason to doubt the general accuracy of the accounts of his childhood in works such as *Omoide* (Memories, 1933) and *Ningen shikkaku* (No Longer Human, 1948), in which his antics are already the product of altogether unchildlike calculations to achieve a predetermined effect. The element of calculation is significant: as Harry Levin has pointed out, clowns may be distinguished from other comic figures by their intentionally (rather than inadvertently) putting themselves at odds with the "norm" for comic purposes, their willingness to go out of their way to make themselves look absurd.[7] Dazai found this role most congenial; and the compulsion to entertain, as both creator and star of his own performance, was later to be conspicuous in much of his writing.

Given such predilections, then, it is hardly surprising that Dazai found himself strongly attracted to a story like *Sanshōuo*. Ibuse's careful manipulation of phrasing and tone must have caught his attention as well; while Dazai was never destined to be the master of indirection that Ibuse was, he found in Ibuse's deadpan understatements, lightning shifts between humility and ironic bombast, and unsparing precision a repertory of stylistic techniques that he was later to employ himself with great effect.

Ibuse's work also provided a model in its disregard of then prevalent notions of realism. "Truth" may have been a value above all others for Dazai, but it was never to be confused with mechanical recounting of events. The exaggerations and distortions in Ibuse's early writing, as well as the construction of fanciful settings in which such nonrealism could flourish, are echoed in some of the stories in Dazai's first published collection, *Bannen* (Last Years, 1936),[8] and were to reappear with a new brilliance in the finest of all his comic works, the retellings of Saikaku stories in *Shinshaku shokokubanashi* (New Tales of the Provinces, 1944) and of *otogibanashi* (children's tales) in *Otogizōshi* (Fairy Tales, 1945).

Another distinctive feature of Ibuse's writing that undoubtedly appealed to Dazai was its treatment of the narratorial persona. Although the emotional and psychological forces at work in Dazai's case were quite different from those in Ibuse's, he could not help but be impressed by the ability of Ibuse's narrators to view themselves in a detached, ironic way, and even to expose themselves as comic objects. Their carefully contrived pose of quiet naïveté was neatly congruent to Dazai's own stance as a misfit who saw through the pretenses and deceptions of those around him but was unwilling to confront them (in comic terms, an *eiron*).

The sense of inadequacy underlying the characteristic self-effacing, reticent tone of the Ibusean narrative voice was also to be echoed in Dazai—counterbalanced in Dazai's case, of course, by a streak of narcissism and exhibitionism quite alien to his mentor. In some of the *Bannen* stories, such as *Kare wa mukashi no kare narazu* (He Is Not the Man He Was, 1934) and *Ressha* (Train, 1933), we even see the Dazai persona temporarily relinquishing center stage to other characters, or at least sharing it with them, and taking the Ibusean role of bemused and somewhat discomfited observer of their all-too-human foibles.

The comic element in Dazai's fiction is frequently associated with the term *dōke* (clowning, foolery), which figures prominently in two of his well-known works, *Ningen shikkaku* and the long story *Dōke no hana* (The Flower of Clowning, 1935). *Dōke no hana*, one of the *Bannen* stories, established the theme near the outset of his career. The story portrays the agonies and antics of the author and a few friends in the days immediately following his highly publicized double suicide attempt at Kamakura:

> And they liked to make others laugh, too. Even to the point of hurting themselves, they wanted to make others laugh. All of it must have stemmed from that same emptiness in their hearts, and yet, one level deeper down, can we not perhaps feel the presence of some desperate anticipation? The souls of victims. (1: 25)

> You ladies and gentlemen who seem to have felt such indignation over their all-too-easygoing attitude, as if they failed to realize that someone had actually been killed. . . . How could there be anything "easygoing" here? If only you could understand their sadness as they grew their fragile flowers of clowning, never exposing them to the wind, forever on the edge of despair! (1: 270)

The principal features of the *dōke* mentality are already in place: in his actions, in his writing, Dazai will "make others laugh." The psychological wellsprings of this impulse were vividly portrayed by Dazai himself and have been explored in detail in latter-day analyses: deep-seated feelings of insecurity and estrangement from those around him, and a desperate urge to shield himself from the potential catastrophe lurking in any form of human contact through the deflecting power of a joke.

If the immediate surroundings fail to offer any promising material, the clown must seek something within, even at the cost of self-abasement, and wring a laugh out of it by some process of distortion, burlesque, coy irony—or sheer fabrication. For Dazai, self-abasement was the price as often as not; for holding others up as objects of public ridicule would violate not only the norms of his society, but the emotional forces that motivated the act in the first place. Despite all the evidence that his feelings of weakness and humiliation coexisted with an extraordinarily robust sense of superiority and vanity, he could hardly remain immune to the clown's occupational hazards of depression and loneliness. Dazai was keenly aware that the role of the clown offered a wealth of thematic possibilities above and beyond its narrower and more obvious limits, especially as the wearer of a tearstained mask with a frozen smile; and in *Dōke no hana* and *Ningen shikkaku* (particularly the latter), he plays adroitly on this internal contradiction.

However, even the most sublime performance of a clown, by itself, does not constitute a comedy. The chief literary limitation of the clown lies in the essentially performative nature of his role; most of the nuances, ambiguities, and resonances lie in the acting out, not in the narrative itself. Comic characters are most effective when they are at least partially unaware of the effect their words or deeds will have on the observer, or in other words where they are something less (or something more) than intentional entertainers. No matter how spectacularly a clown succeeds at making an audience laugh, writing about the process need not be very funny; and in Dazai's case it rarely is. Despite the prominence of the *dōke* theme, and a number of illustrations of some choice routines (genuine or fictional), neither of these works has a comic feel to it. As the clown's capacity for genuine suffering is revealed, he is already ceasing to be a comic figure at all; and in both of these works, the clowning is merely one part of a larger scheme in which suffering is portrayed as very real, the life force is almost annihilated rather than celebrated, and exposure of dualities is not a central element.

Even a writer as resourceful as Dazai, then, will soon discover limits to the literary uses of clowning. Ultimately, what made Dazai a comic writer was not his clowning but his ability to show comic dualities in a broad range of styles, settings, and through a broad range of characters, many of whom were neither overt self-portraits nor clowns. On the whole, Dazai's best comic writing is to be found not in those works which portray, or purport to portray, the particulars of his own life, but in works where his image is either absent entirely, or, if present, does not intrude too obtrusively.

Of course, it is impossible to divide Dazai's works into discrete "autobiographical" and "nonautobiographical" categories; as is true for all "autobiographical" fictionists, virtually all of his writing is in some way self-referential, while virtually none of it is a recounting of true-life experiences free of artistic modification. A number of works from his middle years, such as *Fugaku hyakkei* (One Hundred Views of Mount Fuji, 1939), which present more or less accurately incidents from the author's life in a gently playful tone, are sometimes cited as examples of Dazai's comic talents. However, the characters in these stories remain realistically drawn for the most part, and there is little of the caricaturing and exploration of dualities upon which Dazai's finest comic works thrived.

By contrast, in stories like *Kare wa mukashi no kare narazu* and *Shin'yu kōkan* (The Courtesy Call, 1946) the interplay between a first-person narrator and an *alazon* or braggart provides a comic structure throughout. In both stories, the narrator plausibly combines traits of two familiar, though not always compatible, comic types: the *eiron* who creates a gap between reality and appearance by not stating as much as he knows and the dupe who has not got a clue that the gap exists. The braggart's extravagant boasts, moreover, provide the gap between *pretense* and reality as a further duality to be explored—or exploited. In both stories, the narrator—timid, anxious to please (or at least escape embarrassment) but quite at a loss as to how to do so, doubtful that what he sees and hears are what they purport to be—finds himself imposed upon in various ways by the *alazon*, a flamboyant and thoroughly amoral intruder.

In *Kare wa mukashi no kare narazu*, a little man of indeterminate age and background who styles himself a master of the "Freestyle Genius School" (Jiyū Tensai Ryū) of calligraphy suddenly appears and rents a house from the narrator. He has no visible means of support and never pays any rent, but offers an inexhaustible wealth of high-flown and more than slightly dubious talk. By turns unctuously ingratiating, cunning, disarmingly honest, or overbearingly insulting, he always has an intriguing project to talk about—and never does anything. The narrator oscillates helplessly between moods of bemused aggravation and sympathy until one of his tenant's former lady friends finally reveals what should have been obvious all along: the man is an absolute blank who gets all his ideas (as well as all his funds) from his succession of live-in girlfriends. At the end, the narrator, and the reader whom he has taken into his confidence, is left to meditate on the spectacle of one empty man who sought to lodge his own fantasies in the second-hand fabrications of another. As usual in comedy, the deceptions or pretensions of one character are balanced by another character's willingness to be fooled. The deceiver has the best lines and the most grandiloquent gestures, but the deeper comic theme is embedded in the deceived Dazai alter-ego figure, whose knowledge both of others and of himself is shown to be wanting.

Shin'yū kōkan, one of the best known of Dazai's shorter postwar works, purports to be an account of a visit received by the author while an evacuee in his home town in northern Honshu by a "new type of human being" (*ningen no atarashii taipu*), an outrageous and chilling distillation of all the author found repugnant in the "new" postwar Japan. The story's effectiveness depends in no small part upon Dazai's ability to mix grotesque and familiar elements to impart an air of plausibility to his vision and at the same time implicitly remind us how far it is from what ought to be. The "new type" is utterly without a sense of decency; if anything, he seems to represent the triumph of absolute loutishness as a standard of behavior. He is also the social and moral antithesis of the narrator, who predictably finds himself helpless before his guest's unrelenting barrage of brazen demands and coarse braggadocio.

As a vision of humanity stripped of all dignity and beauty, this is one of the first of the black comedies so characteristic of postwar writing (although not necessarily in Japan!). The transgressing "new type of man," far from being enlightened or expelled as in conventional comedy, threatens to overpower reality and impose his pretense on the world—or at least Dazai's little corner of it. Unlike *Kare wa mukashi no kare narazu*, this story does not end on a note of enlightenment; on the contrary, the *alazon*'s parting message to his hapless victim, *Ibaru na!* ("Don't be so stuck up!"), is an ironic coup de grace which precludes any possibility of reconciliation. In fact, there is a strong note of ambivalence to the endings of both stories: in the first, the only real unmasking takes place within "I"'s mind, and its implications are unsettling; in the second, there is no resolution at all. Things are too close —to reality, to Dazai himself—for comfort.

Clowning figures little in either of these stories; instead, a devious but simple-minded outsider inadvertently provides most of the entertainment while Dazai (as character and narrative voice) does the suffering and provides the ironic reflections. This allows for a broader comic treatment than the fictions in which the authorial persona attempts to monopolize all the main roles, and is, in fact, a major reason why Dazai's most successful comic writing is found in the less overtly autobiographical works.

As various critics have pointed out, Dazai's imagination was not suited to the task of fabricating stories; his characteristic method of composition was to take extant material (from the circumstances of his own life, diaries or letters of acquaintances, or older works of literature) and transmute it into something new and entirely his own.[9] Isogai Hideo has gone so far as to suggest that drawing a distinction between Dazai as self-chronicler and taleteller is pointless, since in either case he uses the same remarkable facility with language and artistic shaping of his raw materials to create a personal statement.[10]

While it is difficult to disagree with this analysis, it is equally difficult to ignore the preponderance of non-autobiographical sources in Dazai's best comic works, especially *Shinshaku shokokubanashi* and *Otogizōshi*. Presumably because these are largely comic reworkings of well-known stories from the Japanese tradition, presented with unmistakably Dazaiesque twists, they are sometimes referred to as examples of the author's gift in the genre of *parodei* (parody).[11] This term, problematic enough in its English (and other Western-language) versions,[12] takes on an even vaguer sense in Japanese. Since the classification *parodei* is extended in some cases to include all of Dazai's reworkings, its connection with the familiar Western notions centering on mockery through an inversion of noble and vulgar matter or styles seems tenuous, and the question of who or what, if anything, constitutes the object of the parodic treatment is left unaddressed. Indeed, the point of Dazai's retellings was not to ridicule his original materials, and invidious contrasts of high and low style and subject matter are largely absent from his displacements. If these stories are "parodies" of anything in particular, it is not of the anterior texts but of some element of the author's own character, or of some of the less admirable ways of the world—in other words, the usual objects of Dazai's comic attention.

Perhaps the term *mojiri* (take-off) might serve just as well to describe this kind of writing, but at any rate it is significant that the technique yielded few comic works on a par with *Shinshaku shokokubanashi* or *Otogizōshi* when applied to materials closer to home. By working with materials remote in time and nature from the particulars of his own life, Dazai was freed from the procrustean requirements of "truth" (which inevitably signified suffering) and could freely indulge in the creation of grotesque or ludicrous caricatures and improbable situations conducive to comedy.[13] The greatly expanded range of characters and situations offered all sorts of opportunities to experiment with expressions and speech patterns impossible to work into more contemporary settings, and all the richer in their ironic possibilities owing to the very fact of their remoteness.

Similar possibilities existed with respect to point of view. Although it is possible to see Dazai surrogates in any of these stories, the constraints of the originals are such that they can be only partial, imperfect reincarnations of their creator, and so he is able to view them with an unaccustomed degree of ironic detachment. This tendency is particularly pronounced in the *Otogizōshi* stories, which cross the border from legend to fantasy and the supernatural. Here the author is able to give his imagination the freest possible rein, and, perhaps even more remarkably, goodness and wisdom are offered at least a chance of prevailing over evil and folly, even if only temporarily. This possibility, hopelessly remote in Dazai's "real" world, allows him to adopt a comic vision based on hope and affirmation rather than suffering and despair.

Like much else in Dazai's fiction, the combination of traditional sources and comic tone is foreshadowed in the pages of *Bannen*, especially in the story *Romanesuku* (Romanesque, 1934). Unlike the later works in a similar vein, *Romanesuku* is a tale told by a rather inconspicuous narrator who only rarely assumes the role of an additional Dazai voice; but in most other respects, it is remarkably similar to the major comic tales of a decade later. As an early attempt to project some of his habitual concerns onto an alien textual field, it suffers from a certain heavy-handedness, but its exuberant richness of comic invention more than redeems it.

The story is composed of three segments, each portraying the career of a single character in an atmosphere reminiscent of the vernacular fiction of the Edo period, but at times reflective of Dazai's own circumstances. Each of the three main figures is born into a well-to-do household but soon begins to reject his privileged milieu as sordid, dull, or deceitful—qualities embodied in their respective fathers. Turning their backs upon the course set out for them, each seeks to create an entirely separate identity for himself, through the mastery of wizardry, brawling, and lying, respectively; and, after achieving some success in his chosen field, each ultimately finds himself a victim of his own arcane expertise. The final scene finds them all together around a table in that eternal haven of lost souls, the wineshop, where they tell each other their stories and Saburō the Liar concocts his grandest lie of all: "We are all brothers. From this meeting today, we must never part, even for death. We are artists. . . . Let us write the stories of our lives as models for the world" (1: 200). With this, any lingering doubts are dispelled: the familiar authorial alter ego has reared his head again, in the form of triplets.

The author's penchant for clowning is reflected in a generous helping of physical comedy, even slapstick, especially in the story of the most physical of the three, Jirōbei the Brawler. After painstakingly perfecting an imposing demeanor and then devising and polishing an appropriately intimidating tough-guy line with which to accost potential opponents, he is finally ready to begin the study of actual fighting: "First he studied fist-making. If he put his thumb outside the fist, it might get hurt. After much research, he tried concealing his thumbs in his fists and arranging the first joints of his other fingers in a tight, neat line. This way, he could make a wonderfully strong fist. When he tried hitting his kneecap with these neatly lined-up knuckles, his fist didn't hurt a bit—but his kneecap hurt so badly it almost flew off with the shock" (1: 187).

The account of Tarō the Wizard contains similar slapstick touches, and is capped by the image of the puffy-faced paragon of Tempyō-period male beauty into which Tarō inadvertently turns himself in an attempt to impress the girl next door (his textbook having been of Tempyō vintage). Nevertheless, *Romanesuku* is by no means an all-out farce. Most of its comic impact depends on the quirks and exaggerations of its characters, which echo a variety of habitual Dazai fixations.

One of the most important of these is the theme of *kakō shikō*, the quintessentially Dazaiesque brand of downward mobility expounded in Okuno Takeo's pioneering *Dazai Osamu ron* (On Dazai Osamu, 1956). The emphatically acted-out rejection of a privileged background with its concomitant burdens of guilt, shame, and repression described by Okuno is, of course, a staple theme of Dazai's life and fictions; but when authorial alter egos are placed in a remote and highly fanciful setting, the emphasis can shift away from the emotional aspects of the process to its inherently comic violation of various putatively fundamental rules of human behavior (e.g., that people strive to maximize their wealth, reputation, and comfort, rather than engaging in an active pursuit of poverty, disrepute, and suffering). They become a breed of comic antiheroes, demonstrating in their own downfalls the energy, flexibility, and resourcefulness with which more conventional comic protagonists seek to live out their own realities above and beyond the normal strictures of society.

Tarō the Wizard is born with a yawn on his lips. Despite numerous auspicious signs suggesting that he is a favorite of the gods who will bring unprecedented prosperity to his village, his inveterate laziness ruins his reputation among his neighbors (as well as with his father, who had at first been only too eager to believe that his son was a prodigy). He retreats physically into the recesses of his father's storehouse and spiritually into one of the old books he discovers there, a manual of wizardry. By repeating the magical spell *omoshiroku nai* (it's no fun) over and over, he masters the art of turning himself into various kinds of animals and overcoming his apathy—until the day of his great fiasco, when his powers are lost forever. Reduced to a hopeless figure of ridicule, he must flee his home and sets off on the wanderings which culminate in the fateful meeting in the wineshop.

The other two stories present variations on the same theme. Jirōbei is equally repelled by the prospect of a humdrum, money-grubbing existence in a merchant family; but because he is a more spirited sort than Tarō, his rejection of reality takes the form of fighting instead of escape. Unfortunately, his efforts are doomed to even more spectacular failure; instead of taking on the merchant world he so disdains, he sets out to become a street brawler and loses himself in empty displays of machismo.

Dazai depicts the excesses of Jirōbei's three years of arduous training in painstaking detail, making of its monomaniacal seriousness and its fixation with superficial details of style a travesty of the posture of self-assured spiritual authority which he found so irksome in the Japanese literary establishment. But the same world that celebrated Tarō as a prodigy only to abandon him as a good-for-nothing proves impervious to Jirōbei's elaborately staged transformation. By the time he has forged himself into a consummate fighter, his demeanor has become so imposing that no one dares challenge him. A freak stroke of luck finally allows him to show the world his toughness, still without ever coming to blows, and win the girl he longs for. But the man who tried to stake everything on his fighting ability can use it only on the one person he loves—one day he accidentally kills her while playfully demonstrating one of his knockout punches. In jail he composes a poem which is "half nonsense, half prayer":

> I whispered to the rock
> As my cheeks reddened
> I'm really tough!
> The rock did not answer. (1: 191)

If reality cannot be escaped or fought, then, perhaps it can be denied. This is the premise of Saburō the Liar. Lying or fabrication is one more facet of Dazai's image of the artist, and of himself—a theme later to be reiterated in *Ningen shikkaku*. The figure of Saburō, a meek, introverted schemer from childhood on who drowns a friend when seized with a mindless "fit" and later becomes a successful *gesaku* writer, is the most directly identifiable with the author of the three, and so is drawn in a less caricatured way. More heavily caricatured in this episode is the father, one of the first in Dazai's gallery of beguilingly cantankerous and deceitful old misers. A "scholar of Chinese religion," he taints his only son's existence with a hint of falsehood from its very outset by naming him Saburō (a name conventionally given to the third son in a Japanese family) and, when spanking him, stops after hitting him only three times because "hitting you any more would only make both of us start feeling hungry for no good reason" (1: 192).

Cannier and more cynical than his country brethren, Edo-born Saburō masters the alchemy of turning lies into the "pure gold of truth" (1: 196). He eventually discovers that the best way to employ his unique talent is in the composition of the then-fashionable compilations of "preposterous jokes and deceit" called *sharebon* (1: 195). His magnum opus is *Ningen banji uso wa makoto* (Lies are the truth in the world of men),[14] a tale of a misanthropic master impostor: "This, in effect, was Saburō's I-novel" (1: 196). But his enterprise is also doomed to failure; for his father, the notorious miser, dies leaving behind a mere 500 *mon*, and this "final, disgusting lie" shocks Saburō into trying to mend his ways. A life without lies, though, is nothing more than another lie; there is no recourse but the welcoming oblivion of the wineshop, where the Ultimate Lie, the invocation of art as salvation, awaits.

Romanesuku, with its sight gags and pratfalls, its grotesquely distorted characterizations, and its consistent movement toward paradox rather than resolution, is not so much a satire as a vision of absurdity in which escape and rebellion become futile mirror images of the conditions they seek to reject. In each of the stories, we can see variations on the comic theme of the Grand Project, a bold attempt to create an alternative reality where the hero is in control. Although the shortcomings of the world left behind by Tarō, Jirōbei, and Saburō are obvious, none of the three succeeds in creating a vision that can replace it, because their visions are founded on falsehoods of their own—or perhaps because all such visions are doomed to failure. Since they cannot realize their visions, the only course left is to convey their images to others through their "art."

Dazai himself was keenly conscious of what an imperfect vessel he was to present himself as a "model for the world," a model that offered no answers, full of paradoxes in a world full of paradoxes but not even aware of them. The act of becoming a writer, calling attention to the follies and deceits of the world, and presenting his own conspicuously imperfect life as a "model" would be a dubious proposition at best. Thus there is an inherent ambivalence to his role which, in his more dispassionate moments, is reflected in his work in the form of a highly ironic outlook, presenting the inevitable paradoxes as faithfully as possible, and then attempting to derive as much consolation as possible from the endlessly intriguing details of the show.

This, of course, is an approach more characteristic of such Edo-period figures as Saikaku and Shikitei Sanba than of Japan's modern writers, Dazai included. His association with the self-consciously traditionalist Nippon Roman Ha (Japanese Romantic School) notwithstanding, he was too attached to his own preoccupations to lose himself in the literary past or adopt the Edoesque detached viewpoint.[15] Even those works like *Romanesuku* that echo the tone and flavor of Edo fiction are not simple neo-*gesaku* entertainments but attempts to come to grips with his usual concerns, including a stylized projection of some isolated feature (or features) of his self-portrait as outsider, that take advantage of possibilities of irony and caricature unavailable in a more straightforward I-fiction form.

Given the sense of ambivalence (invoked at the very outset of his career in a famous Verlaine epigraph to the short story *Ha* [Leaves, 1934])[16] which Dazai seems to have elevated into a virtual article of faith, it is not altogether surprising that his 1936 essay "Koten ryūtō dabi" (Classics and Shaggy Dogs) assails Saikaku for indulging in simplistic moralizing even while hailing him as the "most realistic" of all Japanese writers.[17] This, however, may be taken as more of a critique of the tendency toward didacticism in the Japanese literary tradition than a dismissal of Saikaku's work, for Dazai could not fail to have been attracted by Saikaku's stylistic virtuosity as well as his unremitting concentration on the gap between the professed ideals of his age and the day-to-day subterfuges of real life.

At any rate, it is to Saikaku that Dazai turns for inspiration in *Shinshaku shokokubanashi*, a group of twelve tales loosely based on originals found in eleven of Saikaku's collections. In his foreword he proclaims Saikaku the "greatest writer in the world," far superior to the likes of Mérimée and de Maupassant (6: 196). Like his remark almost a decade earlier in "Koten ryūto dabi," this cries out to be taken with a large grain of salt, not least of all in view of the wartime circumstances; in all likelihood, Dazai felt that without such an appeal to nationalistic sentiments his work ran a risk of being refused publication because its content was not discernibly in the "national interest." These circumstances also undoubtedly explain the phrasing of the final section of the foreword:

> It has been almost a year since I started on this work. In that period, a great number of things have happened to Japan. In my own life, too, it is impossible to foretell what will happen when. Thinking that it is of no small importance to have my readers clearly understand what might be called the tradition of the writer's spirit in Japan, I have gone on writing through the days of air-raid sirens. Although I remain dissatisfied with the results, I can at least say that I have written this with conviction, believing it to be a duty imposed upon me as a writer of the divine Shōwa reign. (6: 197)

If Dazai's choice of material has obviously been influenced by the wartime situation, the disingenuousness of his appeal to the sacred tradition which he had mocked mercilessly in "Koten ryūto dabi" is equally obvious. Of all the writers whom he might have invoked as exemplars of the national spirit, Saikaku, who maintained his detached, ironic point of view even in his tales of samurai honor, is certainly among the less compatible with the officially proclaimed ideals of the age. Nor does his invocation of the "tradition of the Japanese writer's spirit" ring true; judging from the actual content of the work, he seems to be using the Saikaku legacy as a shield to conceal his real concerns from the same authorities he sought to placate in his foreword.

In the same introduction, Dazai declares: "I have given these stories the title *Shinshaku shokokubanashi*, with the feeling that I should like to have it understood as 'My Saikaku.' This is assuredly not a translation of Saikaku into modern Japanese" (6: 196). It is, instead, a collection of Dazai characters donning period costume and projecting themselves backwards into Saikaku's samurai and *chōnin* (merchant) worlds, where they demonstrate their ability to remain themselves in surroundings just as restrictive, just as shot through with dichotomies between official dogma and human instinct, as the Japan of 1944. Their stories will be several times longer than the originals, with many new episodes and some new characters added, told in a form and style that make an occasional obeisance to Saikaku but are unmistakably Dazai's own.

Moreover, Dazai informs us, *Shinshaku shokokubanashi* is by no means to be taken as an attempt to cover the entire range of Saikaku's output. "His" Saikaku is the social observer, the somewhat jaded but indulgent chronicler of a broad panorama of follies and foibles, the Saikaku of works such as *Saikaku shokokubanashi* (Saikaku's Tales of the Provinces, 1685), *Seken mune san'yō* (This Scheming World, 1692), *Nippon eitaigura* (The Japanese Family Storehouse, 1688), and *Buke giri monogatari* (Tales of Samurai Honor, 1688). The celebrated erotic fictions hold no appeal for Dazai: "I can't even accept them as being very good. In fact, it seems to me that their conceptions are trite" (6: 196). Perhaps, as at least one critic has suggested, they fell outside the province of "moral questions" with which he chose to concern himself.[18] At any rate, Dazai's view of love consistently centers on the deceptions and egoism that people inflict upon each other, and upon themselves, rather than on physical impulses, and he has no inclination to emulate Saikaku's "realism" in this respect when it comes into conflict with his own.

Whether within the sphere of Saikaku's tales of samurai and *chōnin* manners or the somewhat more fantastic tales he adopted from *Honchō nijū fukō* (Twenty Cases of Unfilial Children in Japan, 1686) and *Shin Kashōki* (New Stories of Humorous Accounts, 1688), Dazai remains above all to his own self true. With the exception of *Akai taiko* (The Red Drum) and *Nyozoku* (The Highwaywomen), all of the stories in *Shinshaku shokokubanashi* involve some kind of decline and fall, or start out at the bottom and stay there.

Unlike Dazai's more closely autobiographical variations on the theme of downward mobility, such as *Shin'yū kōkan,* where the impulse is (at least professedly) rooted in feelings of shame or inadequacy somehow related to the author's background as a member of a privileged class or to his inability to understand and cope with the society around him, the downward motion in *Shinshaku shokokubanashi* can be viewed in an entirely different light; for the identification between author and characters is considerably more tenuous, and there is ample margin for caricature. Most of the suffering that occurs here is of the purely comic (i.e., unreal) sort, unless the reader chooses to look past the caricatures to the historical Dazai and his standard fictional self-image. Because the self-reflective capacity of these characters is severely limited, they are freed from the burdens of shame and self-doubt, and their downward motion becomes gratuitous, even perverse—in short, the kind of vanity or folly familiar as the subject of countless comedies the world over, and far removed from the kind of pathos-laden decline and fall evoked in the traditional Japanese aesthetic of *mujō.*

Perhaps the purest expression of this pattern is the *rōnin* (masterless samurai) Harada Naisuke, the main figure in the story *Hin no iji* (The Obstinacy of Poverty). He has already touched bottom by the time the story begins and is intent on doing his best to remain there. His fierce-looking countenance masks a habitually weak and ineffectual personality; but when good fortune threatens to pay one of its infrequent calls, he can summon surprising resources to drive it away. One New Year's Eve, it seems that he and his wife will be spared their usual desperate evasions of bill collectors when she receives a "cure-all" of ten gold pieces from her brother, a doctor with a whimsical bent; but Naisuke manages to fall to the occasion:

"If I just accept this, I might die from an overdose of good fortune," said Naisuke with a perfectly straight face. "Are you trying to kill me?" He glared at his wife with bloodshot eyes, and then snickered. "Of course, you wouldn't be that kind of demon. I'll drink. If I don't drink, I'll die. Hmm, it's starting to snow. I'd like to have a talk with my elegant friends—we haven't had the chance for such a long time. Go and round them up for me." (6: 200–201)

But even though everything he touches seems to turn into dross, we later realize that Naisuke's incompetence is rather selective. When considerations of samurai honor complicate the search for some missing (and later surplus) money and threaten to spoil his drinking party, it is Naisuke who, after appropriately exaggerated gestures of indifference to all matters pecuniary, devises the eminently practical scheme that satisfies all the requirements of pride, discretion, and fairness, finally enabling his guests to go home. Like a slum-dwelling Rip Van Winkle, he is capable of doing things as well as the next man, if not better—provided only that there is no possibility of any benefit in it for him.

In Saikaku's version, Naisuke's character is merely sketched out in a few brief details at the very beginning of the story:

Right next to homes where the cries of vendors of New Year's delicacies and decorations echo and New Year's *mochi* is being pounded lives a man who doesn't even clean the soot from his house, who doesn't shave until the night of the twenty-eighth, and who glowers at the errand boy sent from the rice shop, brandishing his red-lacquered scabbard and crying "I told you to wait until the New Year—can't you just wait?," a man who wends a wayward path through today's world, where all dealings are straight and proper.[19]

After this introduction, Saikaku's focus immediately shifts to Naisuke and his *rōnin* compatriots, attempting to maintain the trappings of samurai dignity on the shortest of purse strings, and there it remains. For Dazai, however, these first few lines suggest a way of recasting the story in his own fashion:

Long ago in a miserable thatched cottage near Fuji Chaya in the Shinagawa district of Edo, there lived a big middle-aged man by the name of Harada Naisuke, with a frightfully heavy beard and bloodshot eyes. It happens that men with a fearsome-looking visage become intimidated by the sternness of their own face, and Harada Naisuke, whose glaring eyes and imposing face made him look like no mean personage, was a totally good-for-nothing fellow, who when practicing fencing would shut his eyes tight, emit a horrible shriek, and charge off in the wrong direction, crash into a wall, and holler "I give up!," earning for his troubles the nickname of The Wallbreaker, or being treated to a made-up tale of woe from an unscrupulous young clam vendor, raise his voice in bitter sobs and buy up the boy's entire stock, only to receive a tongue-lashing from his wife, be fed nothing but clams for the next three days, and end up writhing with stomach cramps. (6: 199)

While he maintains the improvidence of Saikaku's character, Dazai endows his Naisuke with qualities that emphasize opportunities wasted, potential unfulfilled. What interests him above all is the theme of the "good-for-nothing fellow" (*dame na otoko*). This he develops by adding illustrative anecdotes and a running commentary, explaining among other things that Naisuke's condition is not a form of madness (as his wife suspects) but rather a matter of character. He is at pains to show Naisuke as a person with a distinctive and interesting psyche, while the other characters are flat (and somewhat ludicrous) background figures. In Dazai's hands, the story takes on a double structure, in which the general comic theme of pretense desperately struggling to prevail in an unforgiving world coexists, somewhat uneasily, with a conspicuously more perverse form of futility, the deliberate and persistent pursuit of failure, poverty, and loss of status.

Dazai's attempt to inject his own concerns into another writer's structure can make for a somewhat less neat scheme than Saikaku's, but in *Hin no iji* and several of the other outstanding stories from *Shinshaku shokokubanashi*, he is able to find elements in the Saikaku originals that lead plausibly enough into his own themes and thus to fuse the two elements into an organic whole (or at least harmonize them). The downward impulse is presented even more forcefully in *Hadakagawa* (Naked River), Dazai's version of a tale dating back to *Taiheiki* (Record of the Great Peace, ca. 1372), which Saikaku used as the first story in his *Buke giri monogatari* under the title *Wagamono yue ni Hadakagawa* (Because It's Mine, Naked River). Saikaku begins with a warning about the destructive power of loose tongues; but he makes the figure intended to embody this moral an insubstantial one, limiting his description to the epithet *saikaku rashiki otoko* (a clever-looking fellow) and a few lines of dialogue. He devotes the bulk of his attention to more uplifting personages, a penny-wise samurai named Aoto who loses and then seeks to retrieve some coins from the Nameri River in Kamakura, and one of the gang of laborers engaged in searching for the coins, whose honesty and filial piety reveal his samurai lineage. Dazai, however, limits the laborer to a nameless, peripheral role and a single rather long-winded speech on filial piety; and he emphasizes the conflict between Aoto (here fleshed out into a figure of mindless, self-important rigidity) and the *saikaku rashiki otoko*, whom he endows with a name, Asada, and an identity as an irreverent dropout and gambler in his middle thirties:

> It is said that human vanity reaches its height at about the age of thirty-four or thirty-five, but even if that were not the case, this Asada, priding himself on his slightly distinguished lineage and upbringing, was arrogant and disdainful toward his superiors despite his having fallen into the ranks of laborers. He was a not altogether total fool who loafed on the job, and whenever some bit of chicanery resulted in ill-gotten gains, he would treat the local young bloods to drinks, saying "well, not really . . . ," when they praised him for his generosity. (6: 256).

With Asada, Dazai comes closer to a sympathetic portrayal than he does with any of the other *Shinshaku shokokubanashi* protagonists. The contrast between Asada's generosity, which is comically distorted by his lack of wherewithal, and Aoto's equally absurd pettiness and pretensions throws an ironic light on the relationship between Asada's fallen condition and Aoto's samurai status. Despite his occasional tongue-in-cheek editorializing on behalf of Aoto (another gesture made, no doubt, with a view to the censors), given Dazai's unsparing exposure of Aoto's faults and his depiction of the laborers' patient suffering caused by those faults, we can hear his voice when the laborers tell Asada: "If the world was the way it should be, a smart fellow like you would be up above Aoto" (6: 259). But as long as the world is not the way it should be, Asada will find himself no place more comfortable than the bottom.

In contrast to *Hin no iji* and *Hadakagawa*, in which the downward descent is already a fait accompli at the outset, several stories trace their characters' falls. In most of these stories the characterizations are heavily exaggerated or distorted, and what they gain in comic breadth they sacrifice in depth. *Dairiki* (The Prodigy of Strength) is adapted from *Muyō no chikara jiman* (Musclebound—And Proud of It), a story from Saikaku's *Honchō nijū fukō*. Like Saikaku, Dazai only pays lip service to the premise of enjoining filial behavior and prefers to stress the grotesque nature of a son's outlook and actions. The main character, Saibei, is born into a prosperous provincial merchant family but dedicates himself single-mindedly to sumō. Vaguely reminiscent of Jirōbei the Brawler in *Romanesuku*, but without Jirōbei's psychological motivation or spiritual overtones, he is a creature of pure ego who revels in humiliating his opponents. After the rude shock of learning that strength alone is not enough to win, he apprentices himself to a journeyman professional and quickly acquires enough skill to make himself invincible. Unfortunately, he never acquires a sense of sportsmanship or maturity to go with his prowess, and his triumphant progress in the ring is paralleled by his degeneration as a human being. His obsession with what is, after all, only a game means the loss of merchant-class respectability, and his ruthlessness toward opponents loses him the respect of his wrestling colleagues despite his extraordinary talent. Before long, he finds himself a pariah as well as a champion:

> Mercilessly slapping down his opponents or sending them flying, he caused numerous injuries, repulsively sneering, "In sumō, winning is the only thing," as he coolly exited from the ring. He built up his strength by eating raw meat three times a day, and his face grew big and red like a demon's. When little children playing beside the road saw him, they would scream and fall sick, while the adults would sniff him out from three *chō* away and flee. . . . In all of Shikoku there wasn't a soul who had not heard of him. Saibei thought in his folly that he was now a man of renown. (6: 217)

His parents, after failing to persuade him to give up his disreputable pastime, try marrying him off in the hope that this will divert him, but his sumō fixation turns the ceremony into a fiasco, and the marriage fails to last a single night. By this time his mentor, ashamed of having created a monster, has retired to the life of a Buddhist recluse; but as rumors of Saibei's excesses reach even his mountain hermitage, he finds it impossible to concentrate on his devotions. Returning in disguise, he manages to dump his fierce ex-pupil (only by means of a bit of trickery), leaving him in a "horribly unsightly state, like some giant catfish which had slipped from a gourd, or a wild boar which had fallen from a ladder" (6: 219). Saibei remains unenlightened by the experience, and he drives off his caretakers by kicking them from his bed. His magnificent body withers away to bare skin and bones, and he dies tended only by his parents, a "grand champion among the twenty unfilials of Japan" (6: 219–220).

Saibei's death, the fitting consequence of his infatuation with a dangerous sport, his childish exultation in thrashing his opponents, and his failure to live as a proper son and *chōnin*, is the ultimate expression of the downward course. It is also, of course, the ultimate form of suffering, and one that is normally alien to comedy unless it is offset by some revival or other manifestation of the life force. But Saibei is so grotesquely caricatured that his death has little emotional impact. Unlike Naisuke or Asada, he is not endowed with any redeeming qualities; on the contrary, his strength, self-confidence, obsessiveness, and enjoyment of others' suffering are all more typical of Dazai antagonists such as Aoto. This is one of the few examples in Dazai's fiction where downward mobility seems to be presented without irony or ambivalence, that is, where the author seems to be wholeheartedly endorsing the norms of society vis-à-vis the values of the deviant individual.[20] While *Dairiki* constitutes a testament to Dazai's ability to envision a story without inserting himself into it, the simplicity of its comic structure makes it one of the less satisfying pieces in *Shinshaku shokokubanashi*.

Nyozoku, based on *Harakara no onna oihagi* (Sisters in Highway Robbery) in Saikaku's *Shin Kashōki*, is, like *Dairiki*, a story in the folktale vein, with psychological and social observation largely sacrificed in the interest of broad caricature and comic incongruity. It revolves around a double set of role reversals in the family of Segoshi, a master bandit from the wilds of Michinoku with distinctly unbanditlike qualities of frugality and refined taste. Segoshi, who shuns the highwayman's customary bearskin outfit in favor of silk, is a Nō aficionado and (except when unbearably excited) speaks in a solemn *sōrō* style instead of the inelegant local dialect. His upward aspirations are balanced against the downward progress of his wife, an aristocratic Kyoto beauty whom Segoshi in effect purchases from her impoverished but greedy father. After getting over her initial shock, she gradually becomes reconciled to the situation and even begins to enjoy it: "and later she, too, put on straw sandals and went forth with her husband, calmly helping him perform his evil deeds. By now she had let herself sink to the level of a despicable bandit woman; she still had the face of a beauty, but there was a nasty glint in her eyes, and when she crouched by the well, intently sharpening her husband's sword, one could detect in her figure the horrid air of a she-demon" (6: 276–277).

Her predatory predilections are passed on to her two daughters, who grow up playing robbers instead of house. When their father dies in an avalanche, they don bearskins and false mustaches and continue the family business, but a deus-ex-machina ending cuts their careers short; their mother joins them to go live happily ever after in a nunnery. In this story Dazai has made relatively few changes or additions to Saikaku's version,[21] relying for the most part on the same masculine-feminine and aristocrat-outlaw contradictions. Although the comedy here is broad, the lack of an ironic consciousness seems to have left Dazai without a means of imparting much depth to the story. His happy ending, satisfying as it may be structurally or morally, falls rather flat, especially when compared to the *rakugo*-style punch lines on which a number of the other stories end. While it certainly provides a kind of unmasking of the delusion under which the women had labored, the joyless life of religious retreat that replaces it may not be much of an improvement from a comic point of view.

The improbability of the conventional formula for concluding things happily, or at least satisfactorily, by renouncing the world and devoting oneself to Buddhist piety is reflected more convincingly in *Yoshinoyama* (The Mountains of Yoshino), Dazai's reworking of *Sakura no Yoshinoyama nangi no fuyu* (A Cheerless Winter and the Cherries of Yoshino) from Saikaku's *Yorozu no fumihōgu* (Scraps of Letters, 1696). The story takes the form of a letter ostensibly written by a young ex-*chōnin* to his friends in Kyoto, lamenting the mistake he made in becoming a recluse. Although his original resolution grew out of a frivolous incident, his friends' attempts to dissuade him only make him more intent—in authentic Dazaiesque contrariness—on leaving them all behind. Unfortunately, things go wrong from the very beginning: he discovers that Yoshino is hardly the idyllic retreat so lavishly praised in countless classic poems and that he doesn't look at all elegant with a shaved head. Cold and impoverished, abandoned by his friends, and constantly cheated by the rapacious locals on whom he depends for supplies, he finds that it is only after leaving this miserable world that one experiences its true misery. Unlike Saikaku's letter writer, who yearns for the companionship of a pleasingly plump boy but is ready to hold on for a few more years, Dazai's concludes that "having already renounced the world, I feel as if I would like to renounce it once again—nothing makes sense any more" (6: 321). Even escape offers no escape; it is just another way of lowering oneself, lightly disguised. Dazai strikes a similar note at the end of *Yūkyōkai* (Thou Shalt Not Carouse), his version of *Hito ni wa bōfurimushi dōzen ni omoware* (No More Than a Bug in Their Eyes) in *Saikaku okimiyage* (Saikaku's Parting Gift, 1693), in which three young men are chastened by their meeting with a former partner whose overindulgence in wine, women, and song has left him squalidly down and out. In the Saikaku story, the three resolve to put an end to their womanizing; Dazai turns them all into misers.

Dazai's *Suijin* (The Man of Taste), based on *Uso mo tada wa kikanu yado* (An Inn Where It's Not Cheap to Lie) from Saikaku's *Seken mune san'yō*, falls into an intermediate category between the deeper, darker comedy of *Hin no iji* and *Hadakagawa* and the broader, more farcical tone of *Nyozoku* and *Yoshinoyama*. Here the merchant-class protagonist personifies the weak-willed, irresponsible, self-indulgent, but not wholly unappealing facet of the Dazai alter ego portrayed more fully in a number of Dazai's postwar stories. Already reduced to insolvency at the beginning of the story, he decides to evade the ultimate moment of truth, the settlement of debts on the last day of the year, by leaving his wife to fend off the bill collectors and lying low in a dingy teahouse in the pleasure quarter. The main comic action here involves his pathetic attempt to pass himself off as a wealthy sophisticate on a slumming lark when in reality he is spending his last few coins. His teahouse visit soon turns into a small-scale disaster of its own as he, the shrewd, hard-bitten mistress, and a decidedly overripe geisha half-heartedly play out the increasingly dismal charade, until a pair of strong-arm apprentices finally runs him to ground and strips him down to his underwear as the first installment on his debt.

Like Naisuke and Saibei, this nameless figure is fully deserving of his fate; but for all his faults, or perhaps precisely because of them, there is something charming about him. Certainly it is difficult to ignore his ingenuity and even his audacity. At the same time that we experience the satisfaction of seeing a crude form of justice carried out in the final scene, therefore, we cannot help but feel a bit of sympathy for the man who has now reached his nadir—a point of view underscored by Dazai when he retains the teahouse mistress's final comment from Saikaku's story, "A fool is a man for whom there's still a little hope."

In conventional comic schemes, the kind of downward progress enacted by Dazai's characters is a fate reserved for transgressors and fools, whose ruin or expulsion saves their antagonists from the danger to which the deviant's faults or follies had exposed them. Dazai, however, gives this convention his own distinctive twist: his comic characters are rarely pure embodiments of vice who intend to harm others in their pursuit of self-gratification (although the wrestler Saibei constitutes something of an exception); nor are they portrayed, as are so many of Ibuse's comic figures, as having no consciousness of their own delusions. In almost all cases, they manifest some form of ambivalence or self-contradiction, and are often conscious of it themselves. Naisuke is feckless, but he is also a man of fastidious honor. The letter writer in *Yoshinoyama* may have been foolish in his premature renunciation of the world, but he is also acutely aware of the hopelessly paradoxical longings for the sacred and the profane which coexist in the human soul.

The impoverished samurai of *Hin no iji* and merchant of *Suijin* are at least aware of their own contradictions. All, in other words, are self-contradictory bundles of good and evil, folly and perception.

It is this ambivalent quality that distinguishes them from the other class of comic characters in Dazai's comic scheme, the solemn, self-assured authority figures who profess to know the truth but in reality have only closed their eyes to the endless complexities and contradictions of existence, and so have little tolerance when others show signs of confusion or doubt. Dazai seems to have identified such types as his principal antagonists from very early on, first in the guise of parents and later in other roles. His attack in 1948 on Shiga Naoya, the quasi-official "god of fiction," in an essay, "Nyoze gamon" (Thus I Have Heard) is probably the most direct and vituperative expression of this mentality; but to see its implications for Dazai's approach to comedy, it is more instructive to turn to the relatively early "Koten ryūtō dabi." After briefly musing on the topic of tradition, which he equates with "self-assurance" (*jishin, jiji*), Dazai offers his assessment of its effect on Japanese literature:

> A monistic mode of thought. In other words, without fail, the enlightened look. They never show a moment's confusion. Insisting firmly on one-sided observations, they never doubt unto the final moment. They are always far-seeing masters, not seekers of truth. Invariably, they preach at us. Even Saikaku, the most realistic writer of all, never forgets to weave a simplistic moral into his endings. . . .
>
> Japanese literature is extremely practical. National service writing. It has poems to summon the rain. It avoids the humoresque. Composing manuscripts as if one were tempering a sword. . . .
>
> It has no idea of the idle pleasure of writing. It revels in the mindlessly serious. It does not know of the beauty of nonsense. . . . It has no affection for the rabbit in the moon, but loves the rabbit of *Kachikachiyama*, a vendetta story.
>
> Spectral beings are the essence of Japan's literary classics. . . . This is the only tradition which retains its vividness. Nothing outdated about it. Female ghosts are a symbol of Japanese literature.[22]

For Dazai, "confusion" (*wakuran*) is a perfectly reasonable, legitimate condition, a condition preferable to a smug pose of understanding, for the world and each individual in it are full of irreconcilable contradictions. In many of Dazai's works these contradictions take the form of a conflict between the authorial alter ego and the others who busily go about their daily routines, seemingly directed by some neat but wholly unintelligible master plan. At other times they are subsumed within this character's own personality, in an endless set of variations on the incongruity of the self-effacing, long-suffering servant of humanity and the exhibitionistic, spoiled egotist—or of *fuan* and *kōkotsu*.

This awareness of dualities, ambivalences, and even outright confusion suggests a natural predisposition toward a comic outlook; and even in Dazai's darkest visions, there often seems to be a comic mirror image lurking a short distance below the surface. At its purest, the incongruity is expressed through confrontations between figures like the rigidly doctrinaire, insufferably arrogant Aoto of *Hadakagawa*, so blinded by his own self-assurance that he ignores clear signs that he is being hoodwinked and causing others to suffer, and Asada, who may have his own faults but is not deceived by cant, even when it is backed by all the trappings of authority. In *Dairiki* and *Nyozoku*, too, Dazai manages to exploit this theme by inserting new characters, a sumō master who unsuccessfully attempts to make Saibei see that there is more to life than humiliating his opponents and a hypocritical father-in-law who sells his daughter off to a bandit in order to finance his own social climbing, and reproaches her for being unfilial when she protests. In other instances, as in *Hin no iji* or *Yoshinoyama* (or, for that matter, *Romanesuku*), similar incongruities are portrayed as contradictions within single characters. In either case, contradictions that lead to downward mobility and suffering of a more or less acute nature in Dazai's more autobiographical works are handled differently when the characters are more distanced from their author. In the latter case, the protagonists either defy the laws of literary gravity by becoming comic antiheroes or, in simpler works, come to resemble the more conventional comic figures who meet with a harsh comeuppance because they stray from values held in common by author and audience.

Stories of the latter type, such as *Suijin*, *Dairiki*, and, in a slightly different way, *Nyozoku*, are not entirely free of the didactic tendency for which Dazai had assailed Saikaku in "Koten ryūtō dabi." The wartime factor undoubtedly played a role here; it is also possible to number these stories, like the stories of *Otogizōshi*, among the products of a "middle period" in which Dazai declared a temporary truce in his running battle with the world and strove to play the role of normal, respectable citizen. But even if one discounts the argument that several of the *Shinshaku shokokubanashi* stories are, in fact, antigovernment or antiwar allegories, it is difficult to construe *Hadakagawa* or

Hin no iji as affirmations of the status quo. Even the simpler stories, dwelling as they do on the compelling attractions of food, drink, and wealth at a time when the government propaganda machine was doing its best to persuade the Japanese public that such materialistic thoughts were little short of treasonous, suggest a tacit rejection of authority and dogma more in keeping with Dazai's usual stance.[23] All the same, the simplistic moralizing note on which he concludes these stories does not ring true, and Dazai turned away from it emphatically in *Otogizōshi*.

Significantly, the qualities of "pleasure" (*kyōraku*) and the "humoresque" (*yūmoresuku*) are invoked in Dazai's defense of ambivalence and confusion, revealing his instinctive understanding that comedy was the most appropriate means of challenging the "far-seeing master" mentality in its literary form. In all of the incongruities he explores, even the simplest collisions of pretense and reality, his stance of ambivalence persistently contests what he considered the one-dimensionality of the Japanese literary establishment, even while he implicitly (and, in *Otogizōshi*, explicitly) includes images of Japanese writers in his rogues' gallery of self-important, mindlessly serious caricatures.

Along with Dazai's ability to reshape Saikaku's characters in accordance with his own vision, it is the richness of his language, much of it comic, that endows *Shinshaku shokokubanashi* with a life of its own. With his ear for ironic nuance, his acute sense of timing, his wealth of vivid anecdotes, and his frequent interruptions of the narrative flow with a stream of highly personal commentary, he is able to flesh out Saikaku's spare sketches and shift the focus toward those themes that concern him most. Thus stories such as *Saruzuka* (The Monkey's Burial Mound) or *Ningyo no umi* (The Sea of Mermaids), in which he seems unable or unwilling to impart his own touch, are the least satisfying in the collection; not coincidentally, these stories are also the least comic in tone.

The interest in such otherworldly phenomena as "spectral beings" (*obake*) and ghosts (*yūrei*) expressed in "Koten ryūtō dabi" may not be a trait readily associated with one of Japan's more celebrated writers of autobiographical fiction, but in fact Dazai was already exploring the world of legend and the fantastic in *Bannen*, most notably in *Romanesuku* and *Gyofukuki* (Metamorphosis, 1933). Dazai's major work along these lines, however, and arguably his supreme comic achievement, was the four-story series *Otogizōshi*, written in the final months of the war, that is, shortly after *Shinshaku shokokubanashi* and almost a full decade after "Koten ryūtō dabi." In his introduction, Dazai claims that he began to think about creating his own versions of these traditional children's tales while reading them to his daughter in an attempt to keep her quiet during air raids—although his treatment of one of the stories, *Kachikachiyama* (Crackling Mountain), is precisely foreshadowed in "Koten ryūtō dabi," suggesting that in fact the idea had already occurred to him several years earlier.

Comic themes familiar from *Romanesuku* and *Shinshaku shokokubanashi* abound again here. The old man of *Kobutori* (Talking the Wen Away) and the prematurely old man of *Shitakiri suzume* (Tongue-cut Sparrow) are reincarnations of the standard Dazaiesque dropout figure, turning their backs on all considerations of wealth and respectability, passing their days in idle diversions to their relatives' chagrin. The *tanuki* (a badger-like animal) in *Kachikachiyama* is perhaps Dazai's most extreme portrayal of the blustering, absolutely egotistical but somehow charming rogue male whose inability to doubt his own pretensions ultimately leads to catastrophe. The only exception is the title character in *Urashima-san*, whose aversion to adventure and all other forms of change precludes (or, rather, seeks to prevent) any possibility of downward progress.[24]

The two old men of *Kobutori* constitute one of Dazai's most vivid portrayals of the comic dichotomy between innocent ambivalence and self-important dogmatism. The first likes nothing better than a cup, or several cups, of *sake*, but since his wife and son are both frigid moral exemplars who seem intent on draining away all of his natural joie de vivre, he has no choice but to flee periodically to the mountains, a zone of freedom where he can drink his fill and assuage his loneliness by talking to the birthmark on his cheek and the forest animals. When he happens upon a party being held by a band of good-natured, imbecilic, and obviously inebriated demons one evening, he naturally joins in the revelry. The serious-minded, arrogant second old man is the diametric opposite of the first in every respect, except that he has a similar birthmark. Resenting it as an "obstacle to success," and hearing that the first old man had his taken by the demons after showing them his dancing talents, he determines to lose his own the same way:

> The old gentleman set out with his eyes glaring and his mouth set in a firm grimace, as if he were a warrior sallying forth to battle. "Tonight," he thought to himself, "I shall stir them with a splendid dance, and if by some remote chance they fail to be stirred, I shall smite them all with my metal fan—and why not, for after all they are

only a band of besotted, foolish demons." As he rushed into the depths of the forest, with shoulders set and his metal fan firmly clutched in his right hand, it was impossible to tell whether he was going to dance for the demons, or to drive them away. (7: 287)

Unfortunately, his arthritically formalized performance only disconcerts the demons and sends them flying; the narrator comments that artistic undertakings of this type, in which the performer is swept away by the ambition to produce a masterpiece, are doomed to failure. One more misapprehension, and one more failed scheme turned completely upside down, but as usual Dazai has no interest in pat happy endings, so the first old man is left in the cold bosom of his family, even lonelier than before now that he has lost his heretofore inseparable companion.

The importance to Dazai of some kind of ambivalence or duality in the original which he could remold in his own way is made absolutely clear in his introductory remarks to the last of the *Otogizōshi* stories, *Shitakiri suzume*, in which he devotes two lengthy paragraphs to an explanation of his reasons for abandoning his original plan to include a retelling of *Momotarō* in the series. This tale of an exemplary Japanese superhero and his demon-routing exploits would seem to be just the right thing to rouse a wartime audience. Unfortunately, Dazai tells us, in order to heighten the story's effect, the demons should be portrayed in as loathsome a light as possible, but genuine Japanese demons are actually benign, almost winsome creatures, who may even arouse the reader's sympathy if handled too roughly. And there is an additional stumbling block:

Flawless, absolute strongmen just aren't suited for stories. And furthermore, perhaps because I myself am without strength, I feel that I have some understanding of the workings of the minds of weaklings, but I don't know much about the minds of the strong. . . . I am a writer with a very weak imagination, and unless I have a certain amount of experience with something I cannot write a single line, not even a single word about it. Therefore, even in telling the story of Momotarō, it would be quite impossible for me to present an absolutely invincible hero when I've never seen one. (7: 350–351)

Dazai's Momotarō would be "a crybaby from childhood, a weakling, a timid, completely worthless fellow"; his three traditional companions, the dog, monkey, and pheasant, would be transformed from model loyal retainers into a quarrelsome trio, each with his own irksome flaws. But in the end, he shrinks from such a scenario, for Momotarō is a national standard bearer,

Japan's Number One Hero, not to be tampered with by "a writer who has never experienced Japan's second or third best, let alone number one." Only after a long and self-consciously repetitive passage cautioning that none of the characters in *Otogizōshi* are to be taken as paragons of anything does he finally launch into his depiction of the main figure of *Shitakiri suzume*, a man who, "far from being Japan's Number One, might be called Japan's most worthless man" (7: 352).

While each of the four stories retains some of the characteristics of *Shinshaku shokokubanashi*, *Otogizōshi* is in other respects a very different work. The introduction contains no appeals to the "tradition of the Japanese writer's spirit" or declarations of duty; the narrator now presents himself as the father of two small children, "with threadbare clothing and a foolish-looking face," struggling like countless other citizens to keep going as the bombs fall around him. If these fairy tales for adults can transport their readers temporarily beyond the grim daily realities and provide a bit of amusement, a faint glimpse of something brighter, then they will have served their purpose.

The worldly pursuit of money, reputation, and creature comforts that Dazai had carried over from Saikaku is largely absent here. All of the *Otogizōshi* stories involve some kind of escape, usually with an element of the supernatural, to some ideal realm which contrasts with the emptiness and disappointment of normal life. In *Kobutori*, even the old man's love of *sake* is a reflection of the loneliness and frustration caused by his "exemplary" but arid family life; the woods of Mount Tsurugi are a haven where he can drink in peace and disport with the demons, who offer the companionship his wife and son cannot. In *Urashima-san*, Dazai's reworking of the well-known legend of Urashima Tarō, who saves a tortoise from being tormented by a group of boys and is later rewarded with a journey on its back to the marvelous undersea palace of the dragon king where he is sumptuously entertained by a princess, it is the palace that provides a utopian vision. There are mountains of pearls, and the floors are covered with delicious cherries and euphoria-inducing blossoms; but only the "elegant" (*fūryū na*) visitor from above would even consider the idea of overindulging. There are no disturbances, no walls, and all the inhabitants are free to do as they please. But this is not a carnivalized world of festive license; unlike the pandemonium which would have ensued if most of the characters of *Shinshaku shokokubanashi* had been allowed to follow their own inclinations in such a place, the atmosphere is remarkably subdued. The keynote is *seitei* (divine resignation), the title of the tune which the undersea princess performs on her *koto*. Everyone is contentedly oblivious to what others are doing, and the constraints and cares that made life in the world of humans so difficult are finally dissolved.

A similar atmosphere pervades the home of the sparrows in *Shitakiri suzume*. In the original, a cruel old woman cuts out the tongue of a sparrow that had taken some food she had prepared; when the bird flies off, the woman's husband follows it to its home, where he is greeted by the bird's family and rewarded for his earlier kindness to it. In Dazai's version, when the fortyish "old man" finally arrives there after a long and arduous search and is reunited with the bird of whom he had grown so fond, he simply sighs, not in disappointment at her pitiful state, but in joy and relief, and gazes at the fountain in the garden outside: "There was no need to say anything" (7: 366). A brief visit is enough for him to reaffirm that the indescribable feeling akin to love, the feeling of fulfillment he could never experience in his own home, was not just a passing delusion.

None of these havens, however, proves to be a happy ever after. The old man in *Kobutori* must go back down the mountain to his killjoy wife and insufferably sanctimonious son, and the husband in *Shitakiri suzume* realizes that the home of the sparrows is not to be his home. Urashima, too, eventually leaves his pleasure dome: "Perhaps he had become tired of being free to do anything. He missed that poor life back on land. He even came to think of the people back on land plodding through their mean, humble existences, always having to worry about what everyone else might think, laughing, raging, as charming, as somehow beautiful" (7: 318). There are no human beings in Dazai's utopias except for casual visitors. In a sense, these idealized or liberated worlds exist only so that the characters may return from them to their ordinary worlds. Utopias cannot hold the human spirit for long; it naturally gravitates away from perfection and back toward the confusion, the irreconcilable contrasts of the world of its origin.

In *Otogizōshi* there are no simple conclusions to be drawn. Dazai takes the children's-story convention of pat endings and turns it on its head; each tale finishes with an anticonclusion that negates the sense of the original and deflects our attention in a new direction. Invariably, in these final remarks, Dazai raises more questions than he answers and then returns us as gently as possible to the irreconcilable dilemmas of our own world. But even as the characters' sojourns in these great good places provide them with an ability to endure life with a sense of acceptance and tolerance that they previously lacked, our reading of their stories endows us with some of the same capacity.

Except in *Shitakiri suzume*, each of these anticonclusions is presented as a kind of informal talk, as if the storyteller, after finishing the narrative, wanted to explain to the audience what the story was all about. The conventional didactic ending of *Kobutori*, which stresses the punishment of the second old man for his wickedness, is not appropriate, he tells us, since the man has done nothing evil: "Isn't it true that his dance merely turned a bit odd, through an excess of tension?" (7: 289). Why, then, has the old man suffered this misfortune?

> If an impatient reader were to force such a question upon me, I suppose I would have no choice but to reply along the following lines:
>
> This is a tragicomedy of character. In the depths of human life, we always find this question flowing as an undercurrent. (7: 289)

Perhaps the hint of diffidence should be attended to and this pronouncement disregarded, but as the handiwork of a compulsive communicator, it does invite speculation. Character (*seikaku*), not morality or ability, is what separates the demons and the first old man from his family and the second old man, just as it separates the hard-working, deadly serious writers hailed by the press as "literary demons" (*bungaku no oni, bundan no kisai*) from an avowedly simple-minded writer who can only respond with "confusion" when he discovers that some writers do not seem to mind such labels. It is, in other words, an expression of the same dichotomy identified in "Koten ryūtō dabi." The second old man's extra birthmark is the logical result of his relying on his self-assurance instead of his eyes, but it is nobody's fault.

In the "forgetfulness" that consoles Urashima when he finds himself a lonely old man, in the husband's bitter smile and his comment "I owe my good fortune to my wife; I made things so hard for her" at the conclusion of *Shitakiri suzume*, even in the plaintive "Was it wrong to love you?" that summarizes the *tanuki*'s demise in *Kachikachiyama*, there is a similar note of acceptance, an understanding that we can only reconcile ourselves to the ultimate irreconcilability of things. Contradictory characters, even the contradictions within a single character, must be taken as they are; and it is better to accept them with a smile, however faint, than to bewail them.

Otogizōshi, with its recurrent passages of transcendent serenity and divine resignation, approaches the redemptive condition of high comedy in a way that Dazai's previous works do not. But while each of the main characters displays a certain fecklessness, the most severe shortcomings are associated not with them but with the "normal world" from which they have fled—the nagging family members of *Kachikachiyama* and *Shitakiri suzume*, the incessant "criticisms" that plague Urashima. It is from these that the protagonists have felt it necessary to flee, and their transcendent experiences, rather than alerting and reconciling them to their own shortcomings, instead reconcile them to the shortcomings of others, who remain unaware of them themselves, and so the reconciliation lacks the full impact of high comedy.

The air of compassion and reconciliation is undercut even more conspicuously by Dazai's strikingly vitriolic portrayals of his female characters. The first old man's wife in *Kobutori*, the rabbit in *Kachikachiyama*, and the wife in *Shitakiri suzume* are merciless vixens whose sole pleasure seems to lie in tormenting hapless males. By far the most extreme case is the rabbit. In his introduction to the story, Dazai writes that the gratuitous cruelty of the rabbit's revenge on the *tanuki* makes the traditional version of the tale inappropriate for children and also violates the manly spirit of the Japanese warrior (*bushidō*). After a lengthy and sarcastic analysis of the shortcomings of the traditional version (and of sanitized contemporary versions) of the story, he announces his solution: if the rabbit's behavior is unmanly, it must be female! He makes her a beautiful maiden of sixteen and speculates that females of this type are the cruelest of all human beings; but in the malevolence and duplicity of the rabbit and the simple-minded greed of the *tanuki*, he offers his paradigm for all male-female relations—or, to put it more precisely, a battle of the sexes in which men are woefully overmatched and the outcome is entirely predetermined.

Kachikachiyama is the only one of the *Otogizōshi* stories in which the male protagonist fails to find a haven. The *tanuki* seeks his paradise within the natural realm, in the form of the rabbit's love, but his obtuse insistence on attempting to live out his worst delusions only leads to catastrophe. After the horrid denouement, when the rabbit has finally pounded her victim beneath the waves of Lake Kawaguchi with an oar and exclaimed "Oh, what a sweaty job!," the narrator muses on the meaning of it all. Is it a cautionary tale about the dangers of amorous dalliance or dull-witted obsession? Or is it an amoral comedy of attraction and repulsion, or any of a number of other likely interpretations? The key is to be found in the *tanuki*'s last words: "Was it wrong to love you?"

I think it would be no exaggeration to say that we see here a major theme of the tales of sadness in all the world's literature, ancient and modern. Within every woman lives one of these merciless rabbits, and in all men a goodly *tanuki* is desperately struggling to keep his head above the waves. When the author considers his own extremely ill-starred experience of the past thirty plus years, this much is crystal clear. In your case, too, perhaps. The end. (7: 348)

The "goodly" (*zenryō na*) *tanuki*, like the male protagonists in the other stories, is very much an adherent of the pleasure principle; he has his own share of flaws and is appealing only in relation to the meanness of the female against whom he is played off. Dazai concedes as much in the final scene of *Shitakiri suzume*, but this does not alter the basic pattern: the roles of victim and victimizer, intensified by comic exaggeration and repetition, are explicitly assigned to male and female respectively. The one prominent exception to the pattern, the princess in *Urashima-san*, is a highly idealized figure who—significantly—leaves everybody alone.

The looseness of the *otogibanashi* originals gives Dazai opportunities for heightened comic effects of various sorts. The very act of retelling such well-known tales requires that he recast them in a striking or distinctive way, since the conclusions are more or less foregone. This is very much in the Japanese tradition of taking a well-known literary or historical narrative line as a premise (*sekai*) and applying to it a novel treatment (*shukō*), typically through juxtapositions of familiar plot sequences with unanticipated settings or characters. Each of these incongruous elements may act as a kind of comic commentary on the other. Dazai adds a further personal touch (and establishes another pair of interwoven comic elements) in the exegeses, some of them quite lengthy, with which he begins all and ends all but one of the *Otogizōshi* stories. Passages of this sort are a common enough feature in Dazai's more straightforward autobiographical fictions, many of which begin with a brief first-person introductory passage in which the author presents himself as a concrete raconteur figure rather than a disembodied narrative voice. Usually these passages have the twofold effect of suggesting an identification, genuine or otherwise, between the author, narrator, and protagonist of the story and, through an intimate, conversational tone that often has the feel of a direct address, developing an immediate rapport between author and readers. Additional direct-address passages may appear throughout the story, interrupting the narrative flow to provide a running commentary on the action as it unfolds; at the end, they may also serve to sum things up and dislocate the reader from the world of the story to a final pseudo-conversation with the narrative voice. In the putatively less self-referential *Otogizōshi,* he imparts a note of freshness by whimsically but insistently reminding his readers that the stories will be told on two levels, the familiar one and his own. In *Kobutori* he quotes the first few lines of the children's story version and immediately comments on them: "This old man lived at the foot of Mount Tsurugi in the province of Awa, Shikoku. Or, at least, that is how it seems to me, but I don't have any particular authority for this. Originally this story is supposed to have come from *Tales from Uji,* but it is impossible to cross-check sources in an air-raid shelter" (7: 274).

In the introductions, we are offered an analysis of the shortcoming of the traditional tale's *sekai* and an announcement of the *shukō* that has been devised to rectify it (turning the first old man in *Kobutori* into a henpecked drinker, making *Kachikachiyama* into a battle of the sexes). In *Urashima-san* the *shukō* consists of reversing the traditional relationship between Urashima and the turtle who guides him to the undersea palace, making the latter a wise-cracking, irreverent wag instead of a humble servant and subverting any notion of the former as a heroic figure. Even Urashima's noble gesture in saving the turtle's life is deflated: after all, the turtle reminds him, it didn't take any particular courage for a grown man to rescue him from a group of small boys, and when he ransomed the creature, he set the price at a paltry five cents—a rather undignified price to have put on one's life, although if it had been a beggar being beaten up by a gang of local toughs, Urashima would probably not even have shown a penny's worth of nobility.

The presence of animals or supernatural beings in all the stories enables the author to suspend the strictures of logic and common sense, especially in *Kachikachiyama,* where the time-honored comic theme of the battle of the sexes is enacted in grand style through the superhuman credulity, gluttony, and vanity of the *tanuki* and the inhuman cruelty of the rabbit. The *tanuki*'s repeated attempts to conceal his true age are reminiscent of the geisha's maneuvers in *Suijin;* but in the fantasy world of the *otogibanashi,* he is free to indulge in a series of evasions so absurd in their crude inconsistency that he rapidly loses all semblance of control over them, ultimately succeeding only in confusing himself.

The same kind of freedom is reflected in the language of *Otogizōshi.* In the alternating voices of narrator, commentator, and characters, Dazai employs a rich variety of styles and tones, from the self-consciously bombastic to the chattily familiar. The narrative voice often has tongue kept firmly in cheek, seeming to show admiration for the characters by describing them with insistently repeated stock epithets (as a minor character in an Ibuse story might) even while their pretensions and inconsistencies are being exposed. Because the usual rules of social decorum are suspended, the dialogue sparkles with kaleidoscopic variations of rhythms, moods, and expressions impossible in more "realistic" situations. Many of these involve comic confrontations between characters who, for once, can tell their adversaries exactly what they think; among the most notable of these are the marital squabble between the birds in *Shitakiri suzume*, deftly echoing (and parodying) the running battles between the old man and his wife, and the long passages of conversation between Urashima and the turtle, a kind of extended literary *manzai* (comic duo) act in which the self-styled aristocrat and advocate of "elegance" serves as a straight man for his quick-witted guide:

> "It's so quiet down here. It's almost scary. We're not in hell, are we?"
>
> "Come on, young master, get a hold of yourself," said the turtle, slapping Urashima on the back with a fin. "All royal palaces are this quiet. Did you have some stale idea that they're making an idiotic non-stop racket in the Dragon Palace, as if it were some kind of fishermen's dance back home in Tango? How pathetic! Isn't a quiet retreat supposed to be the very height of what you people call elegance? What a shame. . . . Hey, you still have your sandals on! Come on, take them off, show some manners!" (7: 304)

The *otogibanashi* feature most enthusiastically exploited by Dazai, however, is the assumption of the traditional storyteller's role. The oral quality of the narration is pervasive. The collection begins with a general introduction portraying the attempt of a harried "father" to pacify his restless five-year-old daughter while waiting out an air raid in the family's cramped backyard shelter:

> This father's clothes are shabby, and he has a rather dull-witted look to him, but he is not the kind of man to be dismissed lightly. He is a man who is well versed in the truly curious art of making up stories.
>
> "Once upon a time, long long ago . . .
>
> Even as he reads from the child's picture book in an odd, silly-sounding voice, an entirely different kind of story is taking shape within him. (7: 272–273)

Although this may suggest yet another Dazai self-portrait, the third-person narrative voice places the father within the narrative frame and creates some distance between him and both the author and reader. The introduction to the first story, *Kobutori*, which follows immediately, recapitulates the scene presented in the general introduction, but this time from the father's own point of view:

> I am crouching in an air-raid shelter, and all I have is the picture book lying open on my lap. I'm in no position to check the facts, so all I can do is let my imagination wander. . . . Thinking such petulant thoughts to himself, that peculiar personage, the father, reading the "Once upon a long, long time ago," of the picture book in his corner of the shelter, began a new story in his mind, entirely different from the one in the book. (7: 275)

From this point on, when the narrative voice intrudes to comment on the development of the story, there are many passages where it is unclear whether this voice belongs to the father who is making up the "entirely new" tale, or to a disembodied narrator whose field of vision encompasses the father. But while many passages in which the story-telling "father" speaks directly to the reader explicitly in a first-person voice remain, third-person references to "the father" disappear. Compared to the general introduction, the distance between author and narrator is reduced in the stories, and so is the distance between author/narrator and reader.

In this respect the narrative voices in the *Otogizōshi* stories recall those in many of Dazai's more recognizably "autobiographical" fictions. But while there are characters in *Otogizōshi* who embody some familiar Dazai traits (the drinker, the henpecked husband, the dandy, etc.), the folktale format separates them temporally and spatially from both the author and the narrator immobilized in his shelter, rendering impossible the kind of direct identification between protagonist, author, and narrator so common in other Dazai works. The increased distance also enables the author to devote more attention than usual to the other characters and achieve something approaching a balance between them and the protagonist. The *tanuki* in *Kachikachiyama*, for instance, is not simply a victim of the rabbit's cruelty; it is clear that his own greed, laziness, and obtuseness contribute to his downfall. In *Shitakiri suzume*, the protagonist is an essentially sympathetic character, especially in contrast to his wife; but the sparrow does not hesitate to mercilessly expose his posturing:

> "I was born to, well, to tell the truth."
>
> "But, you never tell anybody anything, do you?"

"They're all a bunch of liars. I became sick of talking to them. Nothing but lies. And what's more, what's even scarier, is that they don't even realize what lies they're telling."

"That's just a lazy rationalization. It seems like everybody with a little bit of education likes to try self-indulgent, lame excuses like that on people. Look at you—you never do anything at all. There's an old saying, 'If you want to sleep, don't wake people up.' You're in no position to be talking about anybody else."

"That's true," said the old man without agitation. "But there should be a place for people like me. It may look like I'm not doing anything, but it's not necessarily so. There are things that nobody but I can do. I don't know if I'll ever get the chance to show what I can do, but if the right time comes, I'll give it all I've got. In the meantime, well, silence and reading are the things."

"I wonder," said the sparrow with a quizzical cock of the head. "The more spineless someone is, the more sour grapes and the more big talk you hear from them. . . . You console yourself by substituting dreams of the past that will never come again for hopes of the future. I feel sorry for you. It doesn't even amount to big talk. It's just perverse grumbling. Look—you aren't doing any good at all." (7: 357–358)

Dazai's assumption of the traditional storyteller's role allows the narrative voice freedom to intrude to an unusual degree and in a variety of ways. The narrative flow is repeatedly broken by long, leisurely digressions on various topics suggested by something in the action, imagery, or language of the tales (turtles, demons, sparrows, folk customs, and the like), playfully parading the narrator's contrived "erudition" or dryly mocking the entire notion of holding these stories up to serious scrutiny. Sometimes, as in the introduction to *Shitakiri suzume*, he even offers exegeses on his own exegeses. At other times he speculates on the motivations of the characters or provides his own assessment, often one that suggests his own situation. Whether the tone runs toward the gently self-deprecating or inflated clichés, it is always edged with an irony which implicitly suggests that there is more than one side to every phenomenon, that nothing is to be taken completely at face value, and that if we cannot reconcile the paradoxes and imperfections confronting us on all sides, we can at least find a way to make life a bit more comprehensible and endurable through them—in other words, the eternal propositions of comedy.

Published two months after Japan's surrender, *Otogizōshi* was the last of Dazai's wartime reworkings of traditional materials. It also stands as his last completed work in which comedy is not subordinated to a powerful sense of despair. The reasons for this turn away from comedy are no clearer in

Dazai's case than in those of earlier writers such as Sōseki and Uno Kōji, but the postwar years, with their traumas and disillusionments, were not conducive to belief in the nonreality of suffering; and amid the signs of the emergence of a new order in Japan which he found as distasteful in its way as the old one had been, Dazai seems to have found it natural to revert to his customary outsider stance.

His closest approach to comedy is found in stories such as *Shin'yū kōkan* and *Toka tonton* (A Sound of Hammering, 1947). In *Shin'yū kōkan* (discussed earlier in this chapter), the main comic element is the "new type of human being," the boorish visitor whose boasting and greed suggest that Japan's much-heralded new era of peace and freedom may in fact end up making a travesty of all recognizable standards of decent social behavior. The imposed-upon "host" who provides the requisite complement to this figure by becoming his victim is, of course, the alter-ego narrator, who embodies a comic duality of his own as a representative of a kinder, gentler presurrender society (!) whose moral superiority he lacks the strength to defend.

Toka tonton consists almost entirely of a letter purportedly written to Dazai by a young man who, starting on the day of Japan's surrender, finds that every time he considers something that might give meaning to his life (patriotism, writing, work, love, social or political activism), he hears a hammering sound that immediately leads to disillusionment. The repeated pattern of inspiration-sound-disillusionment with its Bergsonian mechanical rhythm and the debunking of untenable ideals by this humble sound give the story a somewhat brighter tone than *Shin'yū kōkan*, but in both stories the conditions are extreme: the denial of human dignity in one and of the human capacity to hold ideals (or any values at all) in the other bring us too close to genuine suffering for comfort—or for comedy, except of the darkest kind. Moreover, Dazai's nihilism offers few or none of the certainties (on the part of both author and audience as to the values and ideals) against which the characters' imperfections may be measured, or even any hope that such certainties can actually be found—an accurate reflection, no doubt, of both his own frame of mind and that of many Japanese at the time, but very problematic ground for comedy, in which at least a modicum of this certainty is usually essential.

Today Dazai's name is most readily associated with the somber works of his last years, such as *Shayō* (Setting Sun, 1947), *Buiyon no tsuma* (Villon's

Wife, 1947), and *Ningen shikkaku,* in which his tortured spirit so precisely captured the national mood that he became the ultimate cult writer in a literature replete with cult writers.[25] Yet this was also the period when the vagaries of fate, or at least the devisers of critical terminology, categorized him with such figures as Sakaguchi Ango, Oda Sakunosuke, and Ishikawa Jun under the label Shin Gesaku Ha (Neo-Gesaku School). Perhaps the desperate pursuit of wine, women, and song depicted in these works, and paralleled at least to some extent in the author's own life following his return from wartime evacuation to Tokyo in late 1946, struck the critics as a throwback to the Edo fiction writers' posture of detachment from public affairs; perhaps it was his avowed conviction, shared with Sakaguchi and Oda, that literature exists to entertain as well as enlighten. While the label was an artificial one at best (and has gradually been supplanted by the equally artificial but slightly less misleading Burai Ha or Outlaw School), it is particularly ironic in Dazai's case, as these were the very years when he drew away from the manner and matter of the *gesaku* spirit and turned back toward those familiar staples in so much twentieth-century Japanese fiction, pathos and relentless self-analysis.

For all their renown, these works are the product of a mere three years, and do not represent the full range of Dazai's talent. Even in *Buiyon no tsuma, Shayō,* and *Ningen shikkaku,* Dazai remains adept at the use of comic moments to rescue passages in danger of falling into excessively oppressive gloom or self-indulgence. Had he lived even a few more years, let alone a normal life span, his comic instincts might well have revealed themselves anew. An indication of what might have been is provided by the unfinished newspaper serial *Guddo bai* (Goodbye, 1948), a surprisingly mischievous comedy of sexual manners that was a remarkable departure from his previous postwar work.[26] As the physical and psychic traumas of the postwar years recede into memory, the predominance of the darker side in Dazai's literary image may be expected to recede as well.[27] Consideration of the entirety of his career should lead to a greater recognition of the importance of mirth and reconciliation in the fiction of Japan's premier apostle of suffering. Like *kōkotsu* and *fuan,* like all dualities, the somber Dazai and the mirthful Dazai are both completely separate from each other and ultimately inseparable. Neither can endure without the other. If such paradoxes lead nowhere, Dazai himself was ready to accept the consequences. In his 1937 essay "Shian no haiboku" (Thought Defeated) he had written: "Laughter. Here is something strong. The fireworks at the end of all culture. If we can assume that intellect, thought, mathematics, all forms of cultivation ultimately culminate in sidesplitting laughter, then cultivation . . . but there we are with our fixation on cultivation once again—what a laugh!"[28]

Dazai was well aware of the inconsistencies implicit in his attempt to approach truth and entertain by assuming the self-created role of professional loser. He also recognized what a powerful source of inspiration the comic spirit can be in trying to learn to live with such inconsistencies rather than being defeated by them.

Chapter 4
The Hisashi Phenomenon

Literature has been no exception to the general pattern of dramatically accelerating rates of productivity that has marked the Japanese economy since the high-growth years of the 1950s and the 1960s. Spurred by the burgeoning of print and other mass media (a trend already well under way in the early decades of the twentieth century, with roots that can be traced as far back as the Edo period), the literary text, especially in prose, has increasingly become a mass-production commodity. It is not uncommon for an author to have dozens of books in print at a time, and this does not include uncollected journalistic ephemera. But even by these standards, Inoue Hisashi (b. 1934) stands out. Since his initial appearance on the literary scene in 1969 with the staging of his comedy *Nihonjin no heso* (The Belly Button of the Japanese) and the publication the next year of his first novel, *Bun to Fun* (translated as *Boon and Phoon*), his productivity has been staggering: the 1997 edition of the standard compendium of Japanese books in print lists him as the author of 150 titles, almost all produced within the space of three decades.[1] His sales figures are on a commensurate order of magnitude, and his major novel to date, *Kirikirijin* (The Kirikirians, 1973–1981), has aroused a degree of public interest matched by few other works of the past two decades.

For sheer versatility, the only postwar author to rival him is Mishima Yukio. Beginning with radio and television scripts, Inoue's output sprawls over the fields of drama, fiction, nonfiction, and song. It includes, among many other things, tales of Asakusa striptease theaters and Australian prisoner-of-war camps, autobiographical evocations of boyhood in northern

Honshu, eloquent defenses of Japan's frequently castigated rice farmers, dramatizations of the lives of several major Japanese writers, learned treatises on Japanese grammar and phonology, ingenious parodies of practically everything, fantastic utopian visions with strong science-fiction overtones, and, presumably his most ambitious work of all (at least in quantitative terms), the saga of a man who spent twenty years walking all around Japan, which Inoue has declared will take twenty years to recount.[2]

Although little of this prodigious corpus has been translated, Inoue has managed to attract notice beyond Japan. In 1983 he was the subject of a brief feature in *Time* magazine, which, citing his then-current totals of 56 books published and 12 million volumes sold, proclaimed him "one of the most successful writers in the world today,"[3] and his play *Keshō* (Greasepaint, 1983) has been translated into and performed in several European languages. Like his early creation, the four-dimensional master thief Bun, Inoue operates on such a breathtakingly vast scale that "phenomenon" seems to be the only adequate label for him.

This is not all that Bun and his author have in common. Both use their respective lines of work to upset the established order, often with a gentle tweak and occasionally with scathing frontal assaults full of moral fervor. Both come by their mission from unconventional backgrounds with a strong pop-culture flavor. In this respect, Bun, who suddenly springs to life from the pages of a potboiler by the hack novelist Fun sensei as a "four-dimensional man for whom nothing is impossible,"[4] may qualify as even more of an outsider than Inoue; but the broadcast media for which Inoue wrote during the early phase of his career have been regarded in Japan as an only slightly less appropriate origin for a writer with "serious" literary aspirations. Of course, Nagai Kafū had his brief flings with the *yose* hall and the kabuki theater in his youth; and the postwar decades saw the emergence of increasing numbers of writers (such as Fukazawa Shichirō, Yamaguchi Hitomi, Nosaka Akiyuki, Itsuki Hiroyuki, and Tanabe Seiko) whose backgrounds were as much in popular entertainment or journalism as in the network of university, publishing house, and little-magazine channels through which Japanese writers have conventionally gained entrée to the literary establishment. But while most of his contemporaries have not demonstrated much concern with publicly justifying the artistic standing of their work, Inoue has poured his formidable reserves of energy, as well as a keen intelligence and a massive barrage of learning, into a bold and persistent challenge to deeply ingrained Japanese attitudes regarding the nature and purpose of literature.

Nowhere is this challenge mounted with more force than in the sphere of comedy, and Inoue has willingly taken on the role of Japan's most vocal and articulate exponent of comedy's validity, even its necessity, in literature. As might be expected given his massive volume of production, not all of Inoue's comic works are remarkable; and in much of his work the comic spirit is either not a major informing element or not present at all. But there are few other Japanese writers in whose work comedy figures in such a conspicuous way; and at his best, especially in *Bun to Fun* and *Kirikirijin,* he has created some of the most original and memorable comic fiction of the contemporary or any other period in Japan.

Inoue's reputation as a comic writer has been based largely on what is widely considered the most striking element in his work, his singular facility with language. Unlike Ibuse, his verbal sense is not displayed in a mastery of subtle stylistic nuances or tonal variations; rather, he hears, sees, and feels words as concrete objects with lives of their own which in turn infuse life into and shape the contours of his works. This life makes itself felt most forcefully in the torrent of wordplay that flows from his pen in a kaleidoscopic variety of forms and guises. In Inoue's most inspired writing, comedy and language are inseparable partners. Although his fiction is also rich in other comic elements, the sheer power of language, of words as words, is usually at the center; and to a greater or lesser extent, all of the other elements are subordinated to it.

The prominence of comedy, wordplay, and parody in Inoue's writing inevitably evokes associations with Edo *gesaku,* and characterizations of Inoue as a latter-day *gesaku* writer are equally inevitable. Inoue himself has frequently expressed his admiration for the spirit and style of the *gesakusha,* and has found the *gesaku* milieu a fertile source of inspiration. Among his more notable treatments are the novella *Tegusari shinjū* (The Love Suicide in Manacles, 1972), which won him the sixty-seventh Naoki Prize; a collection of shorter pieces, *Gesakusha meimei den* (Lives of the *Gesaku* Writers, 1979); and the drama *Omoteura Gennai kaeru gassen* (The Inner and Outer Gennai Frog War, 1970), his homage to the progenitor of *gesaku,* Hiraga Gennai.

As suggested in the introductory chapter, *gesaku,* like so many other items of literary terminology, is not without its problems; it is not at all clear that there is much to be gained by lumping together the comic, parodic, and sometimes oppositionist *kibyōshi* and *kokkeibon* with *sharebon* celebrations of pleasure-quarter savoir faire or the didactic *gōkan* of Takizawa Bakin, which, although treated as "entertainments," were unmistakably "serious" works, consciously striving to promote officially sponsored notions of Confucian virtue. At any rate, Inoue's predilections are reflected in the subject matter and style of his fictions and dramas, and his views on what constitutes the true *gesaku* spirit are further elucidated in a number of essays. In "Kyōfushōsha no jiko keisei shi" (The History of a Phobiac's Self-formation, 1977) and "Watashi ni totte no gesaku" (What *Gesaku* Means to Me, 1978),[5] for example, he has described his discovery of *gesaku*, in particular *kibyōshi*, as a pivotal event in his development as a person and writer. The *gesakusha* pose of self-abasing marginal man or disengaged observer clearly held a powerful attraction for him. Born (like Dazai) in a small town in the Tōhoku region, an area commonly considered backward by other Japanese, he spent a youth marked by hardship and instability: after the early death of his father, his family frequently relocated and he was placed in a Catholic orphanage in Sendai at the age of fifteen. Yet many other Japanese writers who have had equally or even more unhappy upbringings have found themselves more comfortable in other artistic roles. Something peculiar to the *gesaku* mentality, something not accessible in other traditions, must have appealed to instincts not shared by his fellow writers.

The first and most obvious factor is the *gesakusha*'s preoccupation with language. Problems of language figure prominently in Inoue's accounts of the feelings of insecurity and inferiority which plagued him in his youth: his family's repeated moves in a region where each locality had its own unique dialectal features left him unable to communicate freely in school, turned him into a laughingstock among his classmates, and eventually led him to take refuge in stuttering. In the orphanage, he sought to overcome his handicap by excelling in a different language, French, with the help of Canadian priests; but this only resulted in a new humiliation when he arrived in Tokyo to enroll at Sophia University and discovered that his Canadian accent was as much of a stigma in French as a Tōhoku accent is in Japanese. This led to another descent into depression and stuttering and a return to Tōhoku, where he discovered a collection of *kibyōshi* in a public library and found himself captivated by their verbal pyrotechnics, spirit of out-and-out nonsensicality, and the audacious willingness to take everything and anything and unhesitatingly turn it on its head:

> At first I was simply stunned by the brilliance of this sorcery; then I laughed out from the bottom of my heart. Of course one could say that this is just futile, totally

non-utilitarian play, but to a phobia sufferer like me, clinging to an all-encompassing order called "virtue," this futility was something truly fresh and novel. Virtue, after all, allows no room for futility. As I laughed, I suddenly began to feel as if I wanted to embrace the whole world.[6]

In the wake of this liberating discovery, he began to regain his equilibrium, gradually overcoming his deep-seated depression and fears. Moreover, he was awakened to the literary possibilities of wordplay and to the equally significant realization that this type of writing had its own place, legitimate even if not revered, in the Japanese tradition, and thus provided both an inspiration and a model for his own writing.

Another appealing aspect of *gesaku* was the writer's role as comic entertainer. Inoue had already learned what it means to be an object of ridicule in the merciless world of schoolchildren; in Edo fiction he saw a way of generating laughter that led to self-gratification rather than humiliation. The formula is stated neatly by Eijirō, the aspiring *gesakusha* protagonist of *Tegusari shinjū*: "Being a jester just means being made a fool of, so it's no fun. I want to make people laugh, to be laughed at, and at the end I want to be looked up to just a little bit. . . . Jesters are just looked down on—they don't get that last twist, so it's no fun."[7] The same idea is later stated even more pointedly by one of Eijirō's confidants: "He just can't help himself. There isn't any why or wherefore to it. Look, suppose that he was able to make a stone laugh—everybody would love it, wouldn't they? He wants to stand off to the side somewhere, watching them loving it, with a big smirk on his face."[8]

Inoue is well aware that there is more to being a *gesakusha* than assuming a pose of disengaged observer and word-juggling entertainer. In another essay, "Okashi na Edo no gesakusha" (The Funny *Gesakusha* of Edo, 1973), he contends that of all the tradition's major figures, only Gennai and Ōta Nanpo are truly worthy of the *gesakusha* label, because their work reflects the sense of frustration and self-loathing that they felt as men unable to achieve their goals (recognition as a man of scientific learning and a technological innovator in Gennai's case, and advancement within the shogunal bureaucratic hierarchy in Nanpo's). In *gesaku* they found an outlet for these frustrations and for their resentment of a social order that had no use for their talents, albeit at the cost of establishing identities as professional outsiders.[9] For Santō Kyōden and the later writers who followed his example, however, writing *gesaku* was a regular occupation; and as a result, their works display a complacency antithetical to what Inoue sees as the true spirit of *gesaku*. Moreover, he asserts, as the development of printing turned *gesaku* into a mass medium, leading writers such as Jippensha Ikku, Shikitei Sanba, Takizawa Bakin, and Tamenaga Shunsui produced their works for the market rather than for themselves, which in turn resulted in a further adulteration of the original spirit.

It would be a gross oversimplification, though, to view Inoue only as a twentieth-century reincarnation of the *gesakusha*. While some of his free-wheeling satires may evoke the desperado spirit of Gennai, his original ambition was to be a novelist and playwright; and he himself concedes that, having succeeded handsomely, he cannot qualify as a genuine *gesakusha*.[10] Even if we discount his definition of the true *gesakusha* type as excessively purist, there are other significant ways in which he differs: the *gesakusha* after Gennai rarely wrote for the stage, and they certainly did not engage in extensive public defenses and explanations of their own work as Inoue has done.

Moreover, for all his wordplay, fantasies, and erotica, Inoue is not an escapist; and he has neither sought to replicate the classic *gesakusha* posture of cool detachment nor followed the common *gesaku* practice of loading texts with in-jokes intelligible only to a small audience of colleagues and cognoscenti. While works such as *Tegusari shinjū* and *Gesakusha meimei den* may be read as pure entertainments, underlying his most frivolous-sounding gags and puns is an urge to upset the established order that echoes the "spirit of resistance to the age" (*jidai e no teikō seishin*) that elevated Gennai's writing above that of his contemporaries. Most of Inoue's comic fiction touches at least peripherally upon real-world predicaments with a satirical directness that would have been impossible under the strict controls of the Tokugawa shogunate. Even when he is merely peppering the landscape with light satirical potshots, it is as an engaged member of society, not as a dispirited drop-out; and in his most powerful comic fiction, notably *Bun to Fun* and *Kirikirijin*, he uses *gesaku* techniques not only to lampoon the existing order but to create a vision of a better one.

Inoue himself provides some useful hints to understanding the ways in which his comic fiction conforms with the *gesaku* tradition, and how it differs, in his brief polemical essay "Kensatsukan e no gyaku kokuhatsu" (A Counterindictment of the Prosecutors, 1974), in which he enumerates what he considers to be the classic elements of *gesaku*. The first item on the list is the spirit of humility (*herikudari no kokoro*). This refers not only to the way in which authors present themselves but also to the way in which they present their material; they must avoid at all costs giving the reader the impression that they are condescending to impart some kind of precious wisdom or engaging in heady excursions through the aesthetic ether. Most of Inoue's criteria, however, are matters of style rather than spirit. Four of them—wordplay or punning (*goroawase*), facetious classical allusion (*koten no mojiri*), clichéd stock phrases (*tsukinami goku no tayō*), and reduplicated words (*jōgo*)—are functions of the *gesaku* preoccupation with language; and two others—exaggeration (*kochōhō*) and the use of extensive lists (*fukiyose no jutsu*)—are also stylistic in nature.

A final, non-linguistic element is crucial, however: this is *shukō*, the parodic treatment that lends shape, depth, and life to the entire work.[11] A *gesaku* narrative, according to Inoue, is an interweaving of a given *sekai* (a basic premise, theme, subject) with a given *shukō* (a transposition of the *sekai* to an unexpected setting). This structural principle appears frequently in a number of Edo forms, including the non-comic kabuki drama;[12] and as a conscious practice, its roots can be traced at least as far back as the *honkadori* (allusive variation) technique of classical Japanese poetry. But in *gesaku*, at least of the type envisioned by Inoue, it is indispensable. He offers the example of Koikawa Harumachi's *Kinkin sensei eiga no yume* (Master Kinkin's Dream of Glory, 1775), in which a *sekai* derived from *Kan Tan* (Han Tan), a Nō play derived in turn from a Chinese legend of a man who briefly dreams that he becomes an emperor, is updated with the *shukō* of merchant-class extravagance and elegance in Edo. An equally good illustration would be his own *Tegusari shinjū*, which takes its *sekai*, the familiar theme of the aspiring pleasure-quarter dandy, from Kyōden's 1785 *kibyōshi*, *Edo umare uwaki no kabayaki* (Grilled Playboy Edo-Style) and transposes it with the *shukō* of would-be *gesaku* writer. The use of such transpositions, of course, is hardly unique to *gesaku*; it is a fundamental technique of all parodic literature. However, where the parodist normally is at pains to make both his *sekai* and his *shukō* readily recognizable, the *gesakusha*, Inoue points out, conceals his *sekai* and presents only his *shukō*. It is up to the reader to divine the hidden *sekai*, and it is only when this is accomplished that the *gesaku* is fully realized.[13]

While any such formula is bound to be somewhat arbitrary and ultimately incapable of neatly encapsulating a phenomenon as multifaceted and amorphous as a literary genre (or what is taken for one), this essay sheds some valuable light on the larger issue of Inoue's comic style. All of the *gesaku* elements he lists figure prominently in his comic fiction. His choice of orthography for his own name signals his *herikudari no kokoro:* "Hisashi" appears in *hiragana,* stripped of the aura of dignity imparted by Chinese characters. His writing abounds with gratuitous gestures of self-deprecation. Occasionally there are bald declarations on the order of "All false modesty aside, I think that I'm really dumb";[14] more often there is a passing comment on the inevitability of the writer's (and particularly the parodist's) sense of inferiority.[15] Sometimes he engages in outright self-mockery, as in this passage from *Kirikirijin,* in which one vain and preposterous writer recalls another: "Furuhashi visualized the bucktoothed face of Inoue ——, a writer who, like Furuhashi himself, lived in the city of Ichikawa. Apparently this Inoue, despite the fact that he didn't know the first thing about English, had become a visiting professor at a national university in an English-speaking country."[16]

Inoue's most powerful expressions of authorial humility, however, are not these overtly self-referential comments, but the caricatures of writers that appear frequently in his works. Far more flamboyant in their vapidity and solipsism than the painfully self-mocking protagonists of Japanese autobiographical fiction, these professional and would-be professional hacks are devastating send-ups not only of the less exalted side of their creator, but of all artists. The willingness of Eijirō, the protagonist of *Tegusari shinjū,* to do anything for a laugh reflects the pathetic, demeaning position of all *gesaku* writers, or of writers in general, while his insatiable vanity, masquerading as ambition, also seems to reflect something about the nature of writers in general, including, of course, Inoue himself. When the figure of the author appears in a more contemporary setting, as in the case of Fun sensei or of Furuhashi Kenji, the central character in *Kirikirijin,* the authorial self-mockery becomes all the more pointed. Eternally hungry, lazy, and despised hacks, pretenders whose dreams of acceptance into the select circle of revered master novelists are forever doomed to founder on the shoals of their own lack of talent and savoir faire, both figures display traits of authorial self-deprecation even as they mirror the pompous posturings of Japan's "serious" writers.

Like the Edo *gesakusha,* Inoue is pressed into a stance of humility by a combination of externally imposed circumstances and personal predilection. It is the strategy of preference for the weak, the insecure: conscious of their marginal social and cultural status, and of the relative disrepute of their calling, they forestall censure by assuming the classic stance of the *eiron*, pretending to know less than they really do, or to be less than they really are. Such modesty, of course, functions as a double-edged sword: by the very act of choosing to be less, *eiron* figures call attention to the differences between themselves and their putative superiors, who are then subjected to invidious comparisons of a type that might not have been palatable, or possible, if presented in more direct terms.

While *herikudari* is more of an overall informing attitude than a major comic element in both Edo *gesaku* and Inoue's fiction, the *eiron*'s role does have an important comic function: the very existence of the lowly observer-narrator is a parodic commentary on his/her field of observation, a reminder that human beings honor ideals and standards more often than they fulfill them. More significantly, this deliberate self-lowering enables writers to engage in a range of comic practices generally counted among the less dignified items in the literary repertory, including several of the items on Inoue's list of *gesaku* ingredients.

Wordplay (*gengo yūgi*) in its various forms is the most conspicuous of these. Inoue employs all of the forms mentioned in "Kensatsukan e no gyaku kokuhatsu," and many more as well. As both the English and Japanese terms suggest, all these devices involve in one way or another a spirit of games, of play. Play, including play with words, is a phenomenon distinct from comedy. According to Johan Huizinga's celebrated study, the comic is in a subsidiary relation to play, but it is also a category that exists outside the sphere of play, concerning itself as it does with antitheses such as wisdom and folly, truth and falsehood, good and evil, and vice and virtue, which in Huizinga's view are extrinsic to play.[17] Nevertheless, it is no coincidence that verbal gamesmanship appears so frequently in comedy, for the all-too-apparent discrepancies between words and the untidy phenomena they purport to represent mirror the kinds of oppositions between real and ideal or misperception and actuality that are found in all comic incongruities.

The common thread that runs through all Inoue's verbal gyrations is an insistence on treating words not as transparent indicators of meanings but as autonomous forces. The aural and visual qualities of Inoue's words often overshadow their meanings, particularly when they can be related to similar qualities in other words. The juxtaposition of related sounds and unrelated meanings, or rather of meanings forced into a relationship by similarities in sound, is the basis of *goroawase* or punning, Inoue's fundamental form of wordplay. This is simply the application to words of the basic comic technique of pointing out apparent similarities in entities not normally thought to be related (or, conversely, of pointing out differences or incongruities in ostensibly related things). Because of the highly arbitrary nature of sound similarities, such linguistic juxtapositions often seem particularly gratuitous or pointless; and while there may be some validity to Jonathan Culler's claim that "the pun is the foundation of letters, in that the exploitation of formal resemblance to establish connections of meaning seems the basic activity of literature,"[18] this view of literature has had few adherents in twentieth-century Japan, where wordplay is perennially relegated to the nether regions of literature, especially in the case of prose. By taking the primacy of words as his starting premise, Inoue is able to frame the issue in a different light: "It is of words that fiction is constructed. That is, words are the only available means by which the writer can share the fictional world with the reader. In this sense, punning is one of the writer's primary weapons. Since the word 'punning' arouses a negative reaction, let us say 'linguistic experimentations.'"[19]

Inoue cites the achievements of the *gesakusha* to justify his claim that expression (*hyōgen*) takes precedence over content (*naiyō*): the existence of puns that are conspicuously heavy-handed or lack any discernible sense (*dajare*) is no indictment of the act of punning itself, Inoue argues; for any form of literary expression has its less illustrious examples along with its masterpieces, and in the works of the Danrin *haikai* poets and some of the *gesakusha* we find punning of a high order.[20] But there were several other factors that brought him to this position. One is his years of experience writing radio scripts (and prior to that, watching vaudeville comedians while working in an Asakusa burlesque theater), which impressed upon him the power inherent in the sound qualities of words and their effects on audiences. Also, as he has frequently repeated, there is the Japanese language itself; with its limited number of phonemes and its equally limited number of ways of combining them, it boasts an extraordinarily large stock of homonyms and near homonyms, creating superb opportunities for wordplay. As he proclaims, "Punning is the destiny of the Japanese language."[21]

Such arguments are likely to convince few of the as-yet unconverted. In Inoue's writing there is no shortage of *dajare*, puns for their own sake, opportunities which the author seems to have been unwilling to pass up simply because they were there. There are also countless elaborate manipulations of sound, rhythm, meaning, and tone, equally lacking in depth but nonetheless impressive as virtuoso displays of verbal ingenuity.

There are also more pointed uses of wordplay, in which sound similarities are employed to lampoon received notions or to expose the follies or pretensions of a character through the nonsensical, irrelevant, or paradoxical effects created by his or her own statements. These are familiar techniques, but in Inoue's hands they are extended to encompass the nature of language itself: using wordplay to point to the disjunction between words as arbitrary, empty signifiers and the phenomena that stubbornly resist our attempts to organize or delimit them through signification, he reminds us of the frailty of our assumptions about the transparency and efficacy of language as a medium of communication, and about the human minds that create and use it.[22] Moreover, whenever he sends words into dizzy spirals of unmeaning, as in the Möbius-strip recursive dialogue between Furuhashi's prospective parents-in-law in chapter 15 of *Kirikirijin*,[23] or fashions an intricate series of puns that results in a total breakdown of communication, he calls into question the conventionalized forms of perception and "knowledge" whose appropriateness we customarily take for granted as *jōshiki* or "common sense," and adds to his comedy a metaphysical edge that approaches Beckettian absurdism, undermining the very grounds of belief upon which our idea systems are based.

But usually he aims at subversion of a different sort. He does not dismiss the possibility of words' being used to reflect "reality" in a meaningful way; instead, he challenges their abuse, the deceptive attribution of false meanings by speakers intent on establishing or maintaining their own authority or power: "My frequent use of various forms of wordplay could be described as a form of defiance of the demonic power of words to possess more authority than the actual things they are supposed to signify—a power which, in almost all cases, is manifested when irrational authority seeks to impose some kind of command on us."[24]

Behind the irrational authority of words lurks a more serious threat: Inoue sees Japan as beset with countless problems stemming from unscrupulous and abusive behavior by people in positions of illegitimate authority, who regularly attempt to advance their interests or buttress their positions by cloaking them in the illegitimate authority of words. When words are abused in this manner, they take on some of the false authority of their abusers. Like all pretenders to unwarranted authority, they are best hoisted with their own petards, and this is most readily accomplished by holding their pretensions and their true capabilities up to scrutiny and letting readers draw their own conclusions. Inoue's deflation of the power of words that have usurped the powers of the things they are supposed to represent is thus also a deflation of human authority. Comic exaggeration both in quality (sound and sense) and in quantity (sequences, repetition) plays a key role this strategy: by reproducing the speech patterns of typical authority figures (politicians, broadcasters, writers) with only a slight bit of exaggeration and distortion, he shows how they exploit their native tongue's ample possibilities for sonorous obfuscation and euphemism to bamboozle their listeners. With just a bit more exaggeration and a generous helping of *goroawase*, he can strip away their pretensions by reducing their speech to near nonsense, simultaneously reducing the speakers themselves to nonsense as well. By treating people like language and language like people, and defamiliarizing the relations between words in the ordered structure of the Japanese language, he seeks to undermine established patterns of relations between members of Japanese society.[25] Wordplay for Inoue, then, is not just an amusement but a means of overturning any phenomenon and creating out of it a new one.[26] It is only natural that when the villagers of Kirikiri establish their utopian ministate, would-be immigrants who show no interest in punning and no understanding of puns are barred from entry.[27]

As is so often the case with wordplay, attempts to render examples of Inoue's verbal ingenuity into English would largely be self-defeating, since the incongruency between English and Japanese and the consequent need for laborious explanations would destroy the spontaneity upon which their effectiveness depends. His favorite resource is the familiar double-entendre pattern of using one set of sounds to represent two (or more) meanings, or the repetition of a given sound pattern in a variety of ostensibly unrelated contexts, as in the numerous changes rung on the name Bun in the third chapter of *Bun to Fun*.[28] A similar principle is seen in the list of Furuhashi's fictional works in *Kirikirijin*: five of the six titles involve the time-honored theme of love suicide (*shinjū*), four of them punning: *Minami Senjū shinjū* (Love Suicide in Minami Senjū), *Shinju shinjū* (The Pearl Love Suicide), *Shinju shinjū* (A Retainer's Love Suicide), and *Shinshū shinjū* (Love Suicide in the Land of the Gods).[29] Other puns depend on breaking existing words into constituent parts which are then recombined and given new associations, such as the cross between an elephant (*zō*) and goldfish (*kingyo*) created by a Kirikiri scientist and dubbed a *zōkin* (dustcloth).[30]

Fortunately, Inoue is fond of working English and other foreign words into his inventory of sound correspondences, as in Furuhashi's malapropic reference to literary *janguru* (jungles) instead of *janru* (genres).[31] The following example of his earthier side may also be cited:

> "The Prime Minister's diarrhea is chronic, you know," said the General Secretary of the Conservative Party. "We all call him 'Gary Cooper' (Gēri Kūpā). If he has diarrhea (*geri*) when he tries to eat (*kuu*), it's a washout (*paa*) get it? So, Gary Cooper—hahaha."
>
> "I beg your pardon." The commentator was glowering. "We would appreciate it if you would save clumsy puns like that for the commercial stations. You are not dealing with 'The Drifters Stand by for Laffs' here. This is Public Broadcasting—a Special News Alert, in fact."[32]

This is precisely the kind of crudity that gives Inoue and all "linguistic experimenters" a bad name, but here it serves to deflate the dignity of the politician and simultaneously provides the announcer with an opportunity to display in only slightly exaggerated form the smugness typical of Japan's public broadcasters.

Inoue's preoccupation with the comic potential of words does not stop with juxtapositions of similar sounds and divergent senses. The other types of linguistic play enumerated in his *gesaku* formula (facetious classical allusion, clichés, reduplications, exaggeration, and lists) are also frequently employed. These, too, have multiple comic functions, sometimes appearing for their own intrinsic appeal and sometimes to shed a satiric light on particular characters. The most prolific (and most flagrant) of these is Furuhashi, whose manifold abuses of language, like the punning techniques mentioned above, expose the discrepancy between the idealized image of the writer as a paragon of originality and verbal talent and himself (and, by extension, Inoue and his more strait-laced colleagues) as the debased realization of that image. His monumental limitations as a writer are reflected not only in his unfailing instinct for the *mot injuste*, but also in his habitual recourse to thinly veiled plagiarism (most often probably unintended), his instinctive reliance on petrified stock phrases, and his ability to generate endless sequences of reduplications. In a more basic sense, they also serve to subvert the notion of meaning per se, especially when they occur in long repetitious series, producing their own extended rhythm which, combined with the diminished level of content conveyed by the clichés and reduplications, creates a numbing effect; before long, the reader realizes that a passage that has started out with all the trappings of serious discourse has degenerated into utter nonsense.[33]

The compilation of lists (*monozukushi* or *fukiyose no jutsu*) is a *gesaku* technique which transfers comic associative play from the dimension of sound to sense; the expansive energy that pulses through these accumulations of terms and images also suggests comedy's penchant for embodying and celebrating irrepressible life forces. In Japan, the gathering together of the names of as many items as possible in a given category is, of course, a practice that is not limited to comedy and antedates the *gesaku* era by a good deal, as the striking examples in Sei Shōnagon's *Makura no sōshi* (The Pillow Book of Sei Shōnagon, ca. 1000) attest. But Inoue's enumerations, which quickly careen from the plausible to the far-fetched, are intended not only to enlighten or please but to overwhelm and benumb; by transcending the exhaustive and arriving at a condition beyond exhaustion, they ultimately subvert both the putative organizing principle of any given list and the listing process itself by reducing them to meaninglessness. Like the stringing together of similar sounds, this often is a rather blunt comic instrument, and much of its effectiveness depends on the writer's ability to strike just the right balance between not at all obvious associations and all too obvious incongruities between the items listed.

Such lists are supplied with great generosity in *Kirikirijin*, Inoue's most verbally exuberant novel, where they range from such matter-of-fact compilations as a dining-hall menu, a country-by-country breakdown of overseas tax havens and the Japanese corporations that use them, and a three-page list of names of dummy corporate offices established in Kirikiri to thematic collections of onomatopoeic expressions, antonyms, homonyms, and ready-made stock phrases, as well as lists of imaginary disease names and futuristic inventions. Given the lavish scale and satiric perspective of the novel in which they occur, however, the lists in *Kirikirijin* function like neither those of Sei Shōnagon, which appear to lack ironic consciousness or a part in an overall textual strategy, nor the tradition of *kibyōshi* and other relatively compact *gesaku* formats so much as they do the "great catalogues" and "encyclopedic compilations" by which the author goes about "piling up an enormous mass of erudition about his theme or in overwhelming his pedantic targets with an avalanche of their own jargon" in the expansive genre that Northrop Frye has labeled Menippean satire.[34]

The rhythmic and phonetic repetitions in some of these lists create a musical quality that easily lends itself to another favorite Inoue device, the patter song, as in the prosecutor's litany of absurd charges in chapter 8 of *Bun to Fun*:

Sono ta neko no hige wo nusunde ikkagetsu!
Niwatori no tosaka nusunde hankagetsu!
Iwashi nusunde hannichi!
Koyashi nusunde mikka!
Moyashi nusunde itsuka!
Okashi nusunde tōka!
Mawashi nusunde hatsuka![35]

(In addition for theft of the cat's whiskers: one month!
For theft of the chickens' combs: half a month!
Theft of sardines: half a day!
Theft of latrines: three days!
Theft of string beans: five days!
Theft of pralines: ten days!
Theft of blue jeans: twenty days!)

Hyperbolic expression (*kochōhō*), Inoue's final stylistic element, is among the most fundamental tools for presenting comic dichotomies of all kinds. Inoue is, needless to say, a particularly enthusiastic practitioner:

In every prison there are bosses called "trusties" . . . having been in and out of jail so many times, they know everything about the place from the rules inside the walls to the lay of the land outside. They know the habits of the mice in the attics and the nicknames of the roaches that scamper across the floors; at New Year's the roaches send them greeting cards, and at Bon festival time and the end of the year they get their regular gifts from the rats.[36]

Under the broad-brimmed white sports hat was ensconced an enormous nose. While the tip of the nose was flat and squashy, the two wings were extraordinarily highly developed, and at first glance one was likely to think that three noses were lined up together on one face. . . . The nose and upper lip were as far apart as Wakkanai and Kagoshima. In other words, he had a long upper lip.[37]

As with the devices mentioned above, some of these exaggerations are simply play for its own sake, and not deployed as part of any comic dichotomy or toward a satirical end. But by departing so conspicuously from the common scale of things, they remind the reader that the normal relationship between words and things is suspended, again subverting the assumed underpinnings of authority and meaning.

A related technique, not included in Inoue's *gesaku* formula but similar in its effects to some of the others, is the frequent use of striking and sometimes nonsensical similes: "If an explorer were ever stopped by a band of Eskimo bandits in the dead of winter not far from the North Pole and stripped of every last thing he had, he would shiver as Furuhashi was shivering now."[38] When these are combined with the listing and classifying impulses, the product is another kind of word game, the simile chain:

"A publishing company without any books?," asked Furuhashi. "That's like a cow without milk—it just sounds meaningless. Like a cigarette without smoke, or a fire without flames, or a fire engine without water, or *sake* without alcohol, or a wedding banquet without a bride and groom, or *Chūshingura* without Ōishi Kuranosuke, or Sadaharu Oh without home runs, or a haunted house without ghosts, or a women's magazine without gossip, or a teenaged girl without pimples, or Marilyn Monroe without her behind, or Sophia Loren without her chest, or a pregnant woman without her belly, or a geisha without sex appeal.[39]

Where typical similes emphasize the similarity of the compared terms, with some attribute of the first term gaining increased intensity by association with the second, Inoue's similes often undercut their implicit raison d'être by being phrased in such an extravagant manner that resemblance matters less than difference. In this example, the intensification is little more than a pretext to indulge in the gesture of the simile. Similes of this sort are subject to almost infinite expansion, reducing the flow of the narrative to a self-repeating loop of near nonsense until the narrator or one of the characters intrudes to point out that the speaker's obsession with driving home his point is making it impossible for him to make any point at all.

Another variation could be called the underwhelming simile:

He was twenty-two-years old, a brilliant student in the French department at Tokyo University. Moreover, he was six feet tall, good looking, and the captain of the school crew. He was more refined than Richard Burton, had more animal magnetism than Steve McQueen, and even if people like Maruyama Akihiro or Peter tried standing on their heads they couldn't match him for sheer sexiness. At the same time, he was more appealingly droll than Atsumi Kiyoshi, more dignified than the august personages of the imperial household, and when he sang he could make tingles run up and down your spine. Frank Sinatra once asked him for lessons—that's how good he was.[40]

Here the intended effect of intensification is undercut by making comparisons to referents whose claims to their imputed qualities are tenuous at best. The inherent comic gap between sexiness and a prominent Japanese transvestite entertainer reflects back upon the subject of the comparison and strengthens his portrayal as an impostor; he is, in fact, a writer whose talents are prodigious but limited entirely to the sphere of plagiarism.

Inoue's preoccupation with the comic qualities of words and their sounds extends beyond the boundary of standard Japanese. Comic dualities exist not just among the words of a single language but between languages; and Inoue periodically inserts bits of English, Chinese, German, and French into his work, usually in a mangled form whose distortions lend a touch of sham sophistication to would-be impressive speakers. Of greater significance, however, is his use of Japanese dialects. In any language, the appearance of dialect speakers in a narrative is frequently a signal that comedy can be expected. By their very nature, dialects are deviants from a standard, and even the most innocuous utterances can take on a ludicrous tone or (even if only inadvertently) create an effect of pretension. But like most comic dichotomies, this one can be worked from either direction; and for Inoue, dialects, as the language of peripheral or marginal communities, occupy a subordinate status vis-à-vis "standard" Japanese and thus offer satiric possibilities of another kind. Above and beyond this, he adds some distinctive twists that upset the usual expectations regarding comic dialect speakers.

The most prominent case of the comic use of dialect in his early fiction is the series of stories written in the early 1970s featuring Father Mokkinpotto, a French priest who lives in Tokyo and is fluent in Kansai dialect.[41] Although endowed by his creator with a formidable array of quirks, foibles, and infirmities, Mokkinpotto's identity as a foreign speaker of a Japanese dialect is essential to his effectiveness as a comic character.[42] For a foreigner to speak Japanese at all is (at least from the perspective of many Japanese) a violation of "common sense" norms, an anomalous situation fraught with comic implications; but if he or she can, then the expectation is that it will be a painfully strained version of schoolbook (i.e., "standard Tokyo") speech, a reflection of the relatively cosmopolitan sphere to which foreigners are assumed to belong, rather than the idiom of some provincial locale. Moreover, since it is a liability for anyone in a position of power or authority to speak something other than standard Japanese, for a European to model his or her speech on a dialect entails a fatal compromise of whatever prestige attaches to Westerner status.

Mokkinpotto himself is all too well aware of his status as a multiple misfit and the role that dialect plays in it. As he confesses to the narrator of the stories, an Inoue-like figure who arrives in Tokyo to enter the French department of a Catholic university after studying with French Canadian teachers at a provincial orphanage, "I'm like you—I learned to speak Japanese in Kansai, and look at what happened. You could say we both started out choosing the wrong teachers, no?"[43] But Mokkinpotto is more than just an extreme variation on the familiar *hen na gaijin* (oddball foreigner) stereotype, and more than a clerical version of the stock role of pedantic authority figure. He personifies the sacred, or at least as much of the sacred as could be aspired to in the Tokyo of the 1950s, in a comic conflict with the profane in the form of his three student charges, one of whom is the narrator. If the faintness of the distinction between these two principles, sometimes degenerating into interchangeability, is a major theme of the stories, the gap between his actual speech and the dignified priestly cadences that one might anticipate is one of the main expressions of the stories' basic comic dichotomy.

It is with his native Tōhoku speech, however, that Inoue has explored the comic possibilities of dialect to the fullest, and also achieved his greatest upset of the comic dialect convention. The stigma attached to speaking an unprestigious idiom, impressed upon him by the linguistic traumas of his youth, figures prominently in his play *Ame* (Rain, 1976) and most notably in *Kirikirijin*, where the backwater utopia's local dialect is elevated overnight to the lofty status of National Language, posing a challenge to the authority of standard Japanese that echoes the villagers' challenges to the political and social center: "Laws, ordinances, money . . . they all come down on a one-way street from the central authority in standard Japanese. Then things change completely. The farmers talk back to the center in their own language. Wouldn't that be better for the center, too? That was the idea behind Kirikirigo."[44]

As in both Thomas More's Utopia and the pleasure quarters which constituted the matrix of so much of Edo *gesaku*, language sets Kirikiri off from the outside world, and underscores its immunity from that world's conventions and restraints.[45] But unlike the Edo sophisticates, the Kirikirians proclaim their linguistic independence not by devising a novel or fashionable idiom, but by clinging to an old one, the northern Honshu dialect, which has long been disdained by other Japanese as *zūzū-ben*, virtually synonymous with backwardness and unintelligibility. To the Kirikirians, though, the "standard Japanese" of Tokyo is simply a linguistic adjunct of the political and economic power grabs of the Tokugawa shogunate and the Meiji Restoration, an artificial patois that mixes elements from various forms of regional speech with a phonetic structure and vocabulary distorted by the continuing preoccupation of the central authorities with the alien cultures of China and the West. The valorization of their own language, Kirikirian, as an authentic reflection of their own way of life is, in other words, integral to the portrayal of Kirikiri as a repository of indigenous virtues left behind in Japan's campaign to achieve an imported vision of "modernity," and the use of an indigenous, marginal point of reference is integral to Inoue's satiric indictment of modern Japan as a society that has lost its way and probably its soul as well.[46]

Its homegrown virtues notwithstanding, the use of dialect in contexts where it is not expected often has a comic effect, especially when it challenges assumptions about the social implications of different types of speech. Although in many cases the incongruity between idiom and content is deployed to ridicule the idiom's lack of grace and the pretensions of its speakers, context can create the opposite effect as well. By turning an idiom normally associated with peasant life into a medium for government proclamations, bureaucratic routine, television broadcasts, learned discourse, and so forth, Inoue brings into focus the pretenses of some of society's more revered institutions; and by the mere gesture of rephrasing in Kirikirian such sacrosanct texts as the imperial Japanese government's declaration of war against the United Kingdom and the United States or Kobayashi Hideo's essay on Mozart, he succeeds in travestying them without recourse to the usual exaggerations and distortions of content.

Like the other linguistic devices employed by Inoue, the use of dialect utterances with ostensibly incongruous meanings or contexts is an example of the *shukō* principle writ small. But here the *sekai* and *shukō* are both easily identifiable, and so the technique is better described as *parodei* (parody), another favorite Inoue term which enjoyed something of a vogue in Japan in the 1970s and 1980s, although its connotations differ in some important ways from those of the English version. In the Western tradition within which the term developed, literary parody is generally understood to take as its objects readily recognizable specific texts, or features characteristic of a particular author or group of authors. By applying the style of the original to unfamiliar content, it creates effects that are usually either innocuously humorous (with the focus on incongruity per se) or satirical (in which the incongruity points back to something inherently ridiculous in the style or substance of the original).[47]

Examples of both types abound in Inoue's fiction. *Bun to Fun* features a versifying thief named Ohaihai no Haisuke, all of whose works are *tōsaku* (plagiarized, literally "stolen" creations). His favorite model-victim is the poet Ishikawa Takuboku:

> *Nusumedomo nusumedomo*
> *waga kurashi raku ni narazaru*
> *jitto te o miru*[48]
>
> (Although I steal and steal
> my life is none the easier—
> I stare at my hands)

Kirikirijin is replete with parodies. For example, the gospel miracle of the loaves and fishes is retold by one of Kirikiri's elder statesmen, substituting riceballs and milk. In a take-off on Dazai's retellings of traditional stories in *Shinshaku shokokubanashi* and *Otogizōshi*, Inoue has Furuhashi the author of *Shinshaku Otogizōshi*. Two famous cartoon series—the international hired-gun adventure *Golgo 13* and the single-parent swordsman saga *Kozure ōkami*—yield "Belgo 17," a baby-toting Hawaii-born stripper and secret agent. In other Inoue parodies, the satiric thrust is sharper. In *Kirikirijin*, Furuhashi stumbles upon a set of translations of outstanding works of Japanese literature in Kirikirian, published as the first installment of a projected set of *Collected Masterworks of Afro-Asian Literature*: Natsume Sōseki's *Botchan*, Kawabata Yasunari's *Yukiguni*, Kobayashi Hideo's *Mozart*, Dazai's *Shayō*, and a digest of "All the Good Parts" (in Kirikirian, *Ee doko bakka*) from the soft-core erotic fiction of Uno Kōichirō. Furuhashi, in one of his more lucid moments, observes that the only authors to survive this treatment with any grace are Sōseki and perhaps Uno, whose creations embody enough of the spirit of *herikudari* to retain something of their original appeal in this rephrasing.

This is very much in keeping with Inoue's stated views on the function of parody. In his essay "Parodei shian" (Parodic Thoughts, 1971), after warning that "parody" has joined the ranks of words whose sense has been dulled by overuse, he offers his own attempt at clearing the air. The result is a functional analysis that releases parody from the sphere of intertextual relations. He first likens parody to a distorting mirror which bends and exaggerates our features at the same time that it reflects: because the reflection simultaneously does and does not resemble the original, we laugh. He then compares it to the antics of monkeys, in particular of those "boss monkeys" whose posturings are a twisted, debased version of the trappings of authority and superiority seen in the human world and whose essential emptiness is quickly revealed when it is transposed to a lower order of being.[49] Thus, when Japanese aircraft drop a series of leaflets on Kirikiri, Furuhashi immediately senses something familiar in the stiff and overbearing style in which they simultaneously charge the villagers with treason against their nation and emperor, offer forgiveness for those who return to the fold, threaten death for those who do not, and attempt to shame them all by invoking the friends and relatives who are purportedly weeping over the tragedy they have caused. After a bravura forty-five-page digression, he realizes that the leaflets are modeled on those dropped by the Japanese government on the insurgent forces in the February Twenty-sixth Incident, an abortive coup attempt in 1936: "In other words, it's that parody stuff, that's so fashionable these days."[50] The gravely intoned intimidations and manipulations of the greatest of all Japan's boss monkeys, the emperor-centered authority of the state, are deflated by being applied to a tiny utopian village.

This, more than humor or textual irony, is the essence of parody for Inoue. If parody is restricted to mimicry of songs, novels, and their creators, it remains a rather uninteresting operation, incapable of rising above the level of its objects. Unless it mounts a challenge to the false grandeur of authority or to false plausibility (*mottomorashisa*) as the Edo *gesakusha* did (and as the techniques and strategies of wordplay do), it fails to realize its full potential. Reality itself, the full spectrum of human actions and attitudes, must be parodied: "All the Great Ones flourishing in our midst and all their followers should be turned into material for parody, because they have a habit of always rushing on and on in the worst direction, taking the Little Ones along with them. We must take every opportunity to pull them down to the same level as the Little Ones, to topple them with laughter, to remind them that in the face of laughter all are equal, all are as nothing."[51]

Despite this invocation of equality, Inoue's description of parody in "Parodei shian" is couched largely in terms of dragging the high down to the lowly, evoking a society of petty beings in which no one is better than anyone else, rather than one in which one person is as good as the next. But in another essay, "Parodei shigan" (The Will to Parody, 1971), he asserts that this lowering is complemented by—and inseparable from—an elevation of the humble, not to replace their deposed superiors but to meet them halfway in a whirling flux of folly, nobility, evil, good will, and permanent impermanence. Inoue identifies this elevating approach as "humor" in distinction to parody, borrowing the categories from Jean Paul Richter.[52] Yet, as he readily acknowledges, the distinction is irrelevant in his own writing, as well as in the comic works of others which he most admires, since "parody" and "humor" lead to the same end. Even if he identifies himself as a parodist, he is inevitably a humorist at the same time, and his seemingly inexhaustible repertory of comic tricks and techniques can work effectively in either direction.

When posed in these terms, Inoue's conception of parody bears less resemblance to the conventional conception than it does to satire. It also distances him from the parodists of Edo *gesaku*, who rarely engaged in the kind of "humorous" heightening upon which he insists. This is only one of the ways in which Inoue's brand of parody differs from that of the *gesakusha*. As a parodic practitioner, he ventures into areas closed to the *gesakusha* and still generally abjured by aspiring producers of art literature in modern Japan, especially in his use of the "mirror" technique. This was, to be sure, a staple of the Edo comic writers—one need look no further than the figure of Enjirō for an example of one of its most frequent types, the hopelessly uncouth interloper who tries to make a name for himself as a gentleman of fashion but succeeds only in making himself a laughingstock. But for the *gesakusha*, even the indirection of the "monkey" technique was risky when applied to subjects placed off limits by the authorities. To throw away the masks and costumes and adopt the "mirror" technique with such a subject, making no effort to conceal the identity of the comic victim and simply turning him into a more extreme version of himself, would be tantamount to flaunting a well-developed self-destructive urge.

For all his attacks on the capricious abuse of authority in the modern age, Inoue enjoys a freedom to employ the distorting mirror far exceeding any that the *gesakusha* could have imagined, and his works abound with portraits of the important and the self-important with their less flattering features reflected in the magnifying contours. Significantly, unlike the would-be antiheroes in the marginal world of the pleasure quarters who are customarily parodied in *gesaku*, Inoue's objects are portrayed as the figures of genuine power and prestige at the center of their society (politicians, police, eminent writers), whose follies and vices undermine the legitimacy of the structures they occupy. Some are transparent send-ups of well-known public figure. In *Bun to Fun*, a writer named Kawamata sensei, author of a celebrated novel entitled *Yosoguni* (No Country), bewails the mysterious disappearance of his beloved prose style and its replacement by a frightfully lumpy syntax derived from English. *Bun to Fun* also gleefully recounts the excesses of a very recognizable Aristotle Onassis and of Dairiki Shōnosuke, a parsimonious tycoon reminiscent of a prominent Japanese newspaper magnate. *Kirikirijin* is dotted with similar figures, such as Miwata Teru, a caricature of a prominent television announcer who opportunistically parlayed the popularity of his long-running weekly program into a seat in the Diet, and "Pawafuru (Powerful) Tarō," a takeoff on a high-handed leader of the Japan Medical Association, who presents himself before a nationwide television audience in the following terms: "You can think of me as the managing director of the Medical Division, Japan Incorporated, with eighty thousand practicing physicians throughout the country. I am Kentarō the great, also known as Powerful Tarō! I'm a genuine VIP—all I have to do is snap my fingers, and the Minister of Health comes running like an errand boy. . . . Haven't you ever heard the saying, 'In the old days the Army, today the Medical Association'?"[53]

More frequently Inoue mirrors general types or institutions rather than specific individuals. Among his favorite targets are, not surprisingly, politicians, especially the bigwigs of Japan's long-entrenched, conservative, ruling party. In *Kirikirijin,* Inoue's years of practice had resulted in a gallery of caustic portraits of political bosses obsessively engaged in the pursuit of their own enrichment and the maintenance and display of power for their own sakes. The infantile bully lurking beneath the haughty and self-righteous exterior is typified by the Japanese Minister of Justice, who puts a stop to a long-winded discourse by a Tokyo University Law professor by throwing a tantrum and an ashtray at him. The same figure reveals the more chilling side of the power-holder's mentality when he proposes that in order to dissuade would-be imitators, the government take "firm steps" against the first defector to Kirikiri (Furuhashi), to wit, stripping him of his Japanese citizenship and copyrights and executing his relatives. A less violent proclivity of the powerful is embodied in the person of the Minister of Home Affairs, who leaves an emergency cabinet meeting and announces to the assembled reporters, "Well, I think I'll go and have some geisha trace the character *no* on my behind."[54]

Other favorite figures thrust before the mirror include (as in *Bun to Fun*) the police, intellectuals, and the inordinately wealthy. One of the more memorable scenes in *Kirikirijin* is a portrait of the archetypal Japanese nouveau riche, a postwar repatriate from Manchuria who was given an unpromising piece of farmland on the outskirts of Tokyo that now produces real-estate deals instead of crops. He still goes out to his field every morning, but he lets his vegetables go to seed because it is easier to buy food at a store than to grow it. He spends his days reading comic books bought from a vending machine, smoking cigars lit with his Cartier lighter, glancing occasionally at his Patek Phillippe watch, and waiting for his daughter to deliver lunch—a bucket of Kentucky Fried Chicken, which she fetches from Tokyo in her MG.[55]

Since he neither attempts to conceal his humble origins nor imposes himself on others (except by flaunting his wealth), the farmer is less contemptible than most of the other parodied characters and is handled more gently. The same is true of Mokkinpotto, whose vocation makes him an easy target but who takes the guiding of souls as an inescapable responsibility imposed by that vocation rather than a source of gratification. In general, Inoue does not aim to destroy or deny the humanity of his victims, or to expel them from their society; he merely seeks to identify and demolish their presumptions, and the harshness of his parodic handling is generally in direct proportion to the magnitude of those presumptions.

If politicians, bureaucrats, and military men who consider themselves omnipotent are the most dangerous representatives of authority in *Kirikirijin*, journalists of both the print and electronic media are depicted as only slightly less pretentious and overweening. The most inviting media targets are the most "authoritative" newspaper and broadcast network, the *Asahi shinbun* and Japan Broadcasting Corporation respectively, along with those Japanese, especially among the intelligentsia, who mindlessly make a fetish of them. In general these caricatures, too, are tempered with a degree of sympathy, especially for the television news announcers who must struggle to maintain the requisite tone of smug gravity as the events they report descend deeper and deeper into the whirl of nonsense.

Arrayed against, or rather moving toward the position of, the subjects of parodic treatment are the subjects of "humorous" treatment, the humble underlings and outsiders. Too obscure to be parodied as recognizable individuals, these people must be either portrayed as types or en masse. The latter approach is taken in *Bun to Fun*, where Bun's 120,000 followers, for all their supernatural powers, represent the common people at their lowest level (the criminal underclass) and triumph through superior virtue and energy. Certainly Inoue's most elaborate such portrayal to date of a "humorous" type is that of the farmers of Kirikiri. Of all classes and occupations, few have been as consistently subjected to derision, comic and otherwise, as farmers and peasants. Their low social status and their rustic appearance and manners have always made them prone to portrayal as comic butts; even when they represent the superior side in comic dichotomies, the best treatment that can generally be expected for such characters is a chance to play the unpretentious *eiron* role. In *Kirikirijin,* though, Inoue endows them with a more dynamic superiority. Driven to secession from Japan by the government's policy of creating "flourishing agricultural administration and moribund agriculture" in the name of "modernization,"[56] the Kirikirians display the resourcefulness, solidarity, and irrepressible vitality that have always been essential to the survival of agricultural communities, here elevated to heroic proportions.

Along with these familiar agrarian virtues, Inoue's peasants boast a distinctly unusual sophistication which makes them more than a match for the Japanese authorities. The closest approximation of a presiding entity in Kirikiri is a body called the *gujin kaigi* (assembly of fools), a group of physically disabled villagers who debate constitutional law, formulate policy, conduct trials, attend to all other governmental functions, and trade risqué quips while making the rounds of the village in a charcoal-burning bus called the *kokkai gijidōsha,* which doubles as the national mass transit system and triples as a movable revel of drinking and singing. All of this would amount to little more than a repetition of the well-worn motif of rustic burlesque, except that among the *gujin* are several world-class thinkers who repeatedly humiliate their Japanese counterparts (usually representatives of Tokyo University or the bureaucratic elite) with their superior mastery of recondite points of international law, economic theory, or forensic medicine, invariably expounded in their "backward" dialect and frequently punctuated with salty asides. They also include several of the main architects of the technical and scientific innovations by which Kirikiri strives to make itself a showcase of humane progress.

The other inhabitants of Kirikiri, if less accomplished, also embody neglected native virtues, providing a much-needed antidote to the excesses and distortions of a modern society rapidly losing touch with basic human values. But Inoue is not a simplistic agrarian or proletarian moralizer; he is always aware of the comic possibilities inherent in a utopia where the technological and ideological sophistication of the inhabitants are inseparable from the earthiness, petty bickerings, and jovial crudity of village life. The daredevil seaplane pilot who evades a squadron of Japanese interceptors to convey the first delegation of foreign representatives (all of them from small powerless communities) to Kirikiri brings his craft to shore while carrying on a colorful stream of risqué banter with the female *gujin* awaiting his arrival, and finally emerges from the cockpit clad in a sweatshirt, loincloth, and rubber boots.

Similar combinations of heightened virtues and human touches characterize many of Inoue's Little People. One of his favorite types, appearing again and again, is the stripper, whose qualities he was able to observe at close range during his youthful stint in Asakusa. As a relatively recent addition to the Japanese scene, lacking the historical and literary cachet of the courtesan tradition, striptease and its practitioners have shared little in the disreputable glamour of the older profession. For Inoue strippers are, quite literally, embodiments of healthy, or at least irrepressible, natural impulses honestly acknowledged, in contrast to the lawmakers, police, and moralists (Mokkinpotto among them) who engage in elaborate displays of disapproval but find the spectacle impossible to resist. Although treated more extensively in some of his other works,[57] the stripper figure reaches her/his greatest height in *Kirikirijin*, where one Abe Maria attains the status of Kirikiri Living National Treasure and is entrusted with the honor of introducing the new nation's flag to the world, a task which she performs, with Furuhashi's assistance, during a nationally televised act in a fashion possible only to those in her profession; later she performs a duet at the globally televised presidential inauguration with President-designate Furuhashi, whose brain has been transplanted into the body of another stripper.

While such antics may suggest that Kirikiri is a utopia where sexism is one social ill that remains alive and well, Inoue portrays striptease, at least in Kirikiri, as a wholesome celebration of life forces, rooted in natural urges rather than economics. This view does not extend to prostitution. No amount of comic heightening can efface the exploitative aspects of sex for pay, and in Kirikiri Inoue replaces it with an egalitarian system of elective casual sex with complex preliminary negotiations faintly resembling the Japanese arranged marriage system. The hapless Furuhashi's pleasure-hunting venture into the Kirikiri geisha district threatens to turn into a disaster when he finds the women acting as customers and himself treated as the prospective merchandise, with all the attendant indignities. After hearing an elaborate historical account of the miseries of the traditional system, however, he acknowledges the fairness of the Kirikirians' innovation, and in short order he even finds true love through it.

Other "humorously" heightened figures, like the quack turned miracle doctor Akahige (a gesture toward the Yamamoto Shūgorō story and Kurosawa film of the same name, but not "parodic" in Inoue's terms), have little comic sparkle. Even at their best, Inoue's forays into the "humorous" rarely match the comic power of his parodies: because there is nothing to juxtapose with his admiration and righteous indignation when he extols their powers and virtues or bemoans their sufferings at the hands of the powerful, there is also little scope for any kind of comic double vision. The Little People are without pretense; there is only the outside observer's presumption that they fall short of some imputed ideal (e.g., of polished behavior), which is only superficially significant anyway. Because there is so little distance between their realities and ideals, they can rarely equal the authority figures as comic characters.

But as the complement to parodic lowering, Inoue's "humorous" heightening does play an essential role in the principle at the very core of his comedy: the process of continuous upset or inversion on a multiplicity of levels. On the most basic level of comedy are the smallest irreducible units, the joke and its dramatized version, the gag. These comic atoms appear in a vast variety of elements and compounds; Inoue, whose livelihood as a broadcast scriptwriter depended directly for many years on his mastery of such elements, claims to have unearthed some 635 of them.[58] Among these, one of the most important is inversion, a point he has epitomized in his characteristic style with the formula *gyagu wa gyaku* (gags are reversals).[59] When a comedian meticulously peels an apple only to throw it away and start devouring the peel, the upset of our expectations may just be for laughs, but the implications are far-reaching indeed:

> From outside to inside, downward instead of upward, left if somebody says "right," backwards if they say "forward," white instead of black, no instead of yes, wrong instead of right, bad instead of good, the river instead of the mountain—everything is bent back upon itself. In the apple gag, it is the absurdity of mixing up the fruit and the peel. This comedy of reversal elicits the spectator's laughter by suddenly tying together the everyday ordinary world of common sense and a world where everything is reduced to the ridiculous. To reveal the true nature of ignoble normality, despicable moralities, and specious manners by transposing the value of the fruit and the peel, to inspire the courage to do battle with all of these exposed shams by laughing them down—whoever can come this far could become another Brecht.[60]

The *gyaku* principle that informs so many of the atomic units can be expanded to function at the highest levels of narratives, their overall themes and structures, as well as at every level in between. Inoue's comic narrative structures are full of upsets, from the simple surprise endings of the *Gesakusha meimei den* stories to the abrupt rise and equally abrupt downfall of Kirikiri. His longer works contain countless subplots, some of which coherently flow into the main action while others are merely illustrative digressions, or diversions for diversion's sake; but any of them is as likely as not to be a highly compressed series of trials and triumphs concluding with a magnificent non sequitur. Upset is also the keynote in Inoue's handling of ideas. While not all of his comedy addresses significant social themes, the upset of authoritarian structures is central to *Bun to Fun* and *Kirikirijin*; and just in case there are any readers who miss this point, he has explained it clearly in a number of essays.[61] In Inoue's most ambitious comedies, upset is relentlessly pursued down to the ontological base: when the chief of detectives in *Bun to Fun* swears allegiance to "common sense" (*jōshiki*) as his sole mainstay, his life, and his god, and then hires a demon to catch the supernatural villain that he cannot catch himself, he neatly undercuts his own self-confident declaration that "Good people are good, bad people are bad . . . and we protect the good and punish the evil."[62]

In *Bun to Fun* the most conspicuous thematic inversion hinges on the figure of the thief, especially as personified by Bun, and the issue of crime and punishment. Inoue's upset of the reader's assumptions about the relative status of thieves and police is foreshadowed even before Bun makes his appearance, when Fun sensei's reveries on food are interrupted by the arrival of a car at his miserable abode and he speculates on the possible identity of the unexpected caller: "It could be a thief, but the last time one of them showed up here and realized that there wasn't a thing worth taking, he just took off in disgust. He left a piece of roast sweet potato behind—guess he felt a little bit sorry for me. If this is another thief, I'm all set! At the very least, I can intimidate him into paying off my overdue rice bills."[63]

Throughout the novel, the figure of the thief, in the form of Bun and his cohort, is elevated in a multiplicity of ways into a paragon of fairness, even justice. He is as likely to give as to take, to be a victim as a victimizer. His arrival leads not to suffering but to mirth. Bun, the ultimate Good Thief, devotes much of his supernatural talent to lightening the burdens of the well-off and the official. He is not exactly a four-dimensional Japanese incarnation of Robin Hood, however, for his aim is to undermine the authority of his victims by depriving them of their presumptions and vanities, not to redistribute their property. He starts with a series of more or less innocuous escapades such as replacing the Statue of Liberty's torch with an ice cream cone and switching the Great Buddhas of Kamakura and Nara. After establishing the general principle that no cow is totally sacred, he gradually begins to devote his energies to hit-and-run attacks on the complacent and the haughty. He is not above stealing from other thieves or frustrating their carefully planned heists, provided only that his victims are master thieves whose eminence in their field makes them worthy of his attention.

Eventually, Bun decides to go for the ultimate heist: he will steal "the thing that is most important to people," that supreme Inouean bugaboo, authority (*ken'i*) in all its multifarious guises: "For some people it's a sleek mustache. For some it's the glory of their past exploits, the doctor's white coat, medals, the Dietman's badge, a literary prize—people are fond of things like that. They accumulate lots of them and then they try to throw their weight around and get other people to do what they want. Money, success, pride, effort and good works—you name it—they're all nothing but ways for people to acquire authority, to acquire power."[64] Each of Bun's ensuing thefts is an upset in itself. He steals the vanity from a gaggle of insufferably snobbish society ladies, reducing their pretentious chatter into a more mundane form of vulgarity. He filches the magnificent mustache of the renowned German philosopher Karl Yappers, causing the professor to lose both his nerve and the love of gratuitous complication that had been the foundation of his philosophical system. He turns arrogant doctors and politicians into paragons of humaneness by relieving them of their egos.

Meanwhile the forces of authority, especially those quintessential agents of repression, the police, are busy carrying out their side of the inversion. Facing the specter of unemployment because Bun has neutralized their principal means of control, their trusties, the prison wardens are forced to take appropriate measures: "If we're thrown out of our heavenly prisons at our age, with wives and children to support, there will be nothing left but family suicide or turning crook. Nobody likes family suicide, so the chances are that we'll turn crook. In which case, it's possible that we just might end up in jail ourselves . . . which means that we better make our prisons nice and comfortable while we have the chance."[65]

The representatives of law and propriety, frustrated by their inability to stop their four-dimensional adversary, contribute to the inversion process by turning to rather unlikely quarters for assistance: a master plagiarist and a demon. They appear to be on the verge of success when Fun sensei is taken hostage by a Fake Bun who slips into existence from the pages of a forged sequel to Fun sensei's novel, but the Original Bun and his 120,000 partners in "crime," each of whom has sprung to life from a copy of the original best-seller, set in motion a decisive reversal of their own by turning themselves in at police stations throughout the country. After a raucous show trial and a brief sojourn at notorious Abashiri Prison, the Original Bun is transferred to one of the new luxury prisons built by the government to ensure that it can exact as much punishment as possible from all 120,000 Buns, each of whom is serving a virtual life sentence. The prisoners are so pampered that their jailers, and then the public at large, decide to join them in penal utopia; and the swiftest and surest ticket in is theft. The final overturning is a televised general revel, with the announcer exclaiming that the entire population has now turned thief (*ichioku sōdorobō*) as people fill the streets stealing whatever they can, turning themselves in, and chanting:

> Let's steal them let's steal them
> Authority, common sense, money, jewels
> All happy together, let's steal them
> Let's follow Bun and steal them!
>
> Nastiness from the nasty guys
> Badness from the bad guys
> Dignity from dignified bodies
> Refinement from refined bodies
> Money from the rich
> Land from the landlords
> Factories from the owners
> Weapons from the soldiers
> Poverty from the poor
> Sadness from the sad
> Sickness from the sick
> Boasts from the boasters
> Learning from the scholars
> Power from the powerful
> And then we'll all be
> Just plain people

> Just plain wonderful people
> All right!
> All happy together, let's steal them
> Let's follow Bun and steal them![66]

There are no gods, prison is heaven, and all, at last, is right with the world.

With its carnivalesque upset of the existing order, its recasting of the lawbreaker as savior, its vision of a utopian counter-society that can be expanded and multiplied until it encompasses the entire world, even its secondary reversal theme of the grotesquely bumbling hack novelist's sudden and inadvertent rise to quasi-heroic status (if not stature), *Bun to Fun* remains, along with the more elaborate *Kirikirijin*, one of Inoue's most daring and powerful realizations of the principle of comic upset. In most of Inoue's comic fictions, the inversions are of a less complex and far-reaching nature. *Tegusari shinjū*, for example, follows Kyōden's *kibyōshi* model so closely that there is no scope for inversion on a grand scale. The basic paradox, that of the man who must do everything that he should not want to do in his attempt to accomplish what he wants to accomplish, is taken directly from Kyōden, as are many of the individual details and incidents. Both Kyōden's Enjirō and Inoue's Eijirō are forced to voluntarily give up their right to inherit fabulous wealth, and both strive to win entirely unwarranted reputations for debauchery in order to advance "careers" for which they are all too evidently unsuited. When the ineptitude of their quest for recognition as sophisticates finally brings them the disrepute they long for, it takes a form that neither man anticipates or wants.

In Eijirō's case, however, the inversion takes on added irony: while Enjirō's pratfalls do nothing to advance his cause as a would-be great lover, Eijirō's finally establish him as what he always wanted to be, a source of laughs—but as a mere laughingstock instead of a comic writer. By seeking to make himself look like a *gesakusha*, he unwittingly turns himself into a *hōkan*, the simple jester whose style he had disdained because it lacked the all-important "final reversal" (*saigo no hikkurikaeshi*) that is the *gesakusha*'s definitive moment of triumph. In the end, he is granted a *saigo no hikkurikaeshi* of his own, but not one of his own creation: when his carefully faked double suicide attempt under the cherry blossoms in Mukōjima miscarries and culminates in his death, he realizes that his name is now certain to become known throughout Edo—and just before expiring asks for Osuzu, the woman he married and then left as part of his image-building campaign, but could not help loving.

The reversal of Eijirō's story, however, is enveloped in a larger and purer reversal, the story told before and after Eijirō's through the voice of the narrator Yoshichi. Like Eijirō, he aspires to *gesaku* stardom, even after he is warned by no less an authority than Kyōden himself that there is no future in it and; also like Eijirō, he makes the painful discovery that it is far easier to go through the motions of acting like a *gesakusha* than to endure the torments of self-doubt and hard work required to write like one. After Eijirō's funeral, Yoshichi repairs to a nearby tavern with two friends and, in a scene reminiscent of the conclusion to Dazai's *Romanesuku*, they attempt to sort out what it all means. Yoshichi, perhaps emboldened a bit by alcohol, resolves to take up where Eijirō fell. Fully aware that writing frivolities that triumph over realities is a personal hell, as well as economically hopeless and physically dangerous, he resolves to struggle on from this day forward with laughter as his only weapon under a new name: Jippensha Ikku. His friends respond to this display of bravado by announcing new pen names of their own, Kyokutei Bakin and Shikitei Sanba—together with Ikku the greatest writers of the later *gesaku* period. The last *hikkurikaeshi* of all, the resurrection and triumph of the *gesaku* spirit, is the one that matters most.

In the stories found in *Mokkinpotto shi no atoshimatsu* (The Fortunes of Father Mokkinpotto, 1974), too, the inversions are of a less extreme sort. While the Catholic church, with its claims to exclusive authority in matters of sanctity and salvation, may offer a tempting target for challenge or even ridicule, Inoue undermines its claims from within through the figure of Mokkinpotto rather than overturning it from outside. The principal vehicle for this undermining, of course, is the figure of the cleric himself. Mokkinpotto represents the power of the church and holds in his hands the fate of the students; but the prestige that he might normally expect to enjoy as a foreigner, scholar, and holy man is fatally compromised not only by his inelegant Kansai dialect, but by his appearance, personality, and actions, all of which make him an unlikely authority figure. The youthful narrator Komatsu describes him as an "extremely unprepossessing, sharp-eyed, big-nosed Frenchman, horribly filthy," with a head of hair reminiscent of an uncharted African jungle, a soutane shiny with wear and grime, and black fingernails which look like breeding grounds for some mysterious strain of bacteria. Appearances notwithstanding, he is the head of the French department at S—— University; but "if you didn't know this," observes Komatsu, "you'd mistake him for a foreign beggar, and feel like giving him a handout."[67] Moreover, when Mokkinpotto and the other clerical figures in the stories exercise their power, it is almost always benign, not arrogant or abusive. For a less than worldly scholar-clergyman, he shows an almost indecent willingness to cut a deal; but even when he engages in duplicities, they take the form of "holy swindles" intended to help his charges out of their scrapes. For all his superficial exoticism, Mokkinpotto is strongly reminiscent of a familiar Japanese authority figure, the surrogate parent who provides food and shelter for his charges, finds them jobs through his network of connections, and cleans up after them (*atoshimatsu o suru*) when they get themselves into trouble.

Such troubles, alternating with Mokkinpotto's damage control efforts, constitute the main action of the stories. Although the priest is the most interesting figure, he disappears from the scene for long intervals; in fact, less attention is devoted to him than to the students and their misadventures. But even when Mokkinpotto is off stage, the students maintain the focus on the inversion of the sacred and the profane, which quickly eclipses the more obvious Japanese-foreigner dichotomy as the primary theme. Komatsu and his friends are blessed with, if nothing else, an inexhaustibly fertile talent (born out of their desperate poverty, combined with a youthful spirit of mischief which cannot resist testing the limits of their mentor's Christian forbearance) for devising schemes and swindles, most of which involve taking advantage of their cover as pious Catholic students in one form or another and exploiting the clergy and parishioners, whose gullibility and good faith seem equally inexhaustible.

In one episode they try to support themselves by peddling stolen Bibles. In another, when they are caught filching food from a restaurant and cannot provide the furious proprietor with compensation, he demands that they produce "the guy in charge" (*ichiban erai yatsu*) to take responsibility. Komatsu replies that their top guy is Christ, and the manager bellows, "Okay then, let this bozo Christ come and take care of it!" Their long-suffering benefactor is constrained to come to their aid once more:

> Later that day, Father Mokkinpotto took us to the restaurant.
>
> "Are you the Christ these guys were talking about?" asked the proprietor, wiping his hands on his apron.
>
> Without replying to this question, Father Mokkinpotto produced a billfold from his pocket and said, "Please let me take care of this. But, how about a little discount?"[68]

Their most elaborate perversion of the sacred principle takes place in the third story, *Sei Pitā ginkō no hasan* (The St. Peter's Bank Failure), which details their establishment of a *pachinko* parlor in a monastery where Mokkinpotto, in one of his expedient "holy swindles," has installed them as novices after they have lost their previous home. This time their intentions are only the best, and this is their way of expressing their sincere gratitude toward the good-natured young American friars whom they are deceiving. They decorate the machines with colored lights, and replace their bells with a music box that plays *Ave Maria* when a ball enters a tulip. As usual, they go too far, and their good intentions lead to expulsion when the Father Superior discovers that they have been exchanging engraved pictures of the saints for cash to raise funds for Christmas gifts for the friars.

In the *Mokkinpotto* stories, inversion is revealed episodically rather than through a coherently unified plot structure in which a reversal of fortune issues from conflicts among characters of different status. While the stories are full of gags and comic scenes, many of which involve small-scale upsets, the plot focus is somewhat blurred as it shifts back and forth between the agon of Mokkinpotto versus his all-too-worldly disciples and his own internal contradictions as an unlikely holy man in an unlikely situation. Thematically, all five stories hinge in one fashion or another on the confrontation between the ideals and authority of Catholicism and exigent realities; but the confrontation remains inconclusive, the full-fledged upset deferred indefinitely. Characterization, which is less clear-cut than in other Inoue comedies, also plays a part in this deferral: no matter how often the students try to hoodwink Mokkinpotto (and succeed), they never challenge him or try to undo him; after all, they need him. Besides, being swindlers themselves, they have no claim to moral superiority. Mokkinpotto is not, like so many other comic clerical figures, a sanctimonious false authority set up for the kill; his positive attributes of good will and tolerance are displayed with a quality more common among comic figures who enjoy less powerful positions, a splendid resilience in tight situations.

The stories' closest approach to genuine upset comes when Komatsu takes a job at a theater in Asakusa with the imposing name of Furansu-za (French Theater). When Mokkinpotto brings several fellow priests to visit and discovers that it is a burlesque house and not, as Komatsu had led him to believe, a Japanese equivalent of the Comédie Française, he quickly gets over his humiliation and anger, produces his wallet, and comes to the point:

"At any rate, I have to save you from this hell. How much do you need to be born again?"

"But, I like it here!"

"Well, you don't have to come back to school, then. And you can leave the dormitory, too. All right? How much?"

"Could I have 10,000 yen? That would be enough."

Father Mokkinpotto considered this for a moment, and then said in a small voice: "Why don't you make it 5,000, and in return I'll cut your Ave Marias down from 1,000 to 500?"[69]

Unfortunately, his generosity fails to redeem Komatsu from the Furansu-za (all of the cash having "vanished down the female orifice in two nights in Yoshiwara");[70] but he refuses to give up the battle for Komatsu's soul, and so becomes a frequent visitor backstage. One of the strippers takes to calling him "Papa"—he is, after all, a Father—thus sending her gangster boyfriend into a paroxysm of jealousy. Fearing for his mentor's safety as well as his reputation, Komatsu reverses the usual pattern and makes a noble sacrifice in order to rescue his own lapsed rescuer; he quits his job, announcing (untruthfully) that he now has enough money to tide him over for a while, and tries to extract from the cleric a promise that he will never return to that den of sin. Mokkinpotto is wistfully evasive:

"Lately I've come to understand the true greatness of Saint Joanna. In order to keep up the courage of a band of Crusaders surrounded by the Turks, she ripped off her clothes and made herself as naked as the day she was born, knowing full well that she would be pierced by Turkish spears. Perhaps men in every age need women like her."

At this time, Father Mokkinpotto looked very, very big to me.[71]

But almost immediately Komatsu reverts to his usual escapades, and Mokkinpotto resumes his role as guardian of morality.

The only other hint of upset occurs in the fifth story, *Mokkinpotto-shi no sandogasa* (Father Mokkinpotto's Actor's Sedge Hat), when the three students dragoon Mokkinpotto into appearing on stage with a seedy troupe of traveling entertainers. After performing his specialty (sermonizing) during a variety interlude, he disappears with a female audience member who, in accordance with a long-standing custom in entertainments of this sort, has "purchased" his attentions. When he reappears to face the reproach of his charges, he humbles them yet again by reminding them that "it is presumptuous of you to take your own yardstick as an absolute and try to use it to measure the behavior of others."[72] Shortly thereafter his superiors get wind of this unseemly spectacle, and he is whisked away to France, forestalling the possibility of any *saigo no hikkurikaeshi*. As in the earlier stories, the sacred principle, although it perpetually teeters on the verge of collapse under the incessant pressure of vital worldly forces, is never quite displaced. Tension is maintained and resolution suspended indefinitely, and so there is no large-scale inversion of the kind seen in *Bun to Fun* or in *Kirikirijin*.

In *Kirikirijin*, as in *Bun to Fun*, inversion is woven integrally into the structure of the novel on all levels. The principal manifestations are the establishment and nature of the nation of Kirikiri itself: Inoue elevates a small, weak community populated by ostensibly inferior or even ludicrous inhabitants to the status of a model society, in this case one that combines the classic utopian attributes of Arcadian throwback to a simpler way of life, close to nature, and a futuristic society where life is prolonged and made comfortable by advanced technology. Kirikiri is Japan's ultimate backwater, clinging to a pre-industrial economy centered on non-mechanized agriculture. The village has the audacity to push its way into the community of nations while it manages its affairs like a television caricature of a farm village and conducts its government operations inside a charcoal-burning bus. The villagers' open acceptance of the less delicate physical aspects of life would be enough to make the vast majority of their erstwhile fellow countrymen blush, wince, or sneer. They are, in short, the "backward" past that the rest of Japan prides itself upon having escaped.

But to Inoue, this pride, like most other forms of pride, is more worthy of deflation than admiration. If Kirikiri appears small, weak, and backward as a nation, its individual citizens have none of these characteristics as human beings. Upset is inscribed in their names, which are given in "reverse" order (surname last); and beneath their rough-hewn exteriors and their fixation with petty details, they are courageous, self-reliant, imaginative, and, also endowed with a generous humanitarian spirit. Beyond their qualities of character, they also have practical talents even less commonly associated with rustics: as meticulous and resourceful planners, shrewd and sophisticated manipulators of public opinion, and well-informed, thoughtful experts on a wide range of subjects, they repeatedly demonstrate their superiority to the ostensibly more "sophisticated" Japanese.

Of course, all these qualities would be of little use in the Kirikirians' national enterprise except that they are backed, courtesy of historical accident, by a secret cache of 40,000 tons of gold. But unlike the Japanese, whose resources are even greater, they know what should be done with their wealth and how to go about doing it: the centerpiece of their campaign to acquire worldwide respect (and with it formal recognition), their great national hospital, is meant to serve people of all nations as the most advanced healing facility on earth and also to reestablish medicine as an expression of compassion and benevolence rather than a blind pursuit of wealth and status.

The characters who represent Japan in *Kirikirijin* are the satiric opposites of the villagers, caricatures drawn with an emphasis on arrogance, vindictiveness, and pettiness. The contrast is intensified because so many of them are at the apex of the Japanese status pyramid—in the upper echelons of government, Tokyo University, the major newspapers, the Japan Broadcasting Corporation, the professional intelligentsia, and the like. Smugly confident that since they represent Japan they are automatically in the right, they treat any challenge to their position as impudent if not downright treasonous. The result is a continuous parade of childish, duplicitous, rude, and out-and-out foolish behavior. The Kirikirians, for their part, staff their government, bureaucracy, police, and mass media with teenagers and the (sometimes grotesquely) physically disabled, many of them from the poorest and least respectable backgrounds in the community. Almost all of them fulfill their duties perfectly well; and when they appear ludicrous in doing so, the perception stems not so much from inadequacies on their part as from the inflated claims to authority inherent in the roles themselves. The Japanese, for all the massive power they can exert collectively, are inconsequential as individual human beings; the Kirikirians, in their smallness and weakness, are not.

The individual contrasts are paralleled on the communal level, where the Kirikirians' strengths-masquerading-as-weaknesses are implicitly and explicitly contrasted with the situation in Japan and other modern mass societies. The Japan of *Kirikirijin* is all the things that its adversary is not: a big, powerful, and thoroughly modernized nation. Yet it uses its size not to act with magnanimity, but to intimidate the small; and it values its strength not for any worthwhile cause but merely to maintain its own authority through displays of ritual posturing. It prides itself on its economic and technological advancement not because of the benefits they bring, but because of the power and the status of "modernity" they confer, without ever questioning the relevance of their Western-inspired "modernization" to local conditions, let alone its ultimate value.

Another notable manifestation of the principle of upset in *Kirikirijin*, and indeed throughout Inoue's comic fiction, is the sudden reversal to which character relationships are continuously subjected, frequently in the time-honored Japanese pattern of *gekokujō* (the lowly replace the high). Bun the master thief is transformed into a hero while the police anticipate their own imprisonment; the quack Doctor Akahige performs surgical miracles while Powerful Tarō asks the Kirikirians for a heart transplant. Other characters experience extreme and uncanny reversals of fortune: the impecunious Fun sensei suddenly finds himself basking in wealth and renown, and characters like Eijirō who seem destined for success see their carefully constructed plans come to naught.

Reversals of this sort are, of course, not limited to comic characters; but they are particularly frequent in comic narratives, in which (as Bergson has observed) consistency itself is shown to be a false norm, and the capacity to endure instability, even to thrive through reversal upon reversal, is a fundamental trait. Reversals are also particularly important in comedy because of its tendency to rely heavily upon caricatures and types, either flat or in low relief; since the outer appearance and inner reality held up to contrast in any given comic character both tend to be quite simple in themselves, authors can compensate for what such characters lack in inner complexity with changes of role and status. Mokkinpotto, one of Inoue's more rounded comic characters, can indulge his coexisting impulses of generosity and stinginess, and can alternate between humble, devoted shepherd and wrathful patriarch, farcical gullibility and quiet heroic dignity. But his stray sheep, who are largely devoid of such internal contradictions, can only wander back and forth between the peaks of prosperity and vales of disaster. The ultimate example of the instability of fortune in Inoue's fiction is the trajectory of his most extravagantly simple-minded character, Furuhashi, who, following his arrival in Kirikiri, successively finds himself (among other things) an illegal alien, an official state guest, a World Cup Ping-Pong Tournament competitor, a convicted criminal condemned to death, a hospital orderly, a humiliated male geisha, an overjoyed fiancé, a manhunt target, a millionaire winner of multiple literary prizes, and a Poet Laureate. After his dimwittedness and indiscretion lead to the death of Kirikiri's first president, he is designated the successor, is blown up by a grenade, undergoes the world's first successful brain transplant operation, discovers his new self (herself?) to be pregnant, sees his prospects of marriage evaporate, takes his turn on the striptease stage during his presidential inauguration ceremony, meets his own corpse, and is finally assassinated—all within the space of approximately two days.

Fantasy and outright nonsense are frequently mobilized in the cause of upset in *Bun to Fun* and *Kirikirijin*. Bun's four-dimensional exploits and the science-fiction trappings of *Kirikirijin* (firearm implants and other advanced surgery, "greenhouses" of human vegetables cultivated for organ transplants, plant-animal hybrids, etc.) create an atmosphere in which the violation of physical laws goes hand in hand with the transgression of social restraints and demolition of received notions. Just as the signifying power of words is subverted by Inoue's puns, exaggerations, parodies, and other stylistic devices, the notion of purposive human action is repeatedly undermined by long and elaborate streams of gags and anecdotes that violate all rules of logic, and frequently end by petering out into incoherence or simply evaporating. The trappings of rational order are relentlessly pelted with terse crystallizations of paradox such as the description of the watch which Furuhashi receives as a keepsake upon the death of his college professor: "The late professor had always maintained that 'you can't do superior research if you're always concerned about time,' so his watch had neither an hour hand nor a minute hand. But at the same time he also maintained that 'time is always passing, and is not to be wasted,' so his wristwatch had only a second hand."[73]

The physical and structural formalities of the text are not immune from Inouean upset either. In *Bun to Fun* certain page margins are marked off with dotted lines and instructions to the reader to glue them together. The author explains: "Please glue these pages closed. It would not do for your mother to read this passage in which Fun sensei and a young lady sit around a table in the altogether. Although the kinds of things that your mothers will imagine are not going to happen at all, it is unfortunately quite possible (as I noted before) that the great educational value of this book will be misjudged. Adults, especially mothers, are extremely susceptible to various ideas, and it is the duty of children to protect them."[74] Other pages are to be cut out and mailed away, and one of the illustrations is replaced with a note reading "I have helped myself to this picture—Bun."[75] While there is nothing particularly profound or daring about these devices, they do illustrate the breadth of Inoue's inversive program. In an epilogue prepared for an edition of *Bun to Fun* that appeared three years after the novel's composition, he confesses to some dissatisfaction with his handling of the ending, but states, "At that time I wanted to overturn all common sense, all technique. There were any number of other, more novelistic ways to end it, but I chose the ending that was as far as possible from novelistic technique."[76]

Kirikirijin is virtually antinovelistic in its disregard of formal conventions. Considerations of coherence in narrative structure and voice are jettisoned in favor of an extremely loose narrative line that is continually interrupting itself with digressions, digressions within digressions, lists, simile chains, disquisitions on tomato-planting techniques and multinational transfer pricing, and excerpts from legal codes, textbooks, and the like, as well as such ephemera as quiz show questions and restaurant menus. Two pages are occupied by Shandyesque strings of geometrical shapes and typographic symbols purporting to transcribe the proceedings in Furuhashi's mind during one of his frequent losses of consciousness, interrupted in the middle by a notice that two hundred pages of similar material have been deleted. If all this results in a sprawling, unshapely end product, that is very much the author's intention. As he declares midway through a forty-five-page digression on the outrageous circumstances of Furuhashi's youth: "At this point it would be quite possible to return to the main path of the narrative. In fact, that would be the sensible thing to do . . . But . . . I would like to carry on in this senseless vein. After all, this story makes no sense to begin with, and so I who am recording it have no choice but to stray from the path of sense as I wield my brush."[77]

Perhaps the most striking embodiment of all of Inoue's spirit of inversion is the "Doctor of Scatology" who directs the Defecation Research Center of the Kirikiri National Hospital. Located appropriately enough in a forest, symbolically beyond the boundary of civilization, the Center seeks to liberate humanity from its deepest inhibitions and to emulate the freedom of the birds, who feel no constraints about relieving themselves any time, at any place, and in any style that pleases them. As the doctor explains to an astounded Furuhashi, his movement is linked to nudism, the rejection of city life, and all other "natural life" and "simple life" movements: "If you follow the idea of Free Defecation all the way, you end up rejecting clothing, houses, pavement, automobiles, and airplanes. . . . Everyone, rich and poor, will just be human—you can't wear a medal when you're naked, so there will be no great people or lowly people any more. It's the same with nudism. . . . Our paths of approach are different, but we work toward the same goal: anticivilization!"[78]

This is not the only passage in *Kirikirijin* that treats excrement in a positive way. In chapter 9, we are told that the Kirikirians refer to it in reverential terms like those that the Japanese use for their emperor and their various nature deities, and that Kirikiri scientists are experimenting with a system to turn human excrement into a source of "milk, butter, cheese, and *sukiyaki*" by feeding it to cows.[79] The recurrent emphasis on the "lower stratum of the body" and its functions of defecation, digestion, and procreation is one of the many elements in both *Kirikirijin* and *Bun to Fun* that evoke Mikhail Bakhtin's well-known examination of the Renaissance carnival world that finds its supreme literary expression in the endlessly rich and raucous comic fantasies of Rabelais. Other carnival elements are equally prominent, including the festive comic transgression that marks the rebellious communities in both novels and the sheer linguistic exuberance that expresses itself through Inoue's irrepressible torrents of verbiage, lively vernacular idiom, exaggerations, and invention of numerous new words, as well as the combination of popular energy with humanistic values, the encyclopedic scope, frequent in-jokes, and allusions. There is also the continual celebration of the forces of fertility and regeneration, especially the earthy physicality of life that Bakhtin labels "grotesque realism." *Kirikirijin* is full of what Bakhtin considers the most characteristic form of grotesque imagery, the joining of two bodies in one, be they male and female (Furuhashi's brain transplanted into the body of a stripper), living and dying (a terminally ill Kirikirian whose body is frozen in the National Hospital's cryogenics lab to await new life-saving advances in research), or various human, animal, and plant combinations (human bodies that generate and spin cotton, a cat-dog cross or *nyawan*, and a tomato-badger hybrid dubbed a *tonuki*).

Carnival, according to Bakhtin, is a "utopian realm of community, freedom, equality, and abundance"[80] that "does not acknowledge any distinction between actors and spectators" because "its very idea embraces all the people."[81] Comic verbal composition in the form of parodies, both written and oral, is one of its integral components, as is its "characteristic logic, the peculiar logic of the 'inside out' (*à l'envers*), of the 'turnabout,' of a continual shifting from top to bottom, from front to rear, of numerous parodies and travesties, humiliations, profanations, comic crownings and uncrownings."[82] The correspondence with the worlds of *Kirikirijin* and *Bun to Fun*, as well as some of Inoue's critical writings, could hardly be more obvious. But as Bakhtin himself observed in a somewhat offhand way, and as numerous studies have pointed out in more elaborate fashion, the ritual and spectacular manifestations of carnival culture, and even some of its literary manifestations, for all their apparent movement toward subversion of the established order, are in fact strictly limited in their duration; and their transgressions and parodies are licensed by the very forces of authority upon whom their participants heap their mockery.[83] In Victor Turner's words, rituals of status reversal, "by making the low high and the high low, . . . reaffirm the hierarchical principle"[84] and ultimately have the effect of "emphasizing all the more trenchantly the social distinctions within the group."[85] Hutcheon adds that "the parodic text is granted a special license to transgress the limits of convention, but, as in the carnival, it can do so only temporarily and only within the controlled confines authorized by the text parodied—that is, quite simply, within the confines dictated by 'recognizability.'"[86] But although her definition of parody ("imitation with critical ironic distance")[87] is extremely broad, it remains a function of intertextuality; and it is not clear that it can be related in any meaningful way to the non-textual aspects of Inoue's inversive strategy. Moreover, the equally broad sort of "authorization" that she posits has little to do with the kind of tacit consent by sentient authorities that Bakhtin and Turner describe. And it is significant that the *literary* expression of the carnival spirit, although limited to a "laboratory situation,"[88] is not subject to the same constraints of time or authorization that ritual/spectacle expressions are, and so the communities it depicts have the potential to carry their oppositional and transgressive acts to far greater extremes. Inoue willingly exploits this potential to the fullest, not only in the carnivalesque elements so prominent in his style but in the nature of the upsets he depicts. The liberation-minded thieves of *Bun to Fun* and secessionist villagers of *Kirikirijin* are self-authorized transgressors defiantly striving to become the agents of their own liberation, acknowledging no outside powers or temporal limitations. Both narratives center on uprisings in which real power is contested, rather than symbolic ritual displays.

As Turner has observed, "rituals of status reversal" of the type seen in carnival are analogous in some ways to comedy, "for both involve mockery and inversion, but not destruction, of structural roles and overzealous adherents to them."[89] Eco, who draws an even closer connection between the carnival principle and the comic, goes so far as to proclaim that since carnival, and by extension the comic, can exist only as temporary, authorized transgressions of a law "so pervasively and profoundly introjected as to be overwhelmingly present at the moment of its violation," they are doomed to be ineffectual; and even when they manage to exceed the authorized bounds, they only end up producing new sets of rules, which will in turn require new transgressive challenges.[90] If this constraint were to impinge on comic literature in the same way that it is said to do on actual carnivals and other "rituals of status reversal," comic actions would indeed constitute little more than intervals of license between periods of repression, and would, as Bakhtin, Turner, Hutcheon, and Eco suggest, inevitably lead to the restoration of an authoritarian established order (now reinforced by having successfully contained the transgressive gesture). There could be no happy or triumphant endings. But comedy is renowned, and sometimes notorious, for its tendency to end happily even in the most wildly improbable of circumstances. Precisely because comic texts are literary constructs, limited to a "laboratory situation," they pose a less direct threat to existing power/status relations, and thus are not normally subject to the same pressures as carnivals and rituals enacted by actual human beings.[91] Moreover, the author is free to depict transgressive actions that do not depend on authorization, and is also in control of where and when to end the narrative; if he or she prefers not to restore the old order, he or she need not do so. Thus, the natural culmination of transgressive inversion in comedy is a triumphant general revel or *komos*, in which liberation, however transitory, from all restraints and humankind's reunion with the natural order is celebrated. Even in cases where the social order is restored, as in the boy-gets-girl ending of the typical romantic comedy, it takes the form of a reconciliation of conflicting elements, with both of the hitherto contesting parties sharing in the new order; there is no return to the status quo ante of the sort that marks the termination of carnival.

While *komos* is a critical concept derived from Attic Old Comedy, it is also a natural enough development in any comic work that takes as its theme the overturning and replacement of an existing repressive order by a freer, more vital, and less artificial one. Thus it is not surprising to see *komos*-like elements in the conclusions of *Bun to Fun* or *Kirikirijin*, both extended to a global scale courtesy of the twentieth-century miracle of television. In the ending of *Bun to Fun*, as virtually the entire populace seems resolved to join Bun and his partners in crime in liberating themselves through theft and imprisonment, the narrative moves beyond inversion (and its relegitimizing of hierarchical structures) to a condition of leveling in which the former antagonists can be integrated and all hierarchy is abolished. In *Kirikirijin*, the republic's entire brief existence is a kind of ongoing *komos*, as the Kirikirians celebrate their release from centuries of repression and inhibition with a series of festive pageants and open indulgence in earthy eroticism.

And yet, for all the fervent energy (and even fourth-dimensional powers) they pour into their revels, there are finally limits to the ability of Inoue's transgressing communities to achieve a total upset of the old order. The Kirikiri enterprise fails after only a day and a half, inadvertently betrayed by the ever-bumbling Furuhashi and overwhelmed by an onslaught from great powers that can tolerate neither the potential threat it poses to their hegemony over their own restive minority communities nor the notion that people can defiantly take power over their lives and resources into their own hands. And even when there are no such incompetents or hostile outside forces to contend with, another hazard lies in wait for seemingly successful transgressive communities, one rarely encountered by individual comic heroes, who are usually unable to establish their own orders even if they succeed in defying the existing order. As Eco has pointed out, there is always the danger that carnivalization, even as a mere literary gesture, will itself become mannered, and so be reabsorbed by society.[92] In "real life," the ultimate version of carnival is revolution, but "even revolutions produce a restoration of their own . . . in order to install their new social model. Otherwise they are not effective revolutions, only social disturbances."[93]

Inoue clearly understands this; in both novels, an oppressive order is replaced by a new one which, while more humane and ostensibly humbler than its predecessor, is also vulnerable to various challenges and exposures. *Kirikirijin*'s utopian ministate with its great hospital, Inoue's most elaborate vision of the humane order, is constantly held up to comic scrutiny—it is, after all, as much a product of human enterprise as anything else—and its own little vanities exposed. He also understands that the new order established by a successful transgression will in turn breed its own transgressors. Shortly after publishing *Kirikirijin*, he expressed misgivings over bringing Kirikiri's rebellion to an abrupt and rather spiritualized ending, rather than portraying the transgressing community gradually turning into a miniaturized version of the bureaucratic authoritarian order that it strove so hard to break away from. This would have inevitably led to a need for further revolutions within the Kirikiri revolution. (Characteristically, Inoue envisions these subsequent revolts as communal undertakings, too, with the individual emerging only when the last group of two members is ready to split.)[94]

In *Bun to Fun,* Inoue forestalled the possibility of liberation's going sour by ending the narrative in the midst of a celebration of the comic community's successful transgression, with no chance to see it institutionalized or betrayed. But five years after the publication of the novel, in a dramatized version entitled *Sore kara no Bun to Fun* (Bun and Fun Revisited), he added a new ending following the *komos* scene, in which the worldwide Bun community is betrayed and eradicated by Bun clones from dictatorial societies who emerge from deliberately mistranslated versions of Fun sensei's novel and "the world has gone back to just what it was before."[95] Fun sensei is imprisoned in a dungeon where he is allowed only one meal every three days and a bath once in five years. After a fleeting visit from the last real Bun, now a desperate fugitive, Fun vows to come to his aid by writing more novels, even if he has to bite his fingers and write in his own blood on the walls of his cell. Just before the curtain falls he puts a finger to his mouth; once again the ending is less than conclusive, but this time there is no hint of *komos.* Suddenly, one of the most inspired of all Inoue's comic butts has taken on an air of pathos and noble suffering that approaches the tragic.

Nevertheless, it, is significant that the novels themselves do not end with the Buns' demise and the self-induced fission of Kirikiri. The Buns are left on the cusp of their triumph, and Kirikiri goes down fighting. Throughout both novels, the dominant spirit is one of almost uninterrupted defiant festivity, of energy and exuberance—the spirit of *komos* that is emblematic of Inoue's brand of the comic spirit at its boldest and distances it from the restrained, attenuated, or even self-torturing comedy common in so many of the works of his Japanese predecessors. It is in this light that we can best view Inoue's comedy as a whole: underlying each element, be it wordplay, parody, fantasy, or satire, is a grand comic vision that gives life to them all.

Whether grandeur of this sort will suffice to gain Inoue's work acceptance into the canon of modern Japanese art fiction remains an open question. In many ways it fails to provide what most Japanese writers and critics since the days of Tsubouchi Shōyō have found most worthy of approbation. Admirers of the evocative minimalist grace of a Shiga or Kawabata or even the imperial purple of a Mishima are sure to be dismayed by Inoue's luxuriant tangles of verbiage and the obvious glee with which he insists on leaving no rhetorical stone unturned. Equally disconcerting are his blatant disregard of the conventions of illusionist realism in his handling of narrative situations and his lack of concern with deep or subtly nuanced psychological probing. His penchant for maximal inclusion to the detriment of perfection of form has led Ōe Kenzaburō, a professed admirer of Inoue's work and a committed believer in comedy, to characterize *Kirikirijin* as "good literature but not pure literature."[96] Equally damaging, perhaps, is his rejection of the role of solemn and frequently oracular purveyor of a philosophy of life associated with so many art novelists in Japan in favor of the far less lofty role of entertainer.

While he has found articulate advocates in critics such as Yamaguchi Masao, Maeda Ai, Senda Akihiko, and (in English) Masao Miyoshi,[97] Inoue has also shown himself perfectly capable of speaking out on his own behalf in his essays and fiction, and has undertaken occasional guerrilla attacks on his adversaries as well. With respect to language, Inoue argues that because of the reliance on translations of Western models, the dominant schools of modern Japanese drama and fiction have become repositories of monumentally arid and dull prose in which words function exclusively as abstract tokens of ideas and the dimension of sound is ignored. Japanese writers have forgotten that literary art depends upon the "lively dance of words,"[98] and also that the Japanese language, with its limited number of sounds, is ideally suited for exploring connections between sound and sense. Even the most "serious" writers cannot avoid occasionally stumbling into exposure of the rich possibilities for wordplay in Japanese, and thus find themselves betrayed by the spirit of their own language. "I try to make this point clear in my own work," Inoue declares, "which also means that I am making fun of the masterpieces."[99]

Although he has created a number of dramas sympathetically portraying prominent modern writers such as Higuchi Ichiyō, Ishikawa Takuboku, Natsume Sōseki, Miyazawa Kenji, and Dazai Osamu,[100] Inoue uses characters such as Fun sensei and Furuhashi to powerfully satirize what he sees as the shortcomings of modern Japanese literature, not the least of them being its tendency to conflate impenetrability with artistic purity.[101] Fun sensei takes it as a matter of pride that none of his creations has sold more than five copies; and when his *Bun* unaccountably turns into a runaway bestseller, his initial feelings of shock and grief quickly give way to righteous indignation: "This is indecent! . . . How could a novel of mine sell 100,000 copies? . . . People are off their rockers. Are all those housewives out in their housing developments and all those office girls reading this difficult novel while they munch on their roast sweet potatoes? It's a disgrace!"[102] He resolves that his next work will be totally uncompromising, with nothing in its plot or style that might inadvertently pander to the public, a novel so difficult that nobody will buy it, even by mistake. Furuhashi, for all his fantasies of literary glory, boasts no more than 350 or 360 readers, thus possibly qualifying (the narrator notes) as a "serious" rather than a popular writer.[103] And, as Inoue suggests repeatedly in *Kirikirijin*, Furuhashi is not so much a fatuous impostor who violates the norms of Japan's literary establishment as he is an embodiment of the mediocrity and pomposity of that establishment as a whole: although his second novel, written entirely in the present tense, was hailed by critics as the product of a "bold experimental spirit," and "the first Japanese *nouveau roman*," a teenaged reader in Kirikiri easily uncovers the basis of his style, an inability to write in any other tense.

In response to those who regard his unabashed commitment to comedy with discomfort or suspicion, Inoue can, and does, point out that many of the features that make his literature "frivolous" from the modern point of view are actually continuations of a long tradition that includes many of the acknowledged classics of Japanese literature. His interest in exploiting similarities in the sound qualities of words springs from the same instincts that produced the pun-like *kakekotoba* of classical Japanese poetry as well as the *gesakusha*'s bravura displays of verbal agility. His fondness for devices such as elaborate lists and similes reflects a venerable tradition that dates back at least one thousand years in Japan, reaching a peak in the Edo period with Chikamatsu, Saikaku, and the *gesakusha* and surviving into the first pages of Japan's first "modern" novel, Futabatei Shimei's *Ukigomo* (Drifting Cloud, 1887–1889).[104]

Flat characterization is both an integral part of the Japanese tradition and a standard comic technique. Inoue has pointed out that he intentionally keeps his authority figures simple, since they would not be laughable if they were too complicated.[105] By limiting his characterizations to surface elements, he can use them to constitute one side of a *sekai-shukō* dichotomy, or to explore such themes as the relationship between the sacred and profane in the *Mokkinpotto* stories or the pretensions and predicaments of writers in *Bun to Fun*. In a larger sense, the modern concern with complexity and verisimilitude of character is irrelevant to his purposes. Especially in Japanese society, where so much significance is attached to social status as determined by such factors as occupation, age, and rank within one's group, the portrayal of character in terms of types or roles can have as important a function as conventional novelistic scrutinizing of personality traits or psychological motivation.

All of which, of course, is not to say that Inoue's comic spirit represents a total departure from Japanese culture of the last hundred years or a simple return to tradition. It draws inspiration from such twentieth-century antecedents as the fiction of Miyazawa Kenji and Sasaki Kuni, and also is deeply rooted in contemporary forms of popular culture including both the slapstick comedy of the burlesque theater and the radio and television industry in which he began his writing career. To all these precedents he adds his own distinctive contributions, among the most notable of which is a satiric voice of a boldness and eloquence rare in Japan in any age. In his essay "Kigeki ni yoru kigekiteki jiko kyōseihō" (The Comic Method of Comical Self-correction, 1971), Inoue characterizes his role as more like that of a Molière than of the *gesakusha*, calling attention to human foibles and frailties and correcting them with laughter.[106] But where Molière saw human nature as essentially healthy and suggested that society required only to be purged of the occasional infection of hypocrisy or delusion to maintain its equilibrium, Inoue sees healthy and unhealthy elements in a perpetual flux in every human being and in society as a whole. To assail "authority" is to assail human nature itself,[107] for somewhere within each of us lurks a potential petty tyrant, snob, or charlatan:

> In our age people are foolish and presumptuous, dangerously self-confident, politicians vie for power, businessmen shamelessly foul the environment with deadly chemicals, company unions expel militants, scientists devise tools for murder, cars run people over, one person is jealous of the next, writers scribble pulpy novels, critics fail to nurture talent, the talented are overweening, children are skirt-lifters, bankers are bamboozled, merchants are meretricious, farmers are cunning, and I pride myself upon my little stock of gags—and these follies and vanities seem to be accumulating and expanding all the time, leading humanity to ruin. This human folly must be pointed out and corrected somehow, but wouldn't it be better to do it with laughter than with tears and rage?[108]

In Inoue's comic fiction, then, satiric correction characteristically takes the form of a continuous process of overturning the various unhealthy aspects of human nature through ridicule, rather than the enlightenment or expulsion of aberrant individuals. In his most ambitious works, a broad range of types is held up to comic scrutiny; so, implicitly or explicitly, is humanity en masse. On occasion, this breadth of perspective is combined with a shift from Inoue's customary satiric voice of ironic, humorous caricature to direct censure and invective; the result is satire of a very different sort, in which he sheds the buffoon's mask and declaims with savage eloquence. In chapter 24 of *Kirikirijin* when Furuhashi is interviewed on the topic of "What kind of laughter are people looking for today?," he launches into a memorable tirade in a voice that sounds curiously out of character, but gives him the satisfying feeling of "having expressed a real opinion for the first time in a long time": "People aren't looking for anything at all. Creators wrack their brains and come up with all kinds of things, but people just look them all over, and pick out what they like best. This is the public's privilege. The things they like best become the bestsellers, the hit tunes, the TV smashes. Don't you understand? 'People,' that is audiences, don't create a thing on their own, and they have no idea what kind of laughter they're looking for."[109] When his interviewer, "Kurimoto Kazaru" (a caricature of the gossip journalist and television personality Nashimoto Masaru), suggests that this constitutes an "insult to the public," Furuhashi raises the stakes:

> Let them feel insulted. I'm just telling you what I believe. Look—you television people hardly ever criticize your audience. I think that's wrong. *All of you who watch this station's programming are good people. The people who are making the world a bad place are other people.* . . . You make me feel sick. You give me the creeps. What are you doing with the public airwaves you use and all that money you spend on production? You treat the audience like a bunch of nursery-school kids and keep telling them "You're the only ones who aren't doing anything bad." So what happens? The audience, the people, the public, end up turning into real nursery-school kids. And Japan ends up full of people who really believe that "we're the only ones who haven't done anything wrong, in fact we're the only good people. Everything is other people's fault." I'm not asking you to do it all the time, but how about just once in three days, even for just five or ten minutes, telling the audience the truth? For example . . . All you folks who are so crazy about the pandas that have come to Japan—how come you can't find any room in your big hearts for human beings, for foreigners? They say there's no place in the world where it's as hard to become a citizen as Japan. There are tens of thousands of people who have lived here all their lives and want to become Japanese that we call resident alien citizens of someplace or other. There isn't a single foreigner on the faculty of any of the national universities—and we're all yattering away about how this is supposed to be the age of internationalization in Japan. Don't you think there's something kind of strange about all this?[110]

If the ground rules in Japan are such that attempts to identify and correct human folly do not fall into the category of "philosophy" (*shisō*) or "attitude toward life," and if this excludes Inoue's work from consideration as "serious" or high art, he is as usual ready to counterattack with a reversal. What is ostentatiously paraded across the Japanese stage as *shisō*, he charges, is nothing more than a collection of tedious political catchphrases and high-flown pseudo-philosophical obfuscations masquerading as High Culture. Genuine *shisō*, according to Inoue, consists of knowledge (*chishiki*) combined with a sense of values (*kachikan*) or, to put it more crudely, it simply states that "things should be done this way, because it is better."[111] The right way for writers to do what they do is to enliven their work, to remember that art can be entertainment and discovery as well as philosophy, *geijutsu* in the fullest sense of the word, and to take advantage of all available resources, including extravagant language, fantasy, laughter, and nonsense, even if on the surface they appear inimical to the serious presentation of serious issues. If Japanese renditions of Pinter, Beckett, Ionesco, and other modern dramatists make them appear dry and difficult, it is only because the Japanese have chosen to ignore the strong elements of farce and slapstick in these works, and not the fault of the works themselves.[112]

In one of his discussions of comic theory, Inoue notes that comedy's dualistic vision, which juxtaposes outward appearance and inner reality to create a new state of affairs, is analogous to the dialectic method beloved of serious thinkers, and so it is pointless to assail the comic spirit as lacking in *shisō*. But ultimately arguments of this sort do not quite ring true, for they smack of conventional one-dimensional logic rather than dualistic comic logic. Appropriately enough it is Furuhashi, Inoue's fullest realization of human being (and writer) as comic figure, who states the case most tellingly after one of the Kirikirians suggests that his work "seems to have no substance" (*naiyō wa nai yō na mon da*): "That's right. My philosophical position is that I have no philosophy. To put it more plainly, you could call it 'the philosophy of no philosophy,' I guess. . . . Some writers just keep paring away and paring away superfluous words, then they pare away some more. The Shiga Naoya type. Well, I keep paring away and paring away superfluous ideas and then I pare away some more, in just the same way—understand?"[113]

Perhaps "antiphilosophy" or "dephilosophism" might be unsatisfactory as critical terminology, but total *hikkurikaeshi*, the impulse to break through all boundaries and overthrow all principles to approach absolute absurdity, is the principle at the very heart of Inoue's comedy. For the comedian, this is the most realistic, reasonable way to bring some semblance of order to the chaotic swirl of phenomena that, for lack of a better term (language being the imperfect medium it is), we customarily refer to as "life" or "reality."

One of these phenomena is the Inoue phenomenon, and one of the contradictions is that Inoue's upsets and disruptions have been accepted with enthusiasm by so many of the disruptees. No doubt there are many humble readers (and perhaps more than a few self-professedly humble ones) who derive a vicarious pleasure from the upsets. And Inoue knows that a great comic upsetter must also be a great conciliator, balancing his satiric attacks and absurdism with a conviction that correction, and perhaps even salvation, just might be possible. If the bold upset of the Kirikirians ends in death and debacle, as all human undertakings are liable to do sooner or later, their spirits will rise above the earth and above all the follies of fleshly life, patiently awaiting the day when the follies and dichotomies disappear and humanity realizes its potential for genuine peace and harmony. Probably they will wait forever. In the meantime, we have comedy.

Chapter 5
Conclusion

I hope that the preceding pages have served to demonstrate, to the extent that such a demonstration has been necessary, that the comic spirit is indeed present in modern Japanese fiction. It should also be reiterated that the authors discussed here are by no means the only ones who could or should be cited as exemplifying that spirit; Natsume Sōseki, Uno Kōji, or Tanizaki Jun'ichirō among the earlier moderns and Maruya Saiichi or Tsutsui Yasutaka among contemporary novelists might just as easily have been singled out for attention as Ibuse, Dazai, and Inoue.

Having demonstrated that the phenomenon exists, we must consider whether the works discussed might lead to some more or less concrete conclusions about its nature. Since the massed chorus of comedians would remind us that it is one more form of delusion to expect that vast and diverse accumulations of experience can really be ordered into neat and meaningful patterns, we may begin with the observation that these works show the striking variety of forms, themes, and styles that exists within Japanese comedy, and even within the oeuvres of individual authors. The soft-spoken, elliptical allegory of Ibuse's early works gives way to the caustic (but no less allegorical) satire of *Yōhai taichō* and urbane comedies of manners exemplified in *Shūkin ryokō* and *Chinpindō shujin*. Dazai alternates between intensely personal self-mockery, often tinged with intense bitterness, and parodies pointing good-naturedly at a broad range of general human foibles, equally likely to be realized through coarse pratfalls or rarefied high comedy. Inoue offers everything from meticulous antiquarian parody to wildly imaginative fantasy and from straight-ahead conventional narrative structures to bold experiments that flaunt their conviction that in literature, as in life, rules are made to be broken.

But diversity, particularly of the comic variety, inevitably tends toward untidiness, and for purposes of drawing conclusions about the nature of modern Japanese comic fiction, it would be more appropriate to sift through this variegated mass of material in search of whatever features these works might have in common, and what, if anything, these features might suggest about distinctive or characteristic traits of modern Japanese comedy. Unfortunately, gratifying as it would be to be able to point to a "distinctive" or even "unique" "spirit" of Japanese comedy, such an attempt would be as futile in Japan as it would be in any other society whose written history dates back over one thousand years and whose population is counted in tens of millions. Even such broadly recognized phenomena as the "English humor" expounded by Louis Cazamian tend to melt down into shapeless masses upon casual scrutiny: solid, coherent shape can hardly be a salient virtue of any vessel capacious enough to contain *Tom Jones*, *The Pickwick Papers*, *A Handful of Dust*, and Monty Python, each of which has features that can be as readily linked with comic works from other cultures as with each other.

The same applies to *Shūkin ryokō*, *Otogizōshi*, and *Bun to Fun*. Many of the elements in these works (slapstick pratfalls, mistaken identities, battles—or wars—between the sexes, festive affirmation of the life force, social satire, parody, wordplay) are familiar enough in the comic literature of many cultures. But among the various elements of comedy, certain ones tend to turn up more frequently than others in Japanese comedies, owing not so much to factors of "national character" or any intrinsic predispositions on the part of Japanese writers as to certain conditions imposed from without by the pressures of language, culture, literary tradition, or society. To the extent that a common or distinctive quality is to be found in the comic fiction of Ibuse, Dazai, and Inoue, then, it is shaped by a combination of accommodation with and defiance of the circumstances in which they found themselves.

These have been described already (especially in the Introduction). To recapitulate, comedy has not generally been considered an independent literary category in Japan and has not been accorded its own place in the overall artistic scheme; rather, its existence has simply been identified by the presence of humor, or in distinction from the "serious," whether in individual works or in genres (*kyōgen* as vs. Nō drama, *haikai* as vs. *renga* and later *senryū* as vs. *haikai* verse). Of course, even in the Western tradition, where the dichotomy between tragedy and comedy boasts a venerable history, comedy is more often perceived not in terms of an antithetical relation to tragedy but rather in contrast to the "serious," that is, those forms of discourse which disregard incongruities of the sort upon which comedy lavishes so much attention, or at least attempt to proceed as quickly and neatly as possible to their resolution. Those who place a high value on "seriousness" are prone to equate its absence with frivolousness and relegate comic forms of expression to an inferior status. For the most part, however, comedy has been able to maintain itself as a more or less legitimate alternative to the serious, or even a necessary restraint on its excesses. In Japanese high culture, the cult of seriousness—with its aversion to dualities, its preference for the savoring of emotional states over delight in complex intrigue, its discomfort with the pleasure that arises from mirth, and its reluctance to admit works animated by a comic spirit into the canon of high art—has persistently retained such formidable power and prestige that comic artists have had a great deal of trouble in presenting their work as a legitimate alternative. The power of the cult of seriousness is reflected not only in the lack of critical discussion of comedy, but in the tendency either to exclude comic works from that discussion or at best to relegate them to a distinctly secondary artistic status, frequently coupled with a tendency toward association with lower social status.[1]

These unpropitious general circumstances become particularly pronounced in the modern period. In the popular oral-based entertainments, comedy continued to figure prominently enough in traditional forms (most notably *rakugo*) and developed in new directions such as the music-hall comedy troupes of Asakusa and the *manzai* duos of Osaka. But like the new dramatic and poetic genres that were accorded art status in modern Japan, the fictional form called *shōsetsu* neither arose as a comic countergenre nor gave rise to one, and there was no comfortable place for comedy in it. Moreover, unlike earlier forms of fiction such as *monogatari* (prose romances), *setsuwa* (fables), *ukiyo-zōshi* (tales of the floating world), and *gesaku*, which, perhaps because of their relatively low aesthetic and/or social standing, had been relatively open to the exploration of various forms of imaginative play, including the portrayal of comic dualities, *shōsetsu*, especially the influential *shishōsetsu* form, took the disclosure of "truth" as a guarantee of its claims to high-culture status, and its creators were largely disinclined to engage in explorations of that sort.

Any writer who seeks to create comic works within the *shōsetsu* framework will adhere to some patterns common in the general run of *shōsetsu*,[2] many of which have little or no bearing on comedy. But where the characteristics of the *shōsetsu* do impinge on the strategies available to the would-be comic writer, the choice to accommodate will naturally result in the creation of works that occupy a relatively narrow and distinct zone within the overall range of comic possibilities. Throughout most of its hundred-year history, the *shōsetsu* has tended to focus on a single character and reflect the world of its main practitioners (urban intellectuals) in a rather narrow way, in isolation from the social matrix that is the natural seedbed for much comedy. But even on this limited scale, as long as it remained committed to "truth," or at least realism, it reflected a social environment in which statements of self-deprecation are a normal and expected part of public discourse, and public expressions of deprecation of others are frowned upon. In particular, as Futabatei Shimei's *Ukigumo* and Mori Ōgai's *Maihime* (The Dancing Girl, 1890) attest, challenges to authority in various forms, especially parents and the state, have been frequent enough in modern Japanese fiction since its early days; but eminent figures of any sort (generals, pedants, ideologues) have only rarely, and recently, found themselves objects of ridicule or other forms of comic attention.

These characteristics have all played a powerful role in shaping modern Japanese comic fiction. Even in works that transcend the constraints of the *shishōsetsu* and adopt a broader thematic range, one of the most fundamental of all comic strategies, the creation of the inferior term in a comic dichotomy based on character (i.e., a butt) and the expression of overt mockery of that character, would pose major difficulties. The would-be comedian, unable (or unwilling) to support existing norms (and power) by serving as dismissive corrector of deviant behavior or to subvert them by acting as rambunctious upsetter, is left with little choice but to turn in uneasily upon himself—or to deflect his attention to non-human objects, the imperfections inherent in language, or texts that can be parodied.

The first of these has been, if not the most comfortable for the author, at least the strategy most compatible with existing literary expectations; and the most persistently striking feature of modern Japanese comic fiction, especially for readers of translations, has been the conspicuousness of the authorial persona in the multiple roles of narrator, observer, and actor. This would seem to be analogous to the shift of focus "from actor to spectator, from the individual whose oddities are noted to the writer who is taking note" pointed out by Harry Levin in eighteenth- and nineteenth-century British comic writing, in which the author, who had heretofore assumed the stance of a transparent, disembodied observer of eccentric or "humorous" characters, takes on a new, more conspicuous identity, the "role-player" or "collector of hobby-horses," while his characters, formerly objects of ridicule, take on the function of sympathetic authorial mouthpieces.[3] The center of comic attention, in short, moves from what the author sees to his way of seeing things.

Clearly this shift is not restricted to a single culture, or to comic narratives, but is part of an ongoing gravitation in art fiction toward emphasis on authorial identity and away from the creation of characters capable of taking on independent mythic lives of their own. In Japan, the individualized world of the *shōsetsu* supersedes the Edo *katagimono/kokkeibon* tradition with its processions of generic social types (the would-be dandy, impoverished samurai, boorish provincial, etc.) held up for ridicule by an author who, even when assuming a pose of humility, implicitly shares a Hobbesian superiority with his audience. In the comic *shōsetsu*, as in the English case, the emphasis is very much on the observer and the way of observing, but the focus of comic observation is typically a single character (or a very small number of characters) rather than a wide assortment. And when the Japanese comic fictionist accommodates with the indigenous situation, the result is a work that diverges from Levin's pattern in a significant way: even when the protagonist is not a *shishōsetsu*-style authorial persona, the observer, rather than projecting his quirks onto an Other, makes himself the primary or even exclusive object of his own comic observation. The fusion of observer and observed may take any one of a number of forms, including a character within the narrative commenting on itself (Dazai's Urashima), or a first-person narrative voice that comments on its own behavior as a character within the narrative (the *watakushi* in *Tange-shi tei* or *Shūkin ryokō*, Inoue's *Mokkinpotto* stories), or even on itself as narrator (Dazai's *Otogizōshi* stories). Added complexities may be introduced when the observing narrator or character is also an authorial alter ego, or when multiple forms of self-observation occur within a single narrative, as when a character comments on himself in the dialogue and also is commented on by a separate narrative voice.

Thus, in early Ibuse stories such as *Tange-shi tei* and in many of Dazai's *Otogizōshi* and *Shinshaku shokokubanashi* stories, comic unmasking proceeds not by having a character's deficiencies exposed by other characters, but rather by self-revelation, either in the form of a character who consciously reveals his own flaws or an alter ego whose flaws are exposed by the author. The authorial perspective is unmistakably Ibusean or Dazaiesque, both in the mode of expression and in what is singled out for observations, that is, a set of comic foibles which are closely identified with the authorial persona—in the case of Ibuse, a mild-mannered figure underendowed in all areas except powers of observation, struggling to maintain physical and spiritual dignity in a world full of characters enjoying a converse surfeit of self-confidence and insufficiency of self-awareness; in Dazai's, another insecure and easily bruised but honest bungler, but without any of the Ibusean flair for self-effacement. Even in the novels of Inoue, where the author's personality and the circumstances of his life are issues of far less import, the succession of insufferably vain hack writer-protagonists introduces a note of satire that is unmistakably self-directed even as it skewers the pretensions of the modern Japanese literary world at large.

In such a framework, where the self-observed figure may be a comic butt, or hero, or both, the concept of "comic superiority" quickly becomes problematic. As in so many non-comic confessional *shōsetsu*, the putative authorial self-portrait frequently takes on a strong coloring of self-deprecation or self-abnegation as a loser whose inability to live up to social norms exposes him to mockery vis-à-vis the audience as well as from the society within the narrative. In many of these cases, of course, the inferiority is merely a pose, a device that conceals an ironic critique in which the deviant character is set off from the supposedly legitimate norms of a society so that its defects can be displayed all the more clearly. But where this situation usually involves a tacit understanding that author and audience share with the deviant character a superior position vis-à-vis the normative society, the Japanese comic *shōsetsu* is frequently complicated by the author's effort to internalize a comic contrast within a single alter-ego character whose position relative to the reader, even if not to the other characters, is presented as inferior with a minimum of irony. This would serve to confirm (at least for writers like Ibuse, Dazai, and Inoue) the frequently made observation that the comic sensibility is motivated by strong feelings of inadequacy or inferiority on the writer's part, but the unusual way in which it is projected within the frame of the narrative here constitutes a distinctive feature of the comic *shōsetsu*.

Another consequence of Japanese comic fiction's accommodation with its environment is a tendency for its authorial self-mockery (especially in narratives where the comic observer and observed coincide) to be reflected in the downward trajectory of the protagonist's fortunes so common in *shōsetsu*, and a preference for narrative structures in which events are not, and cannot be, concluded happily, be it in the quixotic projects of Ibuse, the missed connections and frustrations of Dazai, or even in the festive but ultimately abortive undertakings of Inoue's Eijirō and Kirikirians. Themes of this sort are common enough in all sorts of non-comic narratives, but in the comic case, they constitute something of an exception: when the exposure of the comic characters' flaws leads to humiliation or expulsion, rather than to correction or acceptance of those flaws and reconciliation with the community whose norms have been transgressed, the "happy ending" commonly associated with comedy is compromised. And when the downward motion also leads to a degree of genuine suffering, as it does with such disconcerting frequency in the writing of Ibuse and Dazai, the even more fundamental comic criterion of mirth is apparently violated.

In the modern comic *shōsetsu*, we may detect the converging of two distinct but related visions of the ultimate futility of human endeavors: the age-old Japanese sensibility of *mujō* and twentieth-century black humor. *Mujō*, a perception of the transience of all living things, traditionally informed expressions of a tragic impulse; only in the instance of a particularly jaded observer such as Kenkō or Saikaku do we see it exploited for its comic potential in visions of folly and vanity whose philosophical (as well as merely social) implications are conducive to mirth rather than despair. In the mid-twentieth century, as the contradictions of human existence came to be perceived as inherently irresolvable, the flawed nature of most comic figures became ever more compatible with narratives that veered away from, rather than toward, the familiar comic "happy ending." In the vision of black comedy, humanity can triumph over the cruelty and senselessness of life only by refusing to acknowledge their all too obvious supremacy—that is, by laughing at them. But where it took two world wars, destruction on a hitherto unimaginable scale, and grotesque new forms of violation of individual dignity by mass society to make such possibilities fully apparent in the West, writers of comic *shōsetsu* such as Ibuse and Uno were already aware of—and exploiting—these possibilities as early as the Taishō period.

Whatever attempts are made at accommodation, certain aspects of comic fiction remain incompatible with the conventional *shōsetsu* pattern; consequently in modern Japan, fiction that seeks to incorporate humor, duality, superiority, suspension of belief in suffering, happy endings, or the celebratory impulse has had to transgress the standards of its own genre. In particular, all these comic qualities in one way or another contravene long-accepted imperatives of honesty and sincerity, seriousness of purpose, monistic pursuit of "truth" and deletion of all but the most essential material, a circumscribed range of themes centering on exploration of the self by an intellect intent on lyrical expression or the quest for a spiritual or philosophical higher truth. For all three writers, the creation of comic *shōsetsu* has meant rejection of the notion that the stylistic sophistication, psychological insight, and implicative depth associated with art fiction are compatible only with the standards of realism and demanded an intentional embrace of dualities, exaggerations, distortions, and outright untruths.

In the works of each author, several methods of departing from the strictures of the conventional *shōsetsu* formula may be seen. The first is to use irony to modify the formula or turn it against itself, whether through the use of *shishōsetsu* narrative structure and the facetious posture of seriousness in some of the early fiction of Ibuse (*Kuchisuke no iru tanima, Tange-shi tei*), Dazai's technique of adapting self-revelation as a tool for exposing others' shortcomings, or Inoue's transmuting of the authorial self-portrait into a withering depiction of the artist as vanity-ridden buffoon. The second is to turn diametrically away from the stylistic and thematic claustrophobia of the *shishōsetsu*. In the place of the language of realism, which commonly sought to pare away all excess verbiage and deploy words as nearly transparent pointers, the comic writers have habitually favored novel forms of expression that intentionally call attention to themselves. Ibuse's resonant deadpan, Dazai's exaggerations, Inoue's puns, the comic counter-language of dialect in works by all three—all are consistently used not only to expose incongruities between perception and reality, but to make us think about the dualities implicit in the very act of using language to portray what we perceive as real. Like the *gesakusha*, the modern comic writers have favored an aesthetic in which words are ends in themselves as well as a means of portrayal, and exuberant indulgence in manipulation of language is a means of establishing the "true" nature of one's identity rather than of obfuscation.

Thematically, all the comic writers find ways to go beyond a small cast of reflexive (and usually young urban intellectual) characters, playing the familiar I-character off against others. Throughout Ibuse's long career, we see a persistent effort to direct his field of vision beyond immediate personal concerns and scenes of life among the intellectuals, first by deflecting attention away from himself with his relatively passive observer-narrators and later leaving them and their psychological baggage behind entirely to focus directly on the broad (if untidy) panorama of society with its wealth of personalities and types (*Shūkin ryokō, Chinpindō shujin*). Even Dazai, who had so much difficulty transcending his personal concerns, was able to create highly effective comic stories by sharing the stage (*Shin'yū kōkan*) or by creating settings remote from his own surroundings, where a variety of characters could be introduced (*Otogizōshi, Shinshaku shokokubanashi*). Inoue, the most versatile of all, seems equally comfortable with self-referential material (*Mokkinpotto*) or with forays deep into remote times and spaces involving all manner of characters and situations, and with *Kirikirijin* the comic *shōsetsu* can finally be said to have definitively shed its long-borne burden of marginality and approached the center of contemporary literary discourse—to the extent that such a center can still be said to exist.

The boldest strategy of all is to abandon the conventions and strictures of realism altogether and enter into the sphere of fantasy or historical allegory (as in Ibuse's *Sanshōuo*, Dazai's *Otogizōshi*, Inoue's *Bun to Fun* and *Kirikirijin*, or the Edo stories of both Dazai and Inoue), where the comic spirit is at its freest. This is a particularly attractive option in Japan, where the creation of more realistic forms such as comedy of manners is impeded by the narrowness of the *shōsetsu* framework and social taboo on overt assumption of superiority.[4]

The text-based incongruity of parody, like fantasy, offers an attractive means of turning away from realism and evading some of the difficulties involved in the expression of incongruity based on character or manners. Despite its distinguished lineage in Japan, parody, with its inherently humorous and dualistic nature, found relatively few practitioners in the modern period until the emergence of writers such as Inoue, Tsutsui Yasutaka, and Wada Makoto in the "parody boom" of the 1970s; but within the bounds of comic fiction, parody has been a particularly prominent feature, whether it takes a specific work as its object (as in numerous passages in *Kirikirijin*) or seems designed to subvert the formal properties of a genre (as in Ibuse's games with *shishōsetsu* narrative voice), or simply reworks familiar traditional themes, perhaps with an overlay of references to the contemporary scene (Dazai).

Of course, none of these features are mutually exclusive, and two or more may overlap in a given work—or even all of them, as in *Kirikirijin*, a veritable encyclopedia of comic techniques. At any rate, the distinctive combinations of comic techniques, themes, and formats chosen by each of the writers under discussion have resulted in an extension of the boundaries of the *shōsetsu*, enabling it to encompass a comic spirit while maintaining an accommodation with the Japanese social and cultural milieu. At the same time, and equally significantly, they reflect a process of accommodation and innovation with respect to the nature of comic literature itself, in which the constituent elements of comedy are rearranged or recast in a different light, thus contributing to the ongoing process of redefinition of what comedy is or can be.

Among the features of Japanese comedy that may be considered distinctive vis-à-vis comedy in general, the most prominent of all are two that have already been mentioned as (by)products of the negotiation between comedy and *shōsetsu*, the internalization of comic incongruities and the adaptation of a *shōsetsu*-style narrative structure to comic ends. When we consider the main dualities in the various stories, even when couched in such familiar terms as youth versus age (*Josefu to joshidaigakusei, Kuchisuke*) or battles between the sexes (*Shūkin ryokō*, many of the stories in *Shinshaku shokoku-banashi*), they generally involve attempts by weak, sensitive, and passive characters to resist pressures, real or imaginary, exerted by characters who represent the diametrically opposite qualities. But where most comic writers would be content to present such clashes from a distance, maintaining a balance between the opposing forces and exposing defects through the workings of external forces (other characters, or the force of circumstance), the Japanese writer typically prefers an imbalanced structure, making the weaker figure both a narrating voice and protagonist and shifting the locus of the comic agon from external conflicts to the workings of the weaker figure's psyche. When the stronger figure embodies flaws that are to be objects of unmasking, the speaking protagonist reveals them directly to the audience while the putative victim remains oblivious to the process. As often as not, the protagonist presents the flaws as his own, apologetically taking upon himself responsibility for those of the antagonist or chastising himself for failing to find an adequate response to them. This gesture is sometimes merely an ironic, indirect means of establishing the protagonist's superior status in a comic dichotomy (or, in Dazai's case, of demonstrating his superiority to the society around him), but frequently in both Ibuse and Dazai it results in a confusion of the issue, a sharing of comic-butt status among the opposed characters, and a diffusion of comic focus. In extreme cases, such as many of Ibuse's early stories, the agon is almost entirely internalized, as the narrative takes the form of a conscious revelation by the protagonist of the process by which his delusions are gradually exposed and dispelled. In some instances such as *Koi* and *Shin'yū kōkan*, the vicarious unmasking of others coexists with, or is even replaced by, the strategy apparently originated by Uno Kōji in which the narrator-protagonist engages in a conscious revelation of his own flaws.

When we consider how the elements postulated in the Introduction as most characteristic of the comic spirit (humor, incongruity, the harmonious/happy ending, the celebratory impulse, the suspension of belief in suffering) are deployed in these fictions, it becomes apparent that, as in any group of works or even within any individual work, some loom larger than others; and some are handled in ways that differ significantly from, or extend, the familiar Western configurations. Of all these elements, humor is at once the most basic and the most stubbornly resistant to analysis. It is not difficult to envision agelastic readers who would dismiss the broad jibes of *Bun to Fun* as nothing worth laughing about, or question whether the darkly delicate attenuations of *Tange-shi tei* and *Koi* or the caustic cruelties of *Kachikachiyama* leave any room for mirth at all. It is difficult, though, to imagine Chinpindō's pratfalls, the merry demons of *Kobutori*, or the incessant gags and ingenious parodies and puns of *Kirikirijin* eliciting such reactions. What this tells us about the nature of Japanese humor, beyond the all-too-obvious conclusion that, like humor elsewhere, it takes a multiplicity of forms, is not clear.

Many of the incongruities that form the basis for humor in these works are rooted in the same delusions and contradictions of character that serve as staples in comedy everywhere: the addled would-be lovers and would-be obstructive avuncular grouch of *Josefu*, the prim woman with a past and her mild-mannered escort in *Shūkin ryokō*, the insufferably self-righteous samurai of *Hadakagawa*, the blustering braggart of *Shin'yū kōkan*, and the hopelessly vain hack writers, obtuse politicians, and bumbling policemen of *Bun to Fun* and *Kirikirijin* would be familiar enough types in narratives throughout the world. And yet some equally familiar characters and situations seem conspicuously absent: the battle of the sexes, that most common and basic of all comic themes, is waged in the grim marital deadlocks of Dazai and the more oblique rivalries of *Shūkin ryokō* and *Chinpindō shujin*; but comedy of romantic intrigue and sexual manners is a distinct rarity. George Meredith's well-known dictum that "where [women] have no social freedom, comedy is absent; where they are household drudges, the form of comedy is primitive; where they are tolerably independent, but uncultivated, exciting melodrama takes its place" is based on a vision of comedy that takes it to be a matter of manners and little more.[5] Even if there were no other evidence to offer, the wordplay and *shukō* so prominent in Japanese comedy would suffice to show that there are any number of other ways to go about the business of incongruity, but by the same token the extensive reliance on these techniques points with mute eloquence to the options not available. The conflict between the rebellious energies of youth and restrictive forces of old age, another staple comic theme, is also relatively uncommon in these texts. Perhaps this is a testament to residual power of Confucian values; when it does appear, as in some early Ibuse stories, it is more likely than not to be in an inverted form, with the prematurely dispirited youthful character vainly seeking to restrain the schemes of his more active and colorful seniors.

Other incongruities are derived not from character contradictions but from structural features. In one of the most common, an author displaces a familiar story or theme with a novel or original presentation; that is, an accommodation, often conscious, is made with the traditional Japanese parodic principle of *sekai* and *shukō*, as in the stock *gesaku* theme of the aspiring playboy turned in on itself in Inoue's *Tegusari shinjū* or the projection of unmistakably Dazaiesque protagonists into familiar folktales in *Otogizōshi*. In many cases, the presence of a narrator who directly addresses the reader is integral to a work's comic structure, as the narratorial commentary provides an incongruous counterpoint to the characters' words and actions. This counterpoint may simply be a matter of a narrator's pointing out delusions and follies that affect the characters, as in *Sanshōuo* or *Bun to Fun;* it may also involve bravura displays of verbal dexterity and other performative features reminiscent of the popular tradition of comic storytelling (*kobanashi*). The oral, performative quality of the first-person direct narrative structures so common in many of these works is also reflected in the pattern of oblique, rambling introduction, leisurely, gradually developed main body, and relatively abrupt ending seen in works such as Ibuse's *Koi* and Dazai's *Otogizōshi*. In Dazai's *Romanesuku* and in Inoue's *Gesakusha meimei den* stories, full revelation of the story's main incongruity is deferred until a punch line ending much like the *ochi* of traditional comic storytelling in which all the thematic elements are finally brought into focus and tied together.

The punchline form of resolution, it should be evident, partakes more of the structure of the joke than of emplotted fiction and drama, in which comic incongruities are progressively developed through action, character, and narrative commentary, and often harmoniously resolved in a more or less conventionalized happy ending, whether through the reconciliation of conflict or the expulsion of incorrigible characters. Since the emplotted structure, even in the relatively loose *shōsetsu* form, offers far richer literary potential, it is the predominant form of comic fiction, if not the very feature that distinguishes comic fiction from the extended joke; and indeed the majority of modern Japanese comic *shōsetsu* fall into this category. At the same time, their structure generally reflects the expectations of the *shōsetsu* form in their tendency to emphasize humorous episodes rather than overall comic shape and especially in their avoidance of the kind of conclusive note supplied by an *ochi* or a happy ending. In Ibuse, things are likely to peter out with an evocative lyrical image. In Dazai, there is more likely to be a conclusion of sorts, but it almost invariably involves the establishment of equilibrium at a new and lower level, an ironic triumph of downward mobility. In the raucous revelry that closes *Bun to Fun*, Inoue provides a rare example of the kind of happy ending standard in Western romantic comedy; but most of his other notable comedies end either with an *ochi* or, more frequently (as in *Kirikirijin*, *Tegusari shinjū*, and several of the *Mokkinpotto* stories) with a catastrophe in which the protagonist's project fails (however redemptively) and repressive forces reassert themselves, rather than on a note of triumph or conciliation.

If we insist on counting "the movement of a story towards an ending characterized by harmony, festivity, and celebration"[6] among the defining qualities of comedy, as so many writers have done over the years, the vast *shōsetsu* corpus will not yield much more than a handful of examples of comedy. It is tempting to relate the aversion to happy endings to the traditional aesthetics of *aware* and *mujō*, which linked beauty with melancholy, sympathized with the sorrows of the defeated rather than celebrating the glories of the victors, and reaffirmed the Buddhist doctrine of the inevitability of decline, fall, and death. But to do so, one would have to disregard other traditional values, such as the sense of delighted wonder connoted by the term *okashi* and smart, dashing elegance associated with the term *iki*, that lend themselves to comedy readily enough. All the explanations we need may be found within the emotional and structural conventions of the *shōsetsu* itself.

The same applies to a comic feature closely associated with the happy ending, the exaltation of the forces of growth, regeneration, and abundance. The triumph of healthy natural impulse over social constraint and all other types of restriction that figures so prominently in traditional forms such as *setsuwa* and *gesaku* is far less common in the *shōsetsu*. When it does appear, it is typically recast in equivocal, far less innocent terms; and characters who defiantly follow their instincts are rewarded with all too credible sufferings of the type often cited as inimical to comedy. Even in the works under consideration here, only *Bun to Fun* and *Kirikirijin* would appear to celebrate life forces with untrammeled gusto.

A number of important pieces, then, seem to be missing from the comic *shōsetsu*—enough, perhaps, to lead us to question whether the comic spirit and the *shōsetsu* form are not after all mutually exclusive. But if *Koi, Tange-shi tei, Shūkin ryokō, Chinpindō shujin, Romanesuku, Hadakagawa, Shin'yū kōkan, Gesakusha meimei den*, the *Mokkinpotto* stories, and even *Kirikirijin* do not conclude in an atmosphere of festive harmony or extol the vitality of their protagonists by showing them prevailing over their adversaries, they do something comparable enough: they celebrate endurance in a hostile world. No matter how often their adversaries or life's impersonal vagaries knock them down, the heroes of these stories are resilient enough to get back up, however groggily; and they reach the ending still on their feet, somehow maintaining their forward momentum against all odds. In their own way, these stories and novels are celebrations of life, and their endings "happy." The celebrations are darker, the happiness more equivocal, to be sure, than those associated with comedy in earlier times, but by reconciling indigenous conventions with conditions that transcend the limits of form and place to characterize much of the twentieth-century experience, these authors have succeeded in creating comedies for their—and our—time.

In his study of Greek culture, Werner Jaeger has observed that Aristophanes brought about a revolution in Attic comedy by transforming it from idle jibes at individuals and their foibles to an intelligent critique of political, aesthetic, and educational systems and ideas.[7] Whether the correlation stems from the writers' own inclinations or from forces beyond their control, the status of comedy has generally been marginal when writers have concerned themselves with margins. When they train their focus closer to the central concerns of their time and place and identify the greatest and most sacrosanct follies and inconsistencies in a bold and vibrant voice, comedy looms large. If we plot the set of points representing the works discussed in this study against time and attempt to extrapolate a pattern from them, it becomes possible to discern an irregularly rising curve as modern Japanese comic fiction moves in from the formal and thematic margins and gradually grows in scope and boldness. Before them came a pair of high points in the form of two satires broader and more powerful than anything that was to appear for decades thereafter, Natsume Sōseki's *Wagahai wa neko de aru* and *Botchan*. In the aftermath of the Naturalist ascendancy, however, comic fiction had to reinvent itself in the shadow of the *shishōsetsu*. Once that genre had assumed the status of an established standard, it gradually became susceptible to a degree of mockery (typically, as we have seen, in the ironic guise of self-mockery), with the first self-conscious steps in that direction taken by Uno Kōji in the mid-Taishō period.

Comic fiction's range was quietly extended by Ibuse, who began by carefully probing around the edges of the lyrical *shishōsetsu*, creating a new comic language of indirection and understatement and, through his participant-narrator, presenting an image of himself as a figure cut off from any identifiable affiliations and thus open to comic treatment without either assuming a position of superiority or offending others. At the same time, he transcended the limitations that a strictly autobiographical approach would impose, slowly shifting at least some of the comic focus away from himself by balancing the participant-narrator figure off against a cast of oddball characters whose simple delusions and pretensions could easily be exposed without giving offense because they were not easily identifiable with any specific group (least of all, any group that readers of fiction would be likely to find too close for comfort).

As Ibuse extends his field of vision beyond immediate personal concerns and scenes of life among urban intellectuals to the broader panorama of daily life, with its inexhaustible lode of comic types and situations, it becomes increasingly evident that in his gentle, unobtrusive way he was including all of Japan, if not all of humanity, in his imaginary village—which turns out to be not so imaginary after all. In his later work, incongruities are presented in a more forthright manner, with some dramatic confrontations between sharply etched characters. But in all save a handful of his most indignant postwar works (especially *Yōhai taichō*), the emotional pitch remains muted; and even when most indignant, he typically prefers to take a somewhat oblique approach to the most disturbing questions and then cover his trail in a cloud of resonant imagery. Much as we may sympathize with his comic figures, especially the self-mocking narrators, and despite all the gentle handling Ibuse usually gives them, most are caricatures of limited, specific types, easily identifiable as Others, and as comic butts whom the reader can view with a distinct sense of superiority. Presenting this comic vision in a fashion that won broad acceptance among critics and readers alike was one of Ibuse's major achievements.

Dazai came to grips with the problem of reconciling comedy and *shōsetsu* in a different way. Although he retains the tendency to caricature, he continues the transition from marginal, eccentric comic characters to more substantial figures. Some resemble familiar types encountered all too frequently in our families, work, or even chance encounters. Others look disturbingly like us—especially if we feel ourselves sharing the doubts and ambivalences that pervade his long series of self-portraits. The darker sides of human nature around which Ibuse had hovered with eloquent reticence are presented more starkly, often inextricably interwoven with a sense of suffering whose painful immediacy gives much of his work a desperate, even tortured tone, and undercuts the duality of his comic vision. The typical Dazai alter ego concentrates all of his considerable resources on achieving the self-defeating goal of downward mobility or, totally immobilized in the face of irreconcilable dichotomies, permits himself to fall victim to the irresistible downward forces exerted by fate, which are usually embodied in the form of his fellow human beings. But when the very bottom is reached, the "laugh at the end of the world" releases the healing power of *seitei*, "divine resignation," redeeming his sardonic anguish and transmuting it into the serene and transcendent grace of high comedy.

Only in the past few decades, with the emergence of Inoue and kindred spirits such as Maruya Saiichi and Tsutsui Yasutaka, has comic fiction emerged from the shadow of the *shishōsetsu* legacy and its burden of hesitancy and doubt, going far beyond its immediate surroundings and the safety of remote margins to take on the full range of modern Japanese institutions and values, mobilizing all the techniques it can find or devise to debunk authority, pretension, and folly wherever it finds them and to hold the conventions of narrative and language themselves up to comic scrutiny. In so doing, these writers have finally made it possible to realize the full potential of comedy in the *shōsetsu* form and to bring the comic spirit in from the margins of modern Japanese fiction.[8]

The comic spirit has made itself felt in diverse ways over the life span of the *shōsetsu*, and in this sense the *shōsetsu* has been something of an exception to the historical Japanese pattern in which comic works appear as parodic or freer versions of works in a preexisting genre and gradually coalesce into a countergenre that takes on a life of its own. Traditionally (whether in the case of *kyōgen*, *haikai*, or *kokkeibon*), this process has been a slow one, and we need not be too surprised that no countergenre to the *shōsetsu* has developed over the hundred years that it has been in existence. Recent years have seen a number of signs and proclamations suggesting the possibility that the art *shōsetsu* itself has become something of a moribund or even endangered species.[9] While this might be taken as another indication that the time is now ripe for the emergence of a parodic/comic countergenre, no form answering to such a description has appeared.

Historically, Japanese comic genres have tended to originate with classes excluded from positions of political, social, and cultural authority, or from members of the dominant class at the point when its power begins to wane. In contemporary Japan, we have a fluid, amorphous class situation: political and economic power are more diffuse than in previous eras, not held by a readily identifiable hereditary elite. If there is a dominant political and economic elite, membership is at least in theory open to a considerably broader section of the populace than in previous eras. Arguably, though, it is still a minority of the total population, and steep barriers persist for groups such as women, *burakumin*, and Koreans born in Japan. These marginalized classes, who traditionally would be likely candidates to develop a new comic form, have so far chosen to work with existing forms, including the *shōsetsu*, adapting them to their own concerns rather than creating new genres. Perhaps because of the aura of moral earnestness associated with their efforts to call attention to their status as victims and a lingering Confucian tradition of righteous indignation, comedy has not been among their most favored weapons. Among currently active writers, those who have most consistently and effectively dedicated themselves to comedy, such as Inoue, Tsutsui, Maruya, and Ōe, are figures who, while acknowledging the significance of peripheral groups and often depicting them in their work, generally do not belong to the these groups themselves, even if, like Inoue and Tsutsui, they began their writing careers on the periphery of "serious" literature. These writers, now all well into middle age, began their educations in the prewar years and started their careers before the supremacy of the art *shōsetsu* began to be called into question. They have continued to take the *shōsetsu* as a point of departure, working to broaden its scope by introducing comic elements, often via parodic or metafictional strategies, rather than attempting to develop some alternative form outside its framework.[10]

Younger writers (and their readers) seem intent on achieving a postmodernistic culmination to the decades-old project of erasing distinctions between fiction with "serious" artistic aspirations and various categories of writing once dismissed as entertainment-oriented "popular" fiction, especially works centrally concerned with social manners and mores (*fūzoku shōsetsu*) and mystery or thriller fiction. Given comedy's gravitation toward the center in "serious" literature and the traditional hospitality to comedy in popular forms (a phenomenon manifest in another category of Japanese popular fiction, the lightly humorous works known as *yūmoa shōsetsu*), a rapprochement between the two would seem to set the stage for an upsurge of comedy in contemporary writing. But in an affluent Japan where the promotion, pursuit, and enjoyment of material gratifications available on a hitherto unimaginable scale have gone far toward reducing any inclinations to soul-searching and where meaningful public discourse seems ever more firmly displaced by mass-media celebrity culture, much of the work of younger writers is pervaded with a sensibility of narcissistic cool that hovers noncommittally on the borders of self-parody. Dichotomies are obscured or unintelligible: there is no harmony to restore, no community to be integrated into, and very little life force to celebrate. Although there have been a number of younger writers such as Shimizu Yoshinori and Mizumura Minae who have produced ingenious fictions that extend the range of comedy and parody into the sensibilities of the Japanese postmodern, much of the writing of their contemporaries invites comic treatment rather than offering it. The surface aimlessness of the *ero-guro-nansensu* subculture of the early Shōwa years, another ambiguous evocation of urban consumption and leisure that failed to develop a full-blown comic expression, comes to mind as a precedent.

Rather than these younger writers, the synthesis of the comic spirit and postmodernistic transgression, decentering, and ludic pastiche has been realized most happily and effectively in Japan in the works of parodic pranksters such as Inoue and Tsutsui. But it is also worth remembering that the flat characterization, satiric exaggeration, and sheer revelry in the play of language that mark their comedy are indigenous Japanese traits that persisted into the early modern period and even gained a measure of new life in

Wagahai wa neko de aru and *Botchan*.[11] Given the prominence of these elements within the tradition, it even becomes possible to conceive of the period from late Meiji to the present as a temporary and artificial interruption in the history of Japanese narrative under the influence of late nineteenth-century realist notions imported from Europe—notions which have proven more enduring in Japan than in their place of origin.[12] In his deliberate disregard of the strictures of illusionist realism, a writer such as Inoue can be seen not only as a pioneer but as, in his own way, as much of an heir to traditional Japanese literary values as writers such as Kawabata, Tanizaki, and Mishima, so much of whose work, despite its frequent association with various aspects of the Japanese tradition in the public imagination, also exhibits striking congruencies with twentieth-century European modernism.[13]

It is tempting to see in this comic resurrection a Japanese analogue to a development postulated in contemporary (apparently Western) literature by Linda Hutcheon: "Perhaps . . . we are witnessing today, in the revival of parodic forms, the preparation of a new linguistic and literary consciousness comparable to the role parody played, according to Bakhtin, in medieval and Renaissance society."[14] Whether this will prove to be the case in Japan or the West is still very much an open question. It does not inspire much confidence that in Japan the boldest and most energetic exponents of comic fiction are older rather than younger. Even Inoue seems to have retreated from the comic audacity and breadth of scope of *Bun to Fun* and *Kirikirijin* in his more recent fiction. This would suggest the disconcerting possibility that the rising curve has already reached its peak, and that the works under discussion in these pages constitute a climactic moment rather than a stage in the development of something larger. But as long as delusion, pretense, folly, and tedium are part of the human experience, and as long as the impulse to celebrate the resiliency of our vital forces in the face of adversity survives, comedy is unlikely to disappear for very long. As a devout believer in the comic spirit, I try not to count on anything in particular, but am hoping for a happy ending.

Reference Matter

Notes

For complete author names, titles of works, and publication data on items cited here in short form, see the Works Cited, pp. 227–239.

Preface

1. Brad Leithauser, "An Ear for the Unspoken," *The New Yorker*, March 6, 1989, p. 105.

2. For a thorough and provocative exploration of this topic, see Edward Fowler, "Rendering Words, Traversing Cultures: On the Art and Politics of Translating Modern Japanese Fiction," *Journal of Japanese Studies*, vol. 18, no. 1, pp. 1–44.

3. Eco, "The Frames of Comic 'Freedom,'" in Tom Seboek, ed., *Carnival*, p. 2.

4. Lee Siegel, *Laughing Matters: Comic Tradition in India*, p. xi.

5. See, for example, Yanagita Kunio, "Gesakusha no dentō," in *Teihon Yanagita Kunio shū*, vol. 7, pp. 186–195; Nakamura Mitsuo, "Warai no sōshitsu," in *Nakamura Mitsuo zenshū*, vol. 10, 107–143; Hamada Taizō, "Warai no keifu," in Hamada Taizō, ed., *Nihon bungaku ni okeru bi to jōnen no nagare—Warai*, pp. 333–359; and Iizawa Tadasu, *Buki to shite no warai.*

6. Isogai Hideo, "Ibuse Masuji—Kindai bungaku ni okeru warai no teichaku," in Nihon Bungaku Kenkyū Shiryō Kankō Kai, ed., *Nihon bungaku kenkyū shiryō sōsho—Ibuse Masuji, Fukazawa Shichirō*, pp. 95–105.

7. James Feibleman, *In Praise of Comedy: A Study in Its Theory and Practice*, p. 271.

8. Susanne K. Langer, *Feeling and Form: A Theory of Art Developed from Philosophy in a New Key*, pp. 335–356.

9. Marleigh Ryan, "Japanese Fiction: Accommodated Truth," *Journal of Japanese Studies*, vol. 2, no. 2, p. 265.

10. It is impossible to resist the temptation to repeat J. R. R. Tolkien's comment on *Beowulf* as quoted by Helen McCullough in her translation of *The Tale of the Heike*, p. 475: "No terms borrowed from Greek or other literatures exactly fit: there is no reason why they should."

11. Masao Miyoshi, *Off Center: Power and Culture Relations between Japan and the United States*, p. 68.

12. It would be interesting and instructive to undertake a critical review of these terms themselves, examining them in the light of the texts to which they have been applied and considering the ways in which they may have shaped the perceptions of Japanese readers and writers over the years (while keeping Western predispositions in mind); but this lies outside the scope of the present study.

13. Among the more vivid examples, and two of the relatively few poststructuralist ventures into coming to terms with comedy, are Jacques Lacan's assertion in "The Meaning of the Phallus" (in Juliet Mitchell and Jacqueline Rose, eds., *Feminine Sexuality: Jacques Lacan and the Ecole freudienne*, p. 84) that "the ideal of typical manifestations of behaviour in both sexes, up to and including the act of sexual copulation, are propelled into comedy" as a consequence of the substitution of an "appearing" of the phallus for its "having"; and Judith Butler's attempt to elucidate and extend this observation in *Gender Trouble: Feminism and the Subversion of Identity* (see pp. 45–47, 50). The critical identification of heterosexuality as inherently comic, if not "comedy" itself, undoubtedly has liberating implications in the context of queer theory but in fact dates back at least to the exceedingly strait-laced (and, presumably, straight) George Meredith; more significantly, it glosses over the larger and more fundamental incongruity between animal drives and social constraints which guarantees that comic potential will be richly inherent in any form of human sexuality.

Chapter 1. Japanese Comedy

1. The existence in Japan of humorous literature as a distinct category has been confirmed by the appearance of various anthologies such as the six-volume *Gendai Nihon no yūmoa bungaku*; a volume devoted to *Warai* edited by Hamada Taizō in the series *Nihon bungaku ni okeru bi to jōnen no nagare*; and a collection of *Kuroi yūmoa* as vol. 6 in the seventeen-volume *Zenshū—Gendai Nihon bungaku no hakken*. The *Warai* volume, unlike the others, contains a sampling of works from the premodern period.

2. On these and other examples of the comic spirit in the Japanese visual arts, see Nobuo Tsuji, *Playfulness in Japanese Art*.

3. Arthur Koestler, *The Act of Creation*, p. 95.

4. Quoted in Robert W. Corrigan, "Introduction: Comedy and the Comic Spirit," in Corrigan, ed., *Comedy: Meaning and Form*, 2nd ed., p. 12.

5. The argument that the atrocities of the twentieth century have made the "nobility" and heroics of tragedy obsolete and led to the appearance of a dark comedy that portrays the essential absurdity of life has been made compellingly by Wylie Sypher; see his essay "The Meanings of Comedy," in Sypher, ed., *Comedy*, pp. 193–201.

6. Langer, p. 331.

7. This summary of *Waranbegusa* is based on Makoto Ueda, *Literary and Art Theories in Japan*, pp. 101–112. For an insightful discussion of *kyōgen*'s comic function in relation to Nō, see William R. LaFleur, *The Karma of Words: Buddhism and the Literary Arts in Medieval Japan*, pp. 133–148.

8. Tsubouchi Shōyō, *Shōsetsu shinzui*, in *Nihon kindai bungaku taikei*, vol. 3, *Tsubouchi Shōyō shū*, pp. 132–134.

9. Natsume Sōseki, *Bungaku ron*, pp. 296–311.

10. Yanagita Kunio, "Warai no bungaku no kigen," in *Teihon Yanagita Kunio shū*, vol. 7, pp. 153–173.

11. Yanagita, "Gesakusha no dentō," pp. 186–187.

12. Kobayashi Hideo, "Nansensu bungaku," in *Kobayashi Hideo senshū*, vol. 1, pp. 157–161.

13. Nakamura Mitsuo, "Warai no sōshitsu," pp. 107–143.

14. Asō Isoji, *Kokkei bungaku ron*; Iizawa, *Buki to shite no warai*; and Hamada, "Warai no keifu."

15. The works of Uchida Hyakken, which appear regularly in Japanese anthologies of modern comic writing, feature what seems to be a highly attenuated form of comedy; and the inclusion of *Narayama bushi kō* (The Ballad of Narayama, 1956), Fukazawa Shichirō's retelling of the *obasute* legend, in the *Kuroi yūmoa* collection suggests a markedly grim conception of the comic, even in an anthology devoted to black humor.

16. *Kojiki*, book 1, verses 14–24. The translation given here is from Robert Borgen and Marian Ury, "Readable Japanese Mythology: Selections from *Nihon Shoki* and *Kojiki*," *Journal of the Association of Teachers of Japanese*, vol. 24, no. 1, pp. 70–71.

17. Yanagita, "Warai no bungaku no kigen," pp. 168ff; Matsumura Takeo, *Nihon shinwa no kenkyū*, vol. 3, pp. 97–102. As Donald L. Phillippi (*Kojiki*, p. 138, n. 11) points out, Ame no Uzume performs a similar act of magico-ritual genital exposure in the *Tenson kōrin* section of *Nihon Shoki*.

18. *Kojiki*, book 2, ch. 51.

19. For a concise overview of this fascinating process, see Haruko Iwasaki, "The Literature of Wit and Humor in Late-Eighteenth-Century Edo," in Donald Jenkins, ed., *The Floating World Revisited*, pp. 47–61.

20. It may provide some insight into the fluid nature of the boundary between official and informal culture in this period when we note that Matsudaira Sadanobu,

the shogunal councillor responsible for the ban on certain forms of *gesaku* during the Kansei Reforms, had himself composed a *gesaku*-style work some years before; see Haruko Iwasaki, "Portrait of a Daimyō: Comical Fiction by Matsudaira Sadanobu," *Monumenta Nipponica*, vol. 38, no. 1, pp. 1–48.

21. Although *Shōsetsu shinzui* is frequently credited with setting the course which modern Japanese fiction would follow, it is not at all clear that it enjoyed much attention or influence at the time of its publication. For a detailed discussion of this question, see Peter Kornicki, *The Reform of Fiction in Meiji Japan*, pp. 35ff.

22. While *shōsetsu* is frequently translated as "novel," the two forms are in fact far from identical; the relatively inconspicuous role played by the comic spirit in the origins and development of the modern *shōsetsu* is just one of the ways in which it differs significantly from the Western form. For a succinct overview of some of the other important differences, see Miyoshi, *Off Center*, pp. 45–50.

23. Jay Rubin, "The Evil and the Ordinary in Sōseki's Fiction," *Harvard Journal of Asiatic Studies*, vol. 46, no. 2, p. 336.

24. This is not to say that the Naturalists were consciously engaged in carrying out Shōyō's theories—if anything, both they and he were products of the same age and circumstances, with Shōyō merely having been somewhat earlier and of a more analytical turn of mind. There was, however, a strong association between the Japanese Naturalist movement and Waseda University, where Shōyō was one of the leading literary figures for many years.

25. Nakamura Mitsuo, "Warai no sōshitsu," pp. 113–115. Many of these observations on the effects of Naturalism and the *shishōsetsu*, and their consequences for comic fiction, were originally made by Nakamura. His exceptionally stimulating and wide-ranging essay has yet to be superseded as a critique of the role of comedy in modern Japanese fiction, and my analysis of this period is deeply indebted to his ideas.

26. Some of the *gesaku* writers, to be sure, may have been willing to adopt a pose of self-deprecation combined with a self-mocking tone, but this was consonant with their social and fictional status as ironic drop-out observers of a social panorama that was the real object of their comic attention. Both social convention and, at times, considerations of material or physical well-being prevented them from displaying an attitude of superiority while indulging in their satirical jibes. This approach is untenable for the modern-day *shishōsetsu* writer, who tends to be wary of the *gesaku* aura of disrespectable frivolity and also serves as his or her own main subject. While strictures against making others the target of public ridicule remain powerful in Japanese society, their effect on the *shishōsetsu* writer is bound to be minimal or moot, given the nature of the genre.

27. Mathew Winston, "Black Humor: To Weep with Laughing," in Maurice Charney, ed., *Comedy: New Perspectives*, p. 32.

28. Linda Hutcheon, *A Theory of Parody: The Teachings of Twentieth-Century Art Forms*, p. 79.

29. Susan J. Napier, in *The Fantastic in Modern Japanese Literature: The Subversion of Modernity*, p. 191, calls *Kappa* "Japan's first full-blown dystopian novel."

30. Although parts of *Botchan* "autobiographically" reflect Sōseki's own experiences as a teacher in a secondary school in Matsuyama, it is not considered a *shishōsetsu* in the sense in which that term is generally employed in Japan. Not only are there significant and obvious differences between character and creator, but Botchan, an innocent little given to self-examination, is played off against a gallery of heavily caricatured Others, and the focus is more on his struggles with them than on Botchan himself. *Botchan*'s predominantly lighthearted tone (darker overtones notwithstanding) would also be out of place in a standard *shishōsetsu*, whereas in *Kura no naka* mirth is grafted onto the conventional *shishōsetsu* ethos of suffering and self-pity.

Chapter 2. Ibuse Masuji

1. While the term "Modernism" and its Japanese counterpart *Modanizumu* are now used primarily with reference to writers associated with the Shin Kankaku Ha such as Yokomitsu and Kawabata, early in the Shōwa period *Modanizumu* was used in Japan in a broader sense to refer to a number of movements including the Shin Kankaku Ha and the Shinkō Geijutsu Ha that sought to develop fiction in directions different from those established by writers of the Meiji and Taishō periods while at the same time rejecting the Proletarians' subordination of artistic values to political programs. It was also used at times to refer specifically to the works of writers associated with the Shinkō Geijutsu Ha, and it is in this narrower sense that both terms will be used here.

2. For a brief but graphic overview of the mass-circulation magazine and *enpon* phenomena, see Miriam Silverberg, *Changing Song: The Marxist Manifestoes of Nakano Shigeharu*, pp. 163–164; and Edward Fowler, *The Rhetoric of Confession: Shishōsetsu in Early Twentieth-Century Japanese Fiction*, p. 141.

3. Despite its rather tantalizing label, upon inspection much of this writing turns out to be disappointingly tame, considerably less erotic and grotesque than some well-known works by writers such as Tanizaki Jun'ichirō and Mishima Yukio. "Nonsense," even more than "erotic" or "grotesque," is such a subjective affair that it would be injudicious for any age or school to press claims of primacy; in this case, at any rate, "nonsense" is more suggestive of a failure to accept conventional standards of seriousness in theme and tone than of an effort to upset notions of rational order.

4. *Ibuse Masuji zenshū* (1964–75; hereafter *IMZS*), vol. 1, p. 37. Citations from this edition will hereafter be given in the text, with the volume and page numbers in parentheses.

5. Among the critics who have associated Ibuse's early fiction with the term *nansensu* are Nakamura Mitsuo, Kawakami Tetsutarō, and Kobayashi Hideo. Nakamura, in his essay "Ibuse Masuji no sakuhin," in *Nakamura Mitsuo zenshū*, vol. 5, pp. 219–227, classes the early Ibuse with Nakamura Masatsune as a leading *nansensu* writer; and in "Ibuse Masuji ron," in *Nakamura Mitsuo zenshū*, vol. 5, pp. 190–219, he cites *Josefu* as a representative piece of Ibuse nonsense. Kawakami, who like Ibuse was connected with the literary magazine *Sakuhin*, founded in 1930, also writes of Ibuse as having been ranked with Nakamura Masatsune as one of the twin stars of *nansensu* literature. He considers this a pointless description, but concedes that there are elements in stories such as *Shigure-tō*, *Tange-shi*, and *Josefu* that make it seem plausible, and even describes Ibuse's postwar *Yōhai taichō* as a "mature" (*jittaika shite seichō shita*) nonsense work. See "Bungaku ron—Ibuse Masuji," in *Kawakami Tetsutarō zenshū*, vol. 5, pp. 477–480. See also Kawakami's afterword to the 1956 Iwanami Bunko collection *Sanshōuo—Yōhai taichō*. Kobayashi, another colleague of Ibuse's on *Sakuhin*, was already rejecting the *nansensu* label for *Tange-shi* in his "Ibuse Masuji no sakuhin ni tsuite," in *Kobayashi Hideo zenshū*, vol. 4, pp. 31–35; he reserved it for works that pleased him less, such as *Josefu*. Sakaguchi Ango, in his early essay "Piero dendōsha," in *Teihon Sakaguchi Ango zenshū*, vol. 7, pp. 11–13, also pairs Ibuse with Nakamura Masatsune but rejects the *nansensu* label for both of them, seeing in their work a "sad laughter" (*kanashiki warai*) rather than the more uproarious spirit of true nonsense—presumably better exemplified by his own *Kaze hakase* (Dr. Wind, 1931). The association of Ibuse's name with that of Nakamura Masatsune is made more plausible by their collaboration on a number of stories published as *Gassaku nansensu monogatari* (Collaborative Nonsense Tales) in 1931; see Kōno Toshirō, "Ibuse Masuji to Nakamura Masatsune," *Gunzō*, vol. 36, no. 12, pp. 252–53.

6. The Bunka Apāto (Culture Apartment) Building, one of the first Western-style apartment buildings for Japanese residents and a landmark in modern Japanese housing design, was completed in the Ochanomizu section of Tokyo in 1923, six years before the publication of *Shigure-tō jokei*.

7. Ibuse Masuji, *Shigure-tō jokei*, *Bungei Shunjū*, vol. 7. no. 11, p. 18.

8. Ibuse Masuji, *Josefu to joshi daigakusei*, *Shinchō*, vol. 27, no. 1, p. 113.

9. Ibid., pp. 110–113. The display of Proletarian consciousness in this story is an interesting element unusual for Ibuse. Scolding his niece for her plan to go on an outing with Joseph, the narrator proclaims that the only point in taking such a trip should be to point out social problems and thus lead people toward "XX." The two characters censored when the story appeared in *Shinchō* may be assumed to have been *kakumei* or "revolution." A dozen more characters taken out of another sentence in the same paragraph obviously expressed the same kind of sentiment. The author may have thought that such gestures, and his narrator's sympathy for the

cause of Irish freedom, would be helpful in getting his work published in 1930. At the same time, the pomposity and naïveté of the self-styled revolutionary narrator and his role as a defender of traditional morality may have been backhanded Ibusean swipes at the Proletarians. A similarly ambiguous treatment of a classic Proletarian theme, a factory strike, is seen in Ibuse's 1930 story *Banshun* (Late Spring, *IMZS* 1: 105–110). The 1929 story *Tankō chitai byōin* (A Hospital in the Coalfields, *IMZS* 1: 61–71) is more openly sympathetic to the cause of the oppressed but stops short of any explicit call to revolutionary action.

10. Kawakami traces the use of a "translation style" *(hon'yaku chō)* in some of Ibuse's early works to his interest in European writers, especially Chekhov, and also characterizes it as a kind of "dialect" (*hōgen*) emanating from subcultures such as Meiji and Taishō student society and emigrant groups rather than the Japanese literary tradition. According to Kawakami, it serves the purpose of adding life to his seemingly ingenuous but still worldly characters ("Bungaku-ron," pp. 478–479). Kamei Katsuichirō claims that the classical and *kanbun* traditions have made the main contribution to the development of Ibuse's style, resulting in his distinctive vocabulary and extreme precision. He also sees a stylistic influence from Western literature skillfully grafted onto the predominant *kanbun* tone in works like *Kuchisuke* ("Ibuse Masuji," in *Kamei Katsuichirō senshū*, vol. 5, pp. 259–261).

11. Of the four stories discussed so far, only *Tange-shi tei* has appeared regularly in Ibuse anthologies over the years. *Shigure-tō jokei* and *Josefu to joshi daigakusei*, like several other early stories, have not been included in later collections of Ibuse's works, suggesting that he was content to let this phase of his career be forgotten. They are now available in vol. 1 of the posthumous *Ibuse Masuji zenshū* (1996).

12. The Shinchōsha volume, *Yofuke to ume no hana*, was published in April 1930 and was Ibuse's first book. Among the sixteen stories included were *Kuchisuke*, *Josefu*, *Shigure-tō*, and *Koi*. The Kaizōsha Ibuse collection *Natsukashiki genjitsu* (Nostalgic Reality) appeared three months later; none of its stories is very well known today.

13. From a July 8, 1963, article in *Shūkan dokushojin*, quoted in Nagata Ryūtarō, ed., *Ibuse Masuji bungaku shoshi*, p. 31.

14. Several of these theoretical proclamations are listed in the entry on the Shinkō Geijitsu Ha in Hisamatsu Sen'ichi et al., eds., *Gendai Nihon bungaku daijiten—zōtei shukusatsu-ban*, p. 575.

15. Among these were Funahashi Seiichi, Hori Tatsuo, Kawabata Yasunari, Kobayashi Hideo, and Abe Tomoji.

16. *Sanshōuo* originally appeared in the magazine *Seiki* under the title *Yūhei* and was published in revised form under its better-known title in *Bungei Toshi* in 1929. Further alterations were made in later reprintings, and as late as 1985 Ibuse created a stir by cutting most of the story's final scene when it was republished in the first

volume of his "self-selected complete works" (*Ibuse Masuji jisen zenshū*, vol. 1, p. 16). *Koi* first appeared in the magazine *Keigetsu*, but the revision which won recognition was published in *Mita Bungaku* in 1928.

17. According to Matsumoto Tsuruo, when *Koi* appeared in *Keigetsu*, a magazine devoted to essays, it was published as a *zuihitsu* (non-fiction), but the revised version later published in *Mita Bungaku* was presented as a work of fiction. See Matsumoto Tsuruo, *Ibuse Masuji—nichijō no moteiifu*, p. 138. In a dialogue with Kawamori Yoshizō, Ibuse reveals that his friend and fellow writer Nagai Tatsuo thought for many years that Aoki Nanpachi, Ibuse's friend in student days and a central figure in *Koi*, was an imaginary character; see Ibuse Masuji and Kawamori Yoshizō, "*Sanshōuo* made," in Ibuse Masuji, *Hito to hitokage*, p. 327.

18. See Kobayashi, "Ibuse Masuji no sakuhin ni tsuite."

19. Saeki Shōichi, "Ibuse Masuji no gyakusetsu." *Shinchō*, vol. 72, no. 3, p. 171.

20. Aside from Ibuse's lack of interest in the attempt to organize a Shinkō Geijutsu Ha Club, one may point to his participation in the magazine *Sakuhin*, which, according to Takami Jun, was founded by a group of non-Proletarian writers dissatisfied with the direction of the Shinkō Geijutsu Ha; see Takami's *Shōwa bungaku seisuishi*, pp. 243–244. Of course, the most eloquent testimony of all is to be found, as usual, in Ibuse's own work.

21. Tōgō Katsumi sees this process starting around 1935 and leading to a definitive shift during the war years; see his "Ibuse Masuji sobyō," pp. 173ff, and "Sensōka no Ibuse Masuji," p. 195, both in Nihon Bungaku Kenkyū Shiryō Kankō Kai, ed., *Nihon bungaku kenkyū shiryō sōsho—Ibuse Masuji, Fukazawa Shichirō*.

22. Ibuse and Kawamori, p. 331.

23. Ibuse was called up by the Army as a correspondent in November 1941. In February of the following year he arrived in Singapore, where he worked for a Japanese-language newspaper and school. In late 1942 he was discharged and returned to Japan. *Hana no machi* (City of Flowers; *IMZS* 3: 31–118), a long story based upon his Singapore experiences, was published as a serial in the *Tōkyō Nichinichi* and *Ōsaka Mainichi* newspapers later that year.

24. See Ban Toshihiko, "Ibuse-san kara kiita koto," part 5, in *Geppō* 7, *IMZS* 7: 3–4, for details of this story.

25. Tōgō, "Ibuse Masuji sobyō," p. 178.

26. Ibid., p. 179.

27. *Noriai jidōsha* (The Charcoal Bus; *IMZS*, 5: 168–181) is another allegorical story in which Ibuse uses a country setting to come to terms with Japan's wartime and postwar experience with devastating effect, but in this case the allegory is so schematic that the comic element is stretched rather thin and lacks the sharpness of *Yōhai taichō*.

28. For an account of the origins of this story, see Kawakami's "*Chinpindō shujin* no chosha Ibuse Masuji e," in *Kawakami Tetsutarō zenshū*, vol. 5, p. 481. According to Ban Toshihiko, Ibuse gathered material for this story by tape-recording goings-on in a Tokyo antique dealer's shop; see "Ibuse-san kara kiita koto," part 4, in *Geppō* 6, *IMZS* 6: 2. Several episodes similar to those in the story are also recounted by Ibuse in the essays "Horidashimono" (Finds, 1950; *IMZS* 10: 356–362) and "Aoyagi Mizuho to kottō" (Aoyagi Mizuho and Antiques, 1972; *IMZS* 14: 162–173).

29. Kamei, "Ibuse Masuji," p. 263; Kobayashi Hideo, "Ibuse-kun no *Kashima ari*," in *Kobayashi Hideo zenshū*, vol. 12, p. 39; and Tōgō, "Ibuse Masuji sobyō," pp. 172–173. For an attempt at a periodization of Ibuse's comic style, see Matsumoto, pp. 138ff.

30. Nakamura Mitsuo, *Nihon no gendai shōsetsu*, p. 102. This essentially accurate observation overlooks one significant point: while the author's persona does tend to become less conspicuous as a comic object, the concern with dogmatism was already apparent in *Sanshōuo*, and it can be seen overshadowing his self-mockery as early as *Josefu to joshi daigakusei*.

31. E. M. Forster, *Aspects of the Novel*, p. 154.

32. "Sakka ni kiku—Ibuse Masuji," *Bungaku*, vol. 20, no. 9, p. 89.

33. For summaries of early Proletarian-oriented critiques by Yodono Ryūzō and Senuma Shigeki, see pp. 297–298 of "Kaisetsu," Ishizaki Hitoshi's comprehensive review of Ibuse criticism in Nihon Bungaku Kenkyū Shiryō Kankō Kai, ed. Ishizaki points out that Senuma later changed his evaluation of Ibuse drastically. The alleged insubstantiality of much of Ibuse's writing, however, continued to draw critical ire into the postwar period; see in particular Terada Tōru's "Ibuse Masuji ron," in ibid., pp. 27–41.

34. Itō Sei, "Ibuse Masuji no sekai," *Tenbō*, no. 39, pp. 42–43.

35. Nihon Bungaku Kenkyū Shiryō Kankō Kai, ed., p. 102.

36. Nakamura Mitsuo, "Ibuse Masuji no sakuhin," p. 221.

37. Kaikō Takeshi and Ibuse Masuji, "Omoi kusshita," *Bungei*, vol. 8, no. 3, p. 176. This observation, which would almost be a truism if applied to *waka* and much of the rest of the Japanese literary tradition, suggests the degree to which Ibuse and Kawabata have retained certain traditional qualities in contrast to the many modern writers who seek to arrive at the truth by revealing as much as possible.

Chapter 3. Dazai Osamu

1. Ibuse Masuji, "Dazai Osamu no koto," as quoted in *Bungei tokuhon Dazai Osamu*, p. 75.

2. Quoted in Sōma Shōichi, *Dazai Osamu to Ibuse Masuji*, p. 127. This book contains much information on the Ibuse-Dazai relationship, especially as it affected Dazai's career.

3. "*Ibuse Masuji senshū* kōki (1)," in *Dazai Osamu zenshū*, 1955–1956 ed., vol. 10, pp. 339–342. Unless otherwise specified, subsequent citations of works by Dazai will be quoted from the 1967–1968 edition of *Dazai Osamu zenshū* (hereafter *DOZS*) and given in the text with the volume and page numbers in parentheses.

4. Sōma, p. 15. According to a Dazai chronology compiled by Yamauchi Shoshi, Ibuse eventually responded to Dazai's request with a story entitled *Yakkyokushitsu sōwa* (A Tale from the Druggist's Room); see Katsura Hidezumi, ed., *Dazai Osamu kenkyū II—Sono kaisō*, p. 337.

5. While Ibuse's stories of this period included several later to be counted among his classics, such as *Koi*, *Yane no ue no Sawan*, and *Yofuke to ume no hana*, there were also some of the now largely forgotten works with a decidedly *nansensu* flavor such as *Kuchisuke no iru tanima* and *Shigure-tō jokei*, both of which Dazai had included in the 1948 Ibuse collection. Ibuse reports that on their first meeting, Dazai showed him one or two stories that he (Ibuse) found very reminiscent of *Pesoko to Yumakichi*, an *ero-guro-nansensu* work he had co-authored with Nakamura Masatsune; see Ibuse, "Dazai Osamu no koto," p. 75.

6. In 1926, at about the time that he was becoming seriously interested in literature, he gave a talk entitled "Yūmoa ni tsuite" (On Humor) at a school public-speaking contest (Katsura, ed., p. 333).

7. Harry Levin, *Playboys and Killjoys: An Essay on the Theory and Practice of Comedy*, pp. 53ff.

8. The very title of this maiden collection suggests Dazai's spiritual affinity with Ibuse; the role of old man seems to have come as naturally to Dazai as it did to Ibuse, although in Dazai's case it was not an old age of serenity and painfully gained experience, but rather that of a man prematurely worn out, already partially dead—and self-consciously aware that somber as his situation was, it was also not without its absurd side.

9. See, for example, Isogai Hideo, "Dazai Osamu ni okeru parodei no mondai," *Kokubungaku Kaishaku to Kyōzai no Kenkyū*, vol. 19, no. 2, p. 69; and Miyoshi, *Accomplices of Silence*, p. 131.

10. Isogai, "Dazai Osamu," pp. 66–68; and Isogai Hideo, "Hōhō no mosaku—*Bannen* o chūshin ni," *Kokubungaku Kaishaku to Kyōzai no Kenkyū*, vol. 21, no. 6, p. 63.

11. See, for example, Isogai, "Dazai Osamu," p. 70; Usui Yoshimi, "Dazai Osamu no warai," in Okuno Takeo, ed., *Dazai Osamu kenkyū I—Sono bungaku*," pp. 103–107; Yoshida Seiichi, "Dazai Osamu to fuokuroa," *Kokubungaku Kaishaku to Kanshō*, vol. 23, no. 12, p. 137; Isogai Hideo, "*Otogizōshi* ron," in Tōgō Katsumi and Watabe

Yoshinori, eds., *Sakuhin ron—Dazai Osamu*, pp. 269–270. Similar observations are made by both Usui and Abe Akira in the symposium article "Shōwa no bungaku—Dazai Osamu," *Gunzō*, vol. 30, no. 7, p. 281.

12. For examples of some of the uncertainties surrounding its origin and use in the Western tradition, see Gérard Genette, *Palimpsestes: La littérature au second degré*, pp. 17–23 *et passim*.

13. As his taste for grotesque characters and tendency toward an intimate, personalized, narrative monologue style in his comic fiction suggest, Dazai was very fond of *rakugo*; see Nagashino Kōichirō, "Dazai Osamu to rakugo," *Kokubungaku Kaishaku to Kanshō*, vol. 48, no. 9, pp. 30–36.

14. Like many another *gesaku* title, this seems to be a takeoff on one that came before it, in this case *Ningen banji uso bakkari* (1813) by Shikitei Sanba (1776–1822).

15. It can also be noted that in the postwar years Dazai was sometimes included among the writers of the so-called Neo-Gesaku School (Shin Gesaku Ha), a hypothetical grouping whose work displays few *gesaku* traits other than choices of tone and subject matter that, for some critics, suggested a lack of commitment to writing as a serious calling.

16. Given by Dazai as "Erabarete aru koto no / kōkotsu to fuan to / futatsu ware ni ari" (there are in me / the ectasy and the anxiety / of being chosen); *DOZS* 1: 5. This is based on Horiguchi Daigaku's translation of the line "J'ai l'extase and j'ai le terreur d'être choise" from the poem "Ah! Seigneur, qu'ai je" in Verlaine's collection *Sagesse* (1881).

17. Dazai Osamu, "Koten ryūtō dabi," in *DOZS*, 1955–1956 ed., 10: 59. Dazai also expressed his admiration for Saikaku as master of short-story technique in a postwar work, *Jūgo nenkan* (Fifteen Years, 1946), in *DOZS* 8: 213–236.

18. Sako Jun'ichirō, "*Shinshaku shokokubanashi* o megutte," *Kokubungaku Kaishaku to Kanshō*, vol. 32, no. 2, p. 84.

19. Ihara Saikaku, *Ōtsugomori wa awanu san'yō*, *Ihara Saikaku shū 2*, *Nihon koten bungaku zenshū*, vol. 39, p. 74.

20. It is not impossible to see Saibei as playing Dazai to Waniguchi's Ibuse as suggested by Koizumi Kōichirō, but this seems gratuitous. Koizumi also claims that *Dairiki*, like several of the other *Shinshaku shokokubanashi* stories, constitutes an implicit critique of Japanese militarism, here embodied in the powerful but childish figure of Saibei; see his "*Shinshaku shokokubanashi* ron—*Dairiki*, *Hadakagawa*, *Giri o meguri*," in *Nihon Bungaku*, vol. 25, no. 1, pp. 36–39. This interpretation is certainly plausible, but it is equally possible to see the story as a more general allegory of the one-dimensional pitted against the natural in various forms. The story is somewhat unusual for Dazai in that the outcast figure is one of the unidimensionals, rather that the customary two-dimensional authorial alter ego.

21. Dazai's principal changes in the story were to make Segoshi a miser rather

than a big spender, to add the figure of the bride's hypocritical, social-climbing father, and to have her make her daughters take up the family profession after their father's death.

22. Dazai, "Koten ryūtō dabi," p. 59.

23. As observed by Nosaka Yukihiro, "*Shinshaku shokokubanashi*," in Tōgō and Watabe, eds., *Sakuhin ron—Dazai Osamu*, pp. 223–224.

24. The conventional interpretation of the story sees Urashima as another Dazai alter ego. But even if one sees no particular significance in his being an eldest brother, it is tempting to consider him as a satirical jibe at Dazai's oldest brother, Tsushima Bunji, who was responsible for maintaining the family's position and property and so showed little admiration for "adventures" of the type indulged in so liberally by Dazai.

25. This image is, if anything, even stronger outside Japan, where translations of *Shayō*, *Ningen shikkaku*, and *Buiyon no tsuma* were, at least until recently, the most easily found of all his works.

26. Because *Guddo bai* was left incomplete at Dazai's death, generally considered to have been a suicide, in 1948, it is easy to conclude from the title that it was meant to be a farewell statement of some sort. In fact, the title refers to the efforts of the protagonist to make a clean start in his life by disentangling himself from affairs with a number of women.

27. The passage of time may have served to accentuate this distinction. Nosaka Yukihiro cites a statement by Dazai's widow, Tsushima Michiko, that *Shinshaku shokokubanashi* was the most widely read of all Dazai's works during his lifetime; see Nosaka, p. 213.

28. Dazai Osamu, "Shian no haiboku," in *DOZS*, 1955–1956 ed., 10: 78. The image is echoed in the phrase *Bunmei no hate no owarai* (The Great Laugh at the End of Civilization) in *Buiyon no tsuma* (*DOZS* 9: 28).

Chapter 4. The Hisashi Phenomenon

1. Nihon Shoseki Shuppan Kyōkai, ed., *Nihon shoseki sōmokuroku—1997*, vol. 4, p. 198.

2. Tsurumi Shunsuke and Inoue Hisashi, "Kirikirikoku wa doko ni aru ka," *Umi*, vol. 14, no. 3, pp. 140–141. The work in question is entitled *Yonsenmanpo no otoko* (The Man of Forty Million Paces); as of 1997, five volumes had appeared.

3. "Magician of Language," *Time*, August 1, 1983, p. 86.

4. Inoue Hisashi, *Bun to Fun*, p. 21.

5. Inoue Hisashi, "Kyōfushōsha no jiko keisei shi," in his *Samazama na jigazō—Essei shū 4*, pp. 9–23; and Inoue Hisashi, "Watashi ni totte no gesaku," in his *Parodei shigan—Essei shū 1*, pp. 133–152.

6. Inoue, "Kyōfushōsha no jiko keisei shi," pp. 20–21.

7. Inoue Hisashi, *Tegusari shunjū*, pp. 26–27.

8. Ibid., p. 62.

9. Inoue notes that Nanpo went on to win renown as a composer of *kyōka* and ultimately achieved his main goal of establishing himself as a bakufu functionary. At this point he had no further use for *gesaku*. See Inoue Hisashi, "Okashi na Edo gesakusha," in *Fūkei wa namida ni yusure—Essei shū 2*, pp. 61–62. A similar argument is put into the mouth of Santō Kyōden in *Tegusari shinjū*, pp. 15–16.

10. In a dialogue with critic Takahashi Yasunari, Inoue refines this idea by half seriously suggesting that a writer like Endō Shūsaku, who divides his energies between comic entertainment literature and works fulfilling the requirements of serious art literature as laid down by the critics, is a true heir to the *gesakusha* mantle, while he himself is compromised because he devotes himself entirely to works of the former type; Inoue and Takahashi, "Gesaku tōzai," *Kokubungaku Kaishaku to Kanshō*, vol. 44, no. 9, p. 18.

11. Although Inoue's list of *gesaku* elements provides a useful guide to his views on comic literature, it is hardly a definitive analysis of the subject; the eminent scholar of Edo literature, Nakamura Yukihiko, for example, makes an even stronger case for the primacy of *shukō*, classifying *fukiyose* and *jiguchi* (puns) as variations on the *shukō* principle; see his *Gesaku ron*, *Nakamura Yukihiko chojutsu shū*, vol. 8, pp. 222–228.

12. For a description of the workings of *sekai* and *shukō* in kabuki, see Barbara E. Thornbury, *Sukeroku's Double Identity: The Dramatic Structure of Edo Kabuki*, pp. 20–28.

13. Inoue Hisashi, "Kensatsukan e no gyakukokuhatsu," in his *Jakku no shōtai—Essei shū 3*, pp. 43–47. Inoue also stresses the importance of *shukō* in "Shukō o ou," in his *Parodei shigan—Essei shū 1*, pp. 97–110; and in "Shibai no shukō ni tsuite," in his *Parodei shigan*, pp. 191–194. The connection between *Tegusari shinjū* and Kyōden's *kibyōshi* is alluded to within the story (p. 47); Kyōden himself also appears briefly as a character early in the story. Incidentally, the dust jacket and flyleaf of *Gesakusha meimei den* feature illustrations that are takeoffs on Kyōden's originals for *Edo umare uwaki no kabayaki*, with a caricature of Inoue replacing that of Kyōden's protagonist Enjirō.

14. Inoue Hisashi, "Dōke no hōhō," in his *Parodei shigan*, p. 117.

15. For example, in Inoue's essay "Parodei shian," in his *Parodei shigan*, pp. 39–45; and *Kirikirijin*, p. 788.

16. Inoue, *Kirikirijin*, p. 330. The reference is to Inoue's sojourn at the Australian National University at Canberra in 1976.

17. Johan Huizinga, *Homo Ludens: A Study of the Play-Element in Culture*, p. 6.

18. Jonathan Culler, "The Call of the Phoneme: Introduction," in Culler, ed., *On Puns: The Foundation of Letters*, p. 8.

19. Inoue Hisashi, "*Farce ni tsuite* ni tsuite," *Kokubungaku Kaishaku to Kyōzai no Kenkyū*, vol. 24, no. 15, p. 14.

20. Ibid., p. 14.

21. Inoue, "Shukō o ou," p. 108.

22. While Inoue has not aligned himself with the structuralist and poststructuralist analyses of the nature and function of language, there are striking resonances between some of the ideas on language expressed in his writings on comedy and those of some structuralist and poststructuralist critiques. Compare, for example, Inoue's remark in "Kigeki wa ken'i o warau" that "my predilection for the abundant use of various forms of wordplay can be thought of as a kind of resistance to that diabolical quality that words have of possessing more authority themselves than do the actual things they signify (which, in almost all cases, arises when some irrational authority is directing some sort of commands at us)" (in *Parodei shigan*, p. 11) with Catherine Belsey's *Critical Practice*: "the 'obvious' and the 'natural' are not *given* but *produced* in a specific society by the ways in which that society thinks and talks about itself and its experience" (p. 3, emphasis Belsey's). Belsey goes on to say, "Because it is characteristic of language to be overlooked, the differences it constructs may seem to be natural, universal, and unalterable when in reality they may be produced by a specific form of social organization" (p. 42).

It may be observed in passing that the poststructuralist/post-Saussurean project, at least by implication, problematizes conventional understandings of how comedy functions. With its claims that "language precedes the existence of independent entities" (Belsey, p. 38) and that all discourse is reducible to a play of indeterminate signifiers where there are no concepts with a fixed or absolute reality anterior to the assignment of a signifier, and no privileged relationships between particular signifiers and signifieds, it offers little room for the comic dualities of reality/delusion or reality/pretense. By insisting that all signification is conditioned by ideology or social formation and thus inherently arbitrary, it seems to create ample ground for a radically new analysis of comedy where the dichotomies are not between false or pretended and (somehow absolutely) real but simply between (relative) discourses. For an attempt in this direction, see Jerry Aline Flieger, *The Purloined Punch Line: Freud's Comic Theory and the Postmodern Text.*

23. Inoue, *Kirikirijin*, pp. 492–493.

24. Inoue, "Kigeki wa ken'i o warau," p. 11.

25. Here Inoue's strategy resembles that of another much-publicized assault on the false authority of language, the deconstructionist project—except that where deconstructionists might use critical techniques to call into question the premises ostensibly underlying a text by exposing the aporia or inadvertent "impasses of meaning" (Terry Eagleton, *Literary Theory: An Introduction*, p. 133) in its language, Inoue intentionally inserts such impasses into the discursive fabric of his imaginative texts

to expose pretenses and follies of characters of his own creation (and by extension certain real-world beings or categories they represent), not with a view to undermining the entire project of establishing determinate meanings but to draw distinctions between legitimate and illegitimate meanings.

26. Inoue, "Kyōfushōsha no jiko keisei shi," p. 21.

27. Inoue, *Kirikirijin*, p. 574.

28. Inoue, *Bun to Fun*, pp. 90–92.

29. Inoue, *Kirikirijin*, p. 135. The fifth of Furuhashi's *shinjū-mono* titles, *Megusare shinjū*, is a takeoff on Inoue's own *Tegusari shinjū*.

30. Ibid., p. 820.

31. Ibid., p. 686.

32. Ibid., p. 236.

33. For example, *Shinshaku otogibanashi*, a facetious allusion to the Dazai stories (Inoue, *Kirikirijin*, p. 688); the exercises in cliché accumulation based on classical Chinese epithets (ibid., p. 473) and elegant variationism (ibid., p. 711); and exploitation of reduplicated forms (ibid., pp. 131–32, 249).

34. Frye, *Anatomy of Criticism*, p. 311.

35. Inoue, *Bun to Fun*, pp. 177–178. Inoue is one of the few Japanese of any age to deliberately employ rhyme in his verses, but the head rhyme in this example is relatively unusual even for him.

36. Ibid., p. 129.

37. Inoue, *Kirikirijin*, p. 489.

38. Ibid., pp. 460–461.

39. Ibid., p. 387. The original is based on the verb *deru* ("put out" books, milk, etc.), but the idioms involved resist a parallel rendition in English.

40. Inoue, *Bun to Fun*, p. 149.

41. Collected under the titles *Mokkinpotto-shi no atoshimatsu* and *Mokkinpotto-shi futatabi*. There is also an English translation of the first title, entitled *The Fortunes of Father Mockinpott*, by Roger Pulvers (Mainichi Daily News, 1986).

42. This is pointed out by Matsuda Osamu in his afterward to the 1974 Kōdansha Bunko edition of *Mokkinpotto-shi no atoshimatsu*, p. 239.

43. Inoue, *Mokkinpotto-shi no atoshimatsu*, p. 14.

44. Inoue Hisashi, "Tochi no kotoba de iikaeshite wa," *Asahi shinbun*, evening ed., November 27, 1981, p. 3.

45. For a perceptive analysis of Kirikiri as a "linguistic utopia," see Maeda Ai, "*Kirikirijin* ron," in *Maeda Ai chosaku shū*, vol. 6, pp. 363–374.

46. This point is made in Umehara Takeshi and Odajima Yūshi in "Kirikirikoku o aruku," *Nami*, vol. 15, no. 7, p. 12.

47. The highly reflexive nature of much twentieth-century literature has prompted a more inclusive redefinition of parody which rejects any essential con-

nection between it and humor or satire; for a detailed exposition, see Hutcheon, *A Theory of Parody*. The narrower traditional sense of the term provides a more precise frame for the discussion of Inoue's parodic fiction, and this is the sense in which I will use it.

48. Inoue, *Bun to Fun*, p. 45. The original is from Takuboku's *Ichiaku no suna* (1910): "Hatarakedo hatarakedo / waga kurashi raku ni narazaru / jitto te wo miru" (Although I work and work / my life is none the easier— / I stare at my hands).

49. Inoue, "Parodei shian," pp. 39–41. The distorting mirror that reflects abuses and deformities and animal society onto which objectionable human traits are projected are the same figures used by Arthur Koestler to illustrate the basic techniques of satire in his *Act of Creation* (pp. 70, 73)—a graphic indication of the strong similarity between Inoue's version of parody and the notion of satire conventionally held in the West.

50. Inoue, *Kirikirijin*, p. 211. One of the villagers disagreees, arguing that the government simply fell back on the old phrases because it was too flustered to think for itself: "To put it strictly, it's a kind of plagiarism, not anything as fancy as a parody" (p. 212).

51. Inoue, "Parodei shian," pp. 44–45.

52. Inoue Hisashi, "Parodei shigan," in his *Parodei shigan*, p. 62.

53. Inoue, *Kirikirijin*, p. 614.

54. Ibid., p. 452.

55. Ibid., pp. 37–40.

56. Ibid., p. 7.

57. Notably a set of stories published in the magazine *Ōru yomimono* and subsequently collected under the title *Isamu yori yoroshiku*.

58. Inoue Hisashi, "Kigeki ni yoru kigekiteki jiko kyōseihō," in his *Parodei shigan*, p. 23.

59. Ibid., p. 19.

60. Ibid., p. 20. On Brecht's use of language for ends very similar to those described here by Inoue, see Eagleton, p. 136.

61. See, for example, Inoue, "Kigeki wa ken'i o warau," pp. 9–12; and "Parodei shian," pp. 39–45.

62. Inoue, *Bun to Fun*, pp. 70–71.

63. Ibid., p. 9.

64. Ibid., p. 138.

65. Ibid., p. 131.

66. Ibid., pp. 196–197. The phrase *ichioku sōdorobō* ("mass thievery," p. 195) echoes the postwar catchphrase *ichioku sōzange* (mass contrition), introduced by Japan's first post-surrender prime minister, Prince Higashikuni Naruhiko, and two parodic products of the fertile mind of the journalist/essayist Ōya Sōichi, *ichioku sōgashi*

(mass starvation) and, at the dawn of the television age, *ichioku sōhakuchika* (mass cretinization).

67. Inoue, *Mokkinpotto-shi no atoshimatsu*, p. 7.

68. Ibid., pp. 49–50.

69. Ibid., p. 32.

70. Ibid., pp. 32–33.

71. Ibid., p. 38.

72. Ibid., p. 230.

73. Inoue, *Kirikirijin*, p. 173.

74. Inoue, *Bun to Fun*, p. 19.

75. Ibid., p. 127.

76. Inoue, "Atogaki" (Afterword) to the 1974 (Asahi Sonorama) edition of *Bun to Fun*, p. 199.

77. Inoue, *Kirikirijin*, p. 183.

78. Ibid., p. 674.

79. Ibid., pp. 311–315.

80. Mikhail Bakhtin, *Rabelais and His World*, tr. Helene Iswolsky, p. 9.

81. Ibid., p. 7.

82. Ibid., pp. 5, 11.

83. Ibid., pp. 89ff. For other examples, see Victor Turner, *The Ritual Process: Structure and Anti-Structure*, pp. 172ff; Umberto Eco, "The Frames of Comic 'Freedom,'" p. 6; and Hutcheon, p. 74.

84. Turner, p. 176.

85. Ibid., p. 172.

86. Hutcheon, p. 75.

87. Ibid., p. 37.

88. Eco, "The Frames of Comic 'Freedom,'" pp. 6–7.

89. Turner, p. 201.

90. Eco, "The Frames of Comic 'Freedom,'" pp. 6–7.

91. Although, of course the subversive potential of certain comedies of festive inversion has not escaped notice and efforts at suppression, as in the celebrated, and celebratory, cases of Beaumarchais's *Le mariage de Figaro* (1785) and Fukazawa Shichirō's *Fūryū mutan* (1960).

92. Eco, "The Frames of Comic 'Freedom,'" p. 6.

93. Ibid., p. 7.

94. Tsurumi and Inoue, "Kirikirikoku was doko ni aru ka," pp. 164–165.

95. Inoue Hisashi, *Sore kara no Bun to Fun*, in *Inoue Hisashi zen shibai*, vol. 2, p. 218.

96. Personal comment to author, May 28, 1992.

97. See Yamaguchi Masao, "Inoue Hisashi no konto no sekai," in *Inoue Hisashi no sekai*, pp. 44–51; Maeda, "*Kirikirijin* ron"; and Senda Akihiko, "Ai to kyūsai no

nansensu" and "Kotoba yami no warai" (both in Senda, *Sekai wa kigeki ni keisha suru*). Miyoshi, in almost identical versions of his essay "Against the Native Grain" in *Postmodernism and Japan* (pp. 157–158) and *Off Center* (pp. 26–27), praises *Kirikirijin* as "one of the most fascinating works" to emerge from what he considers to be the cultural wasteland of post-1970 Japan, although in the latter version he also finds it exceptional "even among Inoue's own works."

98. Inoue Hisashi, "Imi yori oto o—I," in *Parodei shigan*, pp. 69–72. Other pieces in which Inoue assails the linguistic shortcomings of modern Japanese drama and fiction are "Asakusa no kotoba to gekijō no kotoba," in *Parodei shigan*, pp. 13–16, and "Nihon bungaku no kokkei ni tsuite," in *Fūkei wa namida ni yusure—Essei shū 2*, pp. 68–87.

99. Inoue, "Nihon bungaku no kokkei ni tsuite," p. 87.

100. In *Zutsū katakori Higuchi Ichiyō, Nakimushi namaiki Ishikawa Takuboku, Wagahai wa Sōseki de aru, Iihatōbo no gekiressha*, and *Ningen gōkaku*, respectively.

101. Satire, both other-directed and self-directed, is not necessarily the only motive for Inoue's creation of such characters. In a conversation with the American novelist Kurt Vonnegut, he expressed his admiration for Vonnegut's repeated use of the fictional science-fiction author Kilgore Trout in his novels, and commented that "when a novelist appears as a fictional character, it creates another small compartment within the work, another writing of the human image. A device, that is, to show on two different levels that human beings are at the center of the universe" (Inoue Hisashi and Kurt Vonnegut, "Zetsubō ni tachimukau warai," *Asahi shinbun*, evening ed., May 15, 1984, p. 5).

102. Inoue, *Bun to Fun*, pp. 53–54.

103. Inoue, *Kirikirijin*, p. 333.

104. On the *gesaku* element in *Ukigumo*, see Inoue and Takahashi, "Gesaku tōzai," p. 11.

105. Inoue, "Kigeki wa ken'i o warau," p. 11.

106. Inoue, "Kigeki ni yoru kigekiteki jiko kyōseihō," p. 24.

107. A point made by Takahashi in Inoue and Takahashi, "Gesaku tōzai," pp. 14–15.

108. Inoue, "Kigeki ni yoru kigekiteki jiko kyōseihō," pp. 23–24.

109. Inoue, *Kirikirijin*, p. 717.

110. Ibid., pp. 717–718.

111. Inoue Hisashi, "Bokura ni shisō ga nai to iu uwasa wa hontō darō ka," in his *Parodei shigan*, pp. 162–163. He also discusses the role of *shisō* in "Ategotoshitachi no omoshiroi gekijō," "Shieikusupia wa umi de aru," and "Shibai no shukō ni tsuite," all in his *Parodei shigan*. All of these essays deal specifically with the question of *shisō* in the theater, but their conclusions may certainly be taken to apply to fiction as well.

112. Inoue, "Ategotoshitachi no omoshiroi gekijō," pp. 169–170.

113. Inoue, *Kirikirijin*, p. 726.

Chapter 5. Conclusion

1. Comic works by both Natsume Sōseki and Ibuse Masuji have been assailed as, among other things, "high-class *rakugo*" (*kōtō rakugo* or *isshu no kōkyū rakugo*) by unsympathetic contemporaries; see Matsumura Tatsuo's preface ("Kaisetsu") to *Wagahai wa neko de aru* in *Nihon kindai bungaku*, vol. 24, *Natsume Sōseki—I*, p. 27; and Terada Tōru's "Ibuse Masuji ron," p. 29.

2. For a summary of some of the salient ways in which Japanese fiction in both its traditional and modern *shōsetsu* forms differs from the Western-style novel, see Masao Miyoshi, "Against the Native Grain: The Japanese Novel and the 'Postmodern' West" in his *Off Center*, esp. pp. 46–49; and Fowler, *The Rhetoric of Confession*, pp. xvii–xxvii. While Fowler's discussion concentrates on *shishōsetsu*, many of his observations also apply to modern Japanese fiction in general.

3. Introduction to Levin, ed., *Veins of Humor*, p. 13.

4. All three of these strategies have been cited, at least in terms of *warai*, by Isogai Hideo in "Ibuse Masuji" (1950), which, although dated, remains one of the most perceptive critiques of modern Japanese comic fiction. Isogai points out that humorous authors (Ibuse, Uno Kōji, Makino Shin'ichi, Uchida Hyakken, Oda Sakunosuke, and Dazai among others) freely mix truth and falsehood and employ caricature, exaggeration, and fantasy in painting a broad picture of reality (in contrast to the super-realism of Shiga Naoya and his many admirers), and that some (Uno, Ibuse) "seek harmony within ordinary Japanese life" (unlike the slumming, sneering Nagai Kafū or the unworldly Shiga). But he sees later practitioners (Dazai, Oda) as increasingly cut off from common life and self-abusive and characterizes Japanese humor as forlorn (*wabishii*) and besieged again in the postwar years. I hope that a reading of Dazai's comic masterpieces will show that he was able to keep his self-abuse under control at times, and after Inoue it seems unlikely that the defensive posture will be required any time soon.

5. George Meredith, "An Essay on Comedy," in Sypher, ed., *Comedy*, p. 32.

6. T. G. A. Nelson, *Comedy: An Introduction to Comedy in Literature, Drama, and Cinema*, p. 22.

7. Werner Jaeger, *Paideia: The Ideals of Greek Culture*, vol. 1, tr. Gilbert Highet, p. 367.

8. While it would be cruel if not unusual punishment to assign any three writers the burden of representing a phenomenon of this sort in its entirety, and my choice of this particular trio was made long ago, it was reassuring to note that they fit neatly with a recent account which divided the history of comic literature in modern

Japan into three periods: a dark age of hostility and authoritarian repression from the Meiji era through the end of World War II, a (re-)establishment in the early postwar years, and finally an efflorescence beginning in the 1960s marked by a resurgence of two mainstays of comedy, overt satirical challenges to authority and sexual expression (Tsuge Teruhiko, "Warai no bungakushi," *Kaien*, vol. 12, no. 5, pp. 126–132). Although any such scheme inevitably involves a certain amount of overlap between phases, and the careers of some authors including Ibuse and Dazai span more than one period, Tsuge names Ibuse, Dazai, and Inoue among the prominent writers of the first, second, and third phases, respectively.

9. One of the most articulate and persistent voices making this claim has been that of Ōe Kenzaburō; see, for example, his "Japan's Dual Identity: A Writer's Dilemma," in Miyoshi and Harootunian, eds., *Postmodernism and Japan* and his remarks in a dialogue with Kazuo Ishiguro, "The Novelist in Today's World: A Conversation," *boundary 2*, vol. 18, no. 3, pp. 109–122. The decision in 1985 to open the Akutagawa Prize, long the most prominent of Japan's awards for art fiction, to non-fiction works also attests eloquently to the decline in the status of the *shōsetsu*.

10. Examples, aside from Inoue's parodic works, include Tsutsui Yasutaka's metafictional parody of academic literary criticism and of the postmodern novel in *Bungakubu Tadano kyōju* (Professor Tadano of the Literature Faculty, 1990), and Ōe's forays, under the influence of Yamaguchi Masao and Mikhail Bakhtin, into "grotesque realism" in novels such as *Man'en gannen to futtobōru* (1967, trans. as *The Silent*) and *Dōjidai gēmu* (Contemporary Game, 1979). While Ōe has made his belief in the importance of comedy clear in his critical essays, the comedy in his fiction frequently seems less accessible than in the works of his colleagues, although, as Miyoshi suggests in *Off Center* (p. 238), it may simply be that the complexity of Ōe's writing and his "formidable" intellectual status leave readers too intimidated to apprehend it.

11. It could be argued that the form in which the comic spirit has flourished most luxuriantly in recent years in Japan is *manga*, whose popularity easily overshadows that of literature altogether. Perhaps the relative subordination of text to pictures conceals from the academically oriented critic the possibility that *manga* do in fact constitute a kind of comic countergenre to the *shōsetsu*, much as the similarly illustrated *kibyōshi* functioned as a popular comic form in the Edo period.

12. This thesis has been advanced by Takahashi Yasunari; see his "Inoue Hisashi no sekai gekijō," in *Inoue Hisashi no sekai*, p. 41; and Inoue and Takahashi, "Gesaku tōzai," p. 13.

13. See Robert M. Torrance, "Modernism and Modernity," *Journal of the Association of Teachers of Japanese*, vol. 22, no. 2, pp. 206–207.

14. Hutcheon, p. 71.

Works Cited

Unless otherwise indicated, the place of publication of all Japanese-language works is Tokyo.

Asahara Rokurō. *Building to shōben* (Buildings and Urine). Sekirokaku Shobō, 1930.

Asō Isoji. *Kokkei bungaku ron* (On Comical Literature). Tokyo Daigaku Shuppankai, 1954.

Bakhtin, Mikhail. *Rabelais and His World.* Tr. Helene Iswolsky. Bloomington: Indiana University Press, 1984 [1968].

Ban Toshihiko. "Ibuse-san kara kiita koto" (Things I Heard from Mr. Ibuse), part 4, in *Geppō* (Monthly Bulletin) 6, *Ibuse Masuji zenshū* (q.v.), vol. 6, pp. 1–4.

———. "Ibuse-san kara kiita koto" (Things I Heard from Mr. Ibuse), part 5, in *Geppō* (Monthly Bulletin) 7, *Ibuse Masuji zenshū* (q.v.), vol. 7, pp. 1–4.

Belsey, Catherine. *Critical Practice.* London and New York: Routledge, 1980.

Borgen, Robert, and Marian Ury. "Readable Japanese Mythology: Selections from *Nihon Shoki* and *Kojiki*." *Journal of the Association of Teachers of Japanese*, vol. 24, no. 1, pp. 61–97 (April 1990).

Butler, Judith. *Gender Trouble: Feminism and the Subversion of Identity.* New York and London: Routledge, 1990.

Corrigan, Robert W. "Introduction: Comedy and the Comic Spirit," in Robert W. Corrigan, ed., *Comedy: Meaning and Form*, 2nd ed. New York: Harper and Row, 1981.

Culler, Jonathan, "The Call of the Phoneme: Introduction," in Jonathan Culler, ed., *On Puns: The Foundation of Letters.* London: Basil Blackwell, 1988.

Dazai Osamu. *Akai taiko* (The Red Drum), in *Dazai Osamu zenshū*, 1967–1968 ed. (q.v.), vol. 6, pp. 282–293.

———. *Bannen* (Last Years), in *Dazai Osamu zenshū*, 1967–1968 ed. (q.v.), vol. 1, pp. 3–237.

———. *Buiyon no tsuma* (Villon's Wife), in *Dazai Osamu zenshū*, 1967–1968 ed. (q.v.), vol. 9, p. 14–43.

———. *Dairiki* (The Prodigy of Strength), in *Dazai Osamu zenshū*, 1967–1968 ed. (q.v.), vol. 6, pp. 210–220.

———. *Dazai Osamu zenshū* (Complete Works of Dazai Osamu). 12 vols. Chikuma Shobō, 1955–1956.

———. *Dazai Osamu zenshū* (Complete Works of Dazai Osamu). 12 vols. Chikuma Shobō, 1967–1968.

———. *Dōke no hana* (The Flower of Clowning), in *Dazai Osamu zenshū*, 1967–1968 ed. (q.v.), vol. 1, pp. 141–293.

———. *Fugaku hyakkei* (One Hundred Views of Mount Fuji), in *Dazai Osamu zenshū*, 1967–1968 ed. (q.v.), vol. 2, pp. 153–173.

———. *Guddo bai* (Goodbye), in *Dazai Osamu zenshū*, 1967–1968 ed. (q.v.), vol. 9, pp. 471–492.

———. *Gyofukuki* (Metamorphosis), in *Dazai Osamu zenshū*, 1967–1968 ed. (q.v.), vol. 1, pp. 61–70.

———. *Ha* (Leaves), in *Dazai Osamu zenshū*, 1967–1968 ed. (q.v.), vol. 1, pp. 5–21.

———. *Hadakagawa* (Naked River), in *Dazai Osamu zenshū*, 1967–1968 ed. (q.v.), vol. 6, pp. 253–262.

———. *Hin no iji* (The Obstinancy of Poverty), in *Dazai Osamu zenshū*, 1967–1968 ed. (q.v.), vol. 6, pp. 199–209.

———. "*Ibuse Masuji senshū* kōki (1)" (Editor's Postscript to *Collected Works of Ibuse Masuji*), in *Dazai Osamu zenshū*, 1955–1956 ed. (q.v.), vol. 10, pp. 339–342.

———. *Jūgo nenkan* (Fifteen Years), in *Dazai Osamu zenshū*, 1967–1968 ed. (q.v.), vol. 8, pp. 213–236.

———. *Kachikachiyama* (Crackling Mountain), in *Dazai Osamu zenshū*, 1967–1968 ed. (q.v.), vol. 7, pp. 325–348.

———. *Kare wa mukashi no kare narazu* (He Is Not the Man He Was), in *Dazai Osamu zenshū*, 1967–1968 ed. (q.v.), vol. 1, pp. 137–176.

———. *Kobutori* (Talking the Wen Away), in *Dazai Osamu zenshū*, 1967–1968 ed. (q.v.), vol. 7, pp. 274–289.

———. "Koten ryūtō dabi" (Classics and Shaggy Dogs), in *Dazai Osamu zenshū*, 1955–1956 ed. (q.v.), vol. 10, pp. 58–61.

———. *Ningen shikkaku* (No Longer Human), in *Dazai Osamu zenshū*, 1967–1968 ed. (q.v.), vol. 9, pp. 363–470.

———. *Ningyo no umi* (The Sea of Mermaids), in *Dazai Osamu zenshū*, 1967–1968 ed. (q.v.), vol. 6, pp. 229–242.

———. "Nyoze gamon" (Thus I Have Heard), in *Dazai Osamu zenshū*, 1967–1968 ed. (q.v.), vol. 10, pp. 296–326.

———. *Nyozoku* (The Highwaywomen), in *Dazai Osamu zenshū*, 1967–1968 ed. (q.v.), vol. 6, pp. 273–281.

———. *Omoide* (Memories), in *Dazai Osamu zenshū*, 1967–1968 ed. (q.v.), vol. 1, pp. 22–60.

———. *Otogizōshi* (Fairy Tales), in *Dazai Osamu zenshū*, 1967–1968 ed. (q.v.), vol. 7, pp. 271–372.

———. *Ressha* (Train), in *Dazai Osamu zenshū*, 1967–1968 ed. (q.v.), vol. 1, pp. 71–75.

———. *Romanesuku* (Romanesque), in *Dazai Osamu zenshū*, 1967–1968 ed. (q.v.), vol. 1, pp. 177–200.

———. *Saruzuka* (The Monkey's Burial Mound), in *Dazai Osamu zenshū*, 1967–1968 ed. (q.v.), vol. 6, pp. 221–228.

———. *Shayō* (Setting Sun), in *Dazai Osamu zenshū*, 1967–1968 ed. (q.v.), vol. 9, pp. 97–242.

———. "Shian no haiboku" (Thought Defeated), in *Dazai Osamu zenshū*, 1955–1956 ed. (q.v.), vol. 10, pp. 74–78.

———. *Shinshaku shokokubanashi* (New Tales of the Provinces), in *Dazai Osamu zenshū*, 1967–1968 ed. (q.v.), vol. 6, pp. 195–322.

———. *Shin'yū kōkan* (The Courtesy Call), in *Dazai Osamu zenshū*, 1967–1968 ed. (q.v.), vol. 10, pp. 277–298.

———. *Shitakiri suzume* (Tongue-cut Sparrow), in *Dazai Osamu zenshū*, 1967–1968 ed. (q.v.), vol. 7, pp. 349–372.

———. *Suijin* (The Man of Taste), in *Dazai Osamu zenshū*, 1967–1968 ed. (q.v.), vol. 6, pp. 294–304.

———. *Toka tonton* (A Sound of Hammering), in *Dazai Osamu zenshū*, 1967–1968 ed. (q.v.), vol. 10, pp. 320–332.

———. *Urashima-san*, in *Dazai Osamu zenshū*, 1967–1968 ed. (q.v.), vol. 7, pp. 290–324.

———. *Yoshinoyama* (The Mountains of Yoshino), in *Dazai Osamu zenshū*, 1967–1968 ed. (q.v.), vol. 6, pp. 314–322.

———. *Yūkyōkai* (Thou Shalt Not Carouse), in *Dazai Osamu zenshū*, 1967–1968 ed. (q.v.), vol. 6, pp. 305–313.

Eagleton, Terry. *Literary Theory: An Introduction*. Minneapolis: University of Minnesota Press, 1983.

Eco, Umberto. "The Frames of Comic 'Freedom,'" in Tom Sebeok, ed., *Carnival!*, pp. 1–9. Berlin: Mouton, 1984.

Feibleman, James. *In Praise of Comedy: A Study in Its Theory and Practice*. New York: Macmillan, 1939.

Flieger, Jerry Aline. *The Purloined Punch Line: Freud's Comic Theory and the Postmodern Text*. Baltimore: Johns Hopkins University Press, 1991.

Forster, E. M. *Aspects of the Novel*. 1927; reprint, New York: Harcourt, Brace, & World, 1954.

Fowler, Edward. "Rendering Words, Traversing Cultures: On the Art and Politics of Translating Modern Japanese Fiction." *Journal of Japanese Studies*, vol. 18, no. 1, pp. 1–44 (Winter 1992).

———. *The Rhetoric of Confession: Shishōsetsu in Early Twentieth-Century Japanese Fiction*. Berkeley: University of California Press, 1988.

Frye, Northrop. *Anatomy of Criticism*. Princeton: Princeton University Press, 1957.

Gendai Nihon no yūmoa bungaku (Contemporary Japanese Humorous Literature). 6 vols. Rippū Shobō, 1980–1981.

Genette, Gérard. *Palimpsestes: La littérature au second degré* (Palimpsests: Literature to the Second Degree). Paris: Editions du Seuil, 1982.

Hamada Taizō. "Warai no keifu" (The Lineage of Laughter), in Hamada Taizō, ed., *Nihon bungaku ni okeru bi to jōnen no nagare—warai* (Currents of Beauty and Feeling in Japanese Literature: Laughter), pp. 333–359. Gendai Shichō Sha, 1973.

Hisamatsu Sen'ichi et al., eds. *Gendai Nihon bungaku daijiten—Zōtei shukusatsu-ban* (Dictionary of Modern Japanese Literature, Revised Small-Print Edition). Meiji Shoin, 1972.

Huizinga, Johan. *Homo Ludens: A Study of the Play Element in Culture*. Boston: Beacon Press, 1955.

Hutcheon, Linda. *A Theory of Parody: The Teachings of Twentieth-Century Art Forms*. New York: Methuen, 1985.

Ibuse Masuji. *Aogashima taigaiki* (An Account of Aogashima), in *Ibuse Masuji zenshū*, 1964–1975 ed. (q.v.), vol. 1, pp. 289–314.

———. "Aoyagi Mizuho to kottō" (Aoyagi Mizuho and Antiques), in *Ibuse Masuji zenshū*, 1964–1975 ed. (q.v.), vol. 14, pp. 162–173.

———. *Banshun* (Late Spring), in *Ibuse Masuji zenshū*, 1964–1975 ed. (q.v.), vol. 1, pp. 105–110.

———. *Chinpindō shujin* (The Master of Rarity House), in *Ibuse Masuji zenshū*, 1964–1975 ed. (q.v.), vol. 8, pp. 119–249.

———. "Dazai Osamu no koto" (About Dazai Osamu; 1955), in *Bungei tokuhon Dazai Osamu* (A Literary Reader: Dazai Osamu), pp. 74–81. Kawade Shobō Shinsha, 1975.

———. *Ekimae ryokan* (The Inn by the Station), in *Ibuse Masuji zenshū*, 1964–1975 ed. (q.v.), vol. 6, pp. 320–475.

———. *Hana no machi* (City of Flowers), in *Ibuse Masuji zenshū*, 1964–1975 ed. (q.v.), vol. 3, pp. 31–118.

———. *Honjitsu kyūshin* (No Consultations Today), in *Ibuse Masuji zenshū*, 1964–1975 ed. (q.v.), vol. 4, pp. 325–413.

———. "Horidashimono" (Finds), in *Ibuse Masuji zenshū*, 1964–1975 ed. (q.v.), vol. 10, pp. 356–362.

———. *Ibuse Masuji jisen zenshū* (Ibuse Masuji: The Author's Complete Self-Selected Works). 12 vols. Shinchōsha, 1985–1986.

———. *Ibuse Masuji zenshū* (The Complete Works of Ibuse Masuji). 14 vols. Chikuma Shobō, 1964–1975.

———. *Ibuse Masuji zenshū* (The Complete Works of Ibuse Masuji). 30 vols. Chikuma Shobō, 1996– .

———. *In no shima* (The Isle of In), in *Ibuse Masuji zenshū*, 1964–1975 ed. (q.v.), vol. 3, pp. 451–469.

———. *Jon Manjirō hyōryūki* (John Manjirō: A Castaway's Chronicle), in *Ibuse Masuji zenshū*, 1964–1975 ed. (q.v.), vol. 2, pp. 67–144.

———. *Josefu to joshi daigakusei* (Joseph and the College Girl). *Shinchō*, vol. 27, no. 1, pp. 110–120 (January 1930).

———. *Kawa* (The River), in *Ibuse Masuji zenshū*, 1964–1975 ed. (q.v.), vol. 1, pp. 181–226.

———. *Koi* (Carp), in *Ibuse Masuji zenshū*, 1964–1975 ed. (q.v.), vol. 1, pp. 12–17.

———. *Kuchisuke no iru tanima* (Kuchisuke's Valley), in *Ibuse Masuji zenshū*, 1964–1975 ed. (q.v.), vol. 1, pp. 34–60.

———. *Kuroi ame* (Black Rain), in *Ibuse Masuji zenshū*, 1964–1975 ed. (q.v.), vol. 13, pp. 3–298.

———. *Noriai jidōsha* (The Charcoal Bus), in *Ibuse Masuji zenshū*, 1964–1975 ed. (q.v.), vol. 5, pp. 168–181.

———. *Nyonin raihō* (A Female Visitor), in *Ibuse Masuji zenshū*, 1964–1975 ed. (q.v.), vol. 1, pp. 239–260.

———. *Oihagi no hanashi* (Talk about Highway Robbers), in *Ibuse Masuji zenshū*, 1964–1975 ed. (q.v.), vol. 3, pp. 310–327.

———. *Sanshōuo* (Salamander), in *Ibuse Masuji zenshū*, 1964–1975 ed. (q.v.), vol. 1, pp. 3–11.

———. *Sazanami gunki* (Waves), in *Ibuse Masuji zenshū*, 1964–1975 ed. (q.v.), vol. 1, pp. 320–480.

———. *Shigure-tō jokei* (A View of Shigure Island). *Bungei Shunjū*, vol. 7, no. 11, pp. 17–28 (November 1929).

———. *Shiraga* (White Hair), in *Ibuse Masuji zenshū*, 1964–1975 ed. (q.v.), vol. 4, pp. 218–233.

———. *Shūkin ryokō* (The Bill-Collecting Trip), in *Ibuse Masuji zenshū*, 1964–1975 ed. (q.v.), vol. 2, pp. 3–66.

———. *Suri no Sanzaburō* (Sanzaburō the Sneak Thief), in *Ibuse Masuji zenshū*, 1964–1975 ed. (q.v.), vol. 1, pp. 261–272.

———. *Tajinko mura* (Tajinko Village), in *Ibuse Masuji zenshū*, 1964–1975 ed. (q.v.), vol. 2, pp. 236–343.

———. *Tange-shi tei* (Life at Mr. Tange's), in *Ibuse Masuji zenshū*, 1964–1975 ed. (q.v.), vol. 1, pp. 123–140.

———. *Tankō chitai byōin* (A Hospital in the Coalfields), in *Ibuse Masuji zenshū*, 1964–1975 ed. (q.v.), vol. 1, pp. 61–71.

———. *Yane no ue no Sawan* (Sawan on the Roof), in *Ibuse Masuji zenshū*, 1964–1975 ed. (q.v.), vol. 1, pp. 72–79.

———. *Yofuke to ume no hana* (Plum Blossom by Night), in *Ibuse Masuji zenshū*, 1964–1975 ed. (q.v.), vol. 1, pp. 18–33.

———. *Yōhai taichō* (Lieutenant Lookeast), in *Ibuse Masuji zenshū*, 1964–1975 ed. (q.v.), vol. 4, pp. 296–326.

——— and Kawamori Yoshizō. "*Sanshōuo* made" (Until *Sanshōuo*), in Ibuse Masuji, *Hito to hitokage* (People and People's Shadows), pp. 311–331. Mainichi Shinbunsha, 1972.

Ihara Saikaku. *Ōtsugomori was awanu san'yō* (A New Year's Eve Imbalance), in *Ihara Saikaku shū 2, Nihon koten bungaku zenshū*, vol. 39, pp. 74–78. Shōgakkan, 1973.

Iizawa Tadasu. *Buki to shite no warai* (Laughter as a Weapon). Iwanami Shoten, 1977.

Inoue Hisashi. "Asakusa no kotoba to gekijō no kotoba" (The Language of Asakusa and the Language of the Theater; 1971), in his *Parodei shigan—Essei shū 1* (q.v.), pp. 13–16.

———. "Ategotoshitachi no omoshiroi gekijō" (The Interesting Theater of the Dubbers; 1970), in his *Parodei shigan—Essei shū 1* (q.v.), pp. 164–171.

———. "Bokura ni shisō ga nai to iu uwasa was hontō darō ka" (Is the Rumor That We Have No Ideas Really True?; 1970), in his *Parodei shigan—Essei shū 1* (q.v.), pp. 162–163.

———. *Bun to Fun* (Boon and Phoon). Shinchō Bunko, 1974.

———. "Dōke no hōhō" (The Technique of Clowning; 1975), in his *Parodei shigan—Essei shū 1* (q.v.), pp. 111–120.

———. "*Farce ni tsuite* ni tsuite" (Concerning "Concerning Farce"). *Kokubungaku Kaishaku to Kyōzai no Kenkyū*, vol. 24, no. 15, pp. 12–14 (December 1979).

———. *Fūkei wa namida ni yusure—Essei shū 2* (The Scenery Quivered in Tears: Collected Essays 2; 1979). Chūkō Bunko, 1982.

———. *Iihatōbo no gekiressha* (The Iihatōbo Theater Train). Shinchōsha, 1980.

———. "Imi yori oto o—1" (Sound Rather than Meaning: Part 1; 1972), in his *Parodei shigan—Essei shū 1* (q.v.), pp. 69–72.

———. *Isamu yori yoroshiku* (Greetings from Isamu). Bungei Shunjū, 1974.

———. "Kensatsukan e no gyakukokuhatsu" (A Counterindictment of the Prosecutors; 1974), in his *Jakku no shōtai—Essei shū 3* (The Jack's Real State: Collected Essays 3; 1979), pp. 43–47. Chūkō Bunko, 1982.

———. "Kigeki ni yoru kigekiteki jiko kyōseihō" (The Comic Method of Comical Self-correction; 1971), in his *Parodei shigan—Essei shū 1* (q.v.), pp. 17–24.

———. "Kigeki wa ken'i o warau" (Comedy Laughs at Authority; 1971), in his *Parodei shigan—Essei shū 1* (q.v.), pp. 9–12.

———. *Kirikirijin* (The Kirikirians). Shinchōsha, 1981.

———. "Kyōfushōsha no jiko keisei shi" (The History of a Phobic's Self-formation; 1977), in his *Samazama na jigazō—Essei shū 4* (q.v.), pp. 9–23.

———. *Mokkinpotto-shi futatabi* (Father Mockinpott Once Again). Kōdansha Bunko, 1985.

———. *Mokkinpotto-shi no atoshimatsu* (The Fortunes of Father Mockinpott; 1972). Kōdansha Bunko, 1974.

———. *Nakimushi namaiki Ishikawa Takuboku* (Crybaby, Wiseguy Ishikawa Takuboku). Shinchōsha, 1986.

———. "Nihon bungaku no kokkei ni tsuite" (On Humor in Japanese Literature; 1978), in his *Fūkei was namida ni yusure—Essei shū 2* (q.v.), pp. 68–87.

———. *Ningen gōkaku* (A Qualified Human). Shūeisha, 1990.

———. "Okashi na Edo gesakusha" (The Funny *Gesakusha* of Edo; 1973), in his *Fūkei wa namida ni yusure—Essei shū 2* (q.v.), pp. 61–62.

———. "Parodei shian" (Thoughts on Parody; 1972), in his *Parodei shigan—Essei shu 1* (q.v.), pp. 39–45.

———. "Parodei shigan" (The Will to Parody; 1972), in his *Parodei shigan—Essei shū 1* (q.v.), pp. 61–64.

———. *Parodei shigan— Essei shū 1* (The Will to Parody: Collected Essays 1; 1979). Chūkō Bunko, 1982.

———. *Samazama na jigazō—Essei shū 4* (Various Self-portraits: Collected Essays 4; 1979). Chūkō Bunko, 1982.

———. "Shibai no shukō ni tsuite" (On *Shukō* in Plays; 1974), in his *Parodei shigan—Essei shū 1* (q.v.), pp. 191–194.

———. "Shieikusupia was umi de aru" (Shakespeare Is an Ocean; 1971), in his *Parodei shigan—Essei shū 1* (q.v.), pp. 172–176.

———. "Shukō o ou" (In Pursuit of *Shukō*; 1971), in his *Parodei shigan—Essei shū 1* (q.v.), pp. 97–110.

———. *Sore kara no Bun to Fun* (Boon and Phoon Revisted; 1974), in *Inoue Hisashi zen shibai* (Complete Plays of Inoue Hisashi), vol. 2, pp. 131–220. Shinchōsha, 1984.

———. *Tegusari shinjū* (The Love Suicide in Manacles; 1972). Bunshun Bunko, 1975.

———. "Tochi no kotoba de iikaeshite wa" (Talking Back in Local Language). *Asahi shinbun*, evening edition, November 27, 1981, p. 3.

———. *Wagahai wa Sōseki de aru* (I Am Sōseki). Shūeisha, 1982.

———. "Watashi ni totte no gesaku" (What *Gesaku* Means to Me; 1978), in his *Parodei shigan—Essei shū 1* (q.v.), pp. 133–152.

———. *Zutsū katakori Higuchi Ichiyō* (Headachy, Stiff-shouldered Higuchi Ichiyō). Shūeisha, 1984.

——— and Takahashi Yasunari. "Gesaku tōzai" (*Gesaku* East and West). *Kokubungaku Kaishaku to Kanshō*, vol. 44, no. 9, pp. 6–20 (August 1979).

——— and Kurt Vonnegut. "Zetsubō ni tachimukau warai" (Laughter Confronts Despair). *Asahi shinbun*, evening edition, May 15, 1984, p. 5.

Inoue Hisashi no sekai (The World of Inoue Hisashi). Hakusuisha, 1982.

Inoue Hisashi zen shibai (The Complete Plays of Inoue Hisashi). 5 vols. Shinchōsha, 1984–1994.

Ishizaki Hitoshi, "Kaisetsu" (Commentary), in Nihon Bungaku Kenkyū Shiryō Kankō Kai, ed., *Nihon bungaku kenkyū shiryō soshō—Ibuse Masuji, Fukazawa Shichirō* (q.v.), pp. 296–312.

Isogai Hideo. "Dazai Osamu ni okeru parodei no mondai" (The Issue of Parody in the Works of Dazai Osamu). *Kokubungaku Kaishaku to Kyōzai no Kenkyū*, vol. 19, no. 2, pp. 66–71 (February 1974).

———. "Hōhō no mosaku—*Bannen* o chūshin ni" (The Search for a Method: Centering on *Bannen*), *Kokubungaku Kaishaku to Kyōzai no Kenkyū*, vol. 21, no. 6, pp. 60–65 (May 1976).

———. "Ibuse Masuji—Kindai bungaku ni okeru warai no teichaku" (Ibuse Masuji: The Establishment of Laughter in Modern Literature; 1950), in Nihon Bungaku Kenkyū Shiryō Kankō Kai, ed., *Nihon bungaku kenkyū shiryō sōsho—Ibuse Masuji, Fukazawa Shichirō* (q.v.), pp. 95–105.

———. "*Otogizōshi* ron" (On *Otogizōshi*), in Tōgō Katsumi and Watabe Yoshinori, eds., *Sakuhin ron—Dazai Osamu* (q.v.), pp. 264–285.

Itō Sei (Hitoshi). "Ibuse Masuji no sekai" (The World of Ibuse Masuji). *Tenbō*, no. 39, pp. 42–43 (March 1949).

Iwasaki, Haruko. "The Literature of Wit and Humor in Late-Eighteenth-Century Edo," in Donald Jenkins, ed., *The Floating World Revisited*, pp. 47–61. Honolulu: University of Hawaii Press and Portland Art Museum, 1993.

———. "Portrait of a Daimyō: Comical Fiction by Matsudaira Sadanobu." *Monumenta Nipponica*, vol. 38, no. 1, pp. 1–48 (1983).

Jaeger, Werner Wilhelm. *Paideia: The Ideals of Greek Culture*, vol. 1. Tr. from the 2nd German edition by Gilbert Highet. New York: Oxford University Press, 1965.

Kaikō Takeshi and Ibuse Masuji. "Omoi kusshita" (The Mind Gives In). *Bungei*, vol. 8, no. 3, pp. 172–183 (March 1969).

Kamei Katsuichirō. "Ibuse Masuji" (1947; 1956), in *Kamei Katsuichirō senshū* (Selected Works of Kamei Katsuichirō), vol. 5, pp. 252–266. Kōdansha, 1965.

Katsura Hidezumi, ed. *Dazai Osamu kenkyū II—Sono kaisō* (Studies on Dazai Osamu, II: The Recollections). Chikuma Shobō, 1978.

Kawakami Tetsutarō. "Bungaku ron—Ibuse Masuji" (On Literature: Ibuse Masuji; 1953), in *Kawakami Tetsutarō zenshū* (Complete Works of Kawakami Tetsutarō), vol. 5, pp. 477–480. Keisō Shobō, 1970.

———. "*Chinpindō shujin* no chosha Ibuse Masuji e" (To Ibuse Masuji, Author of *Chinpindō shujin*; 1958), in *Kawakami Tetsutarō zenshū*, vol. 5, p. 481. Keisō Shobō, 1970.

———. "Kaisetsu" (Commentary), in Ibuse Masuji, *Sanshōuo—Yohai taichō*, pp. 133–138. Iwanami Bunko, 1956.

Kobayashi Hideo. "Ibuse-kun no *Kashima ari*" (Ibuse's *Kashima ari*; 1959), in *Kobayashi Hideo zenshū* (Complete Works of Kobayashi Hideo), vol. 12, pp. 35–41. Shinchōsha, 1968.

———. "Ibuse Masuji no sakuhin ni tsuite" (On the Works of Ibuse Masuji; ca. 1931), in *Kobayashi Hideo zenshū*, vol. 14, pp. 31–35. Shinchōsha, 1968.

———. "Nansensu bungaku" (Nonsense Literature; 1930), in *Kobayashi Hideo zenshū*, vol. 1, pp. 157–161. Shinchōsha, 1967.

Koestler, Arthur. *The Act of Creation*. London: Arkana, 1989 [1964].

Koizumi Kōichirō. "*Shinshaku shokokubanashi* ron—*Dairiki, Hadakagawa, Giri* o meguri" (On *Shinshaku shokokubanashi*: Concerning *Dairiki, Hadakagawa*, and *Giri*). *Nihon Bungaku*, vol. 25, no. 1, pp. 35–47 (January 1976).

Kōno Toshirō. "Ibuse Masuji to Nakamura Masatsune" (Ibuse Masuji and Nakamura Masatsune). *Gunzō*, vol. 36, no. 12, pp. 252–253 (December 1981).

Kornicki, Peter. *The Reform of Fiction in Meiji Japan*. London: Ithaca Press, 1982.

Kuroi yūmoa (Black Humor). Vol. 6 of *Zenshū—Gendai bungaku no hakken* (Anthology: The Discovery of Contemporary Literature). Gakugei Shorin, 1969.

Lacan, Jacques. "The Meaning of the Phallus" (1958), tr. Jacqueline Rose, in Juliet Mitchell and Jacqueline Rose, eds., *Feminine Sexuality: Jacques Lacan and the Ecole freudienne*, pp. 74–85. New York: Norton, 1983.

LaFleur, William R. *The Karma of Words: Buddhism and the Literary Arts in Medieval Japan*. Berkeley: University of California Press, 1983.

Langer, Susanne K. *Feeling and Form: A Theory of Art Developed from Philosophy in a New Key*. New York: Charles Scribner's Sons, 1953.

Leithauser, Brad. "An Ear for the Unspoken." *The New Yorker*, March 6, 1989, pp. 105–111.

Levin, Harry. *Playboys and Killjoys: An Essay on the Theory and Practice of Comedy*. New York: Oxford University Press, 1987.

———, ed. *Veins of Humor*. Cambridge, Mass.: Harvard University Press, 1972.

Maeda Ai. "*Kirikirijin* ron" (On *Kirikirijin*; 1982), in *Maeda Ai chosaku shū* (Collected Writings of Maeda Ai), vol. 6, pp. 363–374. Chikuma Shobō, 1990.

"Magician of Language." *Time*, August 1, 1983, p. 86.

Maruya Saiichi. *Tatta hitori no hanran*. Kōdansha, 1972. Trans. as *Singular Rebellion*. Tokyo: Kodansha International, 1986.

Matsuda Osamu. "Kaisetsu" (Commentary), in Inoue Hisashi, *Mokkinpotto-shi no atoshimatsu* (q.v.), pp. 236–254.

Matsumoto Tsuruo. *Ibuse Masuji—Nichijō no moteiifu* (Ibuse Masuji: The Motif of the Ordinary). Chūsekisha, 1988.

Matsumura Takeo. *Nihon shinwa no kenkyū* (Studies in Japanese Myth), vol. 3. Baifūkan, 1955.

Matsumura Tatsuo. "Kaisetsu" (Commentary), in *Nihon kindai bungaku taikei*, vol. 24, *Natsume Sōseki—I*, pp. 7–42. Kadokawa Shoten, 1971.

McCullough, Helen, tr. *The Tale of the Heike*. Stanford: Stanford University Press, 1988.

Meredith, George. "An Essay on Comedy," in Wylie Sypher, ed., *Comedy*, pp. 3–57. Garden City, N.Y.: Doubleday, Anchor Books, 1956.

Miyoshi, Masao. *Accomplices of Silence: The Modern Japanese Novel*. Berkeley: University of California Press, 1974.

———. *Off Center: Power and Culture Relations between Japan and the United States*. Cambridge, Mass.: Harvard University Press, 1991.

——— and H. D. Harootunian, eds. *Postmodernism and Japan*. Durham, N.C.: Duke University Press, 1989.

Morris-Suzuki, Tessa. "The Invention and Reinvention of Japanese Culture." *Journal of Asian Studies*, vol. 54, no. 3, pp. 759–780 (1995).

Nagashino Kōichirō. "Dazai Osamu to rakugo" (Dazai Osamu and *Rakugo*). *Kokubungaku Kaishaku to Kanshō*, vol. 48, no. 9, pp. 30–36 (June 1983).

Nagata Ryūtarō, ed. *Ibuse Masuji bungaku shoshi* (A Bibliography of the Works of Ibuse Masuji). Nagata Shobō, 1972.

Nakamura Mitsuo. "Ibuse Masuji no sakuhin" (The Works of Ibuse Masuji; 1960), in *Nakamura Mitsuo zenshū* (Complete Works of Nakamura Mitsuo), vol. 5, pp. 219–227. Chikuma Shobō, 1972.

———. "Ibuse Masuji ron" (On Ibuse Masuji; 1957), in *Nakamura Mitsuo zenshū*, vol. 5, pp. 190–219. Chikuma Shobō, 1972.

———. *Nihon no gendai shōsetsu* (Contemporary Japanese Fiction). Iwanami Shinsho, 1968.

———. "Warai no sōshitsu" (The Loss of Laughter; 1948), in *Nakamura Mitsuo zenshū*, vol. 10, pp. 107–143. Chikuma Shobō, 1972.

Nakamura Yukihiko. *Gesaku ron* (On *Gesaku*). *Nakamura Yukihiko chojutsu shū* (Collected Writings of Nakamura Yukihiko), vol. 8. Chūō Kōron sha, 1982.

Napier, Susan J. *The Fantastic in Modern Japanese Literature: The Subversion of Modernity*. London: Routledge, 1996.

Natsume Sōseki. *Bungaku ron* (Theory of Literature; 1907), in *Sōseki zenshū* (Complete Works of [Natsume] Sōseki), vol. 14, pp. 1–535. Iwanami Shoten, 1995.

Nelson, T. G. A. *Comedy: An Introduction to Comedy in Literature, Drama, and Cinema*. Oxford: Oxford University Press, 1990.

Nihon Bungaku Kenkyū Shiryō Kankō Kai, ed. *Nihon bungaku kenkyū shiryō sōsho—Ibuse Masuji, Fukazawa Shichirō* (Japanese Literature Research Materials Series: Ibuse Masuji, Fukazawa Shichirō). Yūseidō, 1977.

Nihon Shoseki Shuppan Kyōkai, ed. *Nihon shoseki sōmokuroku—1997* (Japanese Books in Print, 1997 Edition), vol. 4, 1997.

Nosaka Yukihiro, "*Shinshaku shokokubanashi*," in Tōgō and Watabe, eds., *Sakuhin ron—Dazai Osamu* (q.v.), pp. 223–224.

Ōe Kenzaburō. "Japan's Dual Identity: A Writer's Dilemma," in Masao Miyoshi and H. D. Harootunian, eds., *Postmodernism and Japan* (q.v.), pp. 189–213.

——— and Kazuo Ishiguro. "The Novelist in Today's World: A Conversation." *boundary 2*, vol. 18, no. 3, pp. 109–122 (Fall 1991).

Okuno Takeo, ed. *Dazai Osamu kenkyū I—Sono bungaku* (Studies on Dazai Osamu, I: The Literature). Chikuma Shobō, 1978.

———. *Dazai Osamu ron* (On Dazai Osamu; 1957). Kadokawa Bunko, 1960.

Philippi, Donald L., tr. *Kojiki*. Princeton: Princeton University Press, 1968.

Rubin, Jay. "The Evil and the Ordinary in Sōseki's Fiction." *Harvard Journal of Asiatic Studies*, vol. 46, no. 2, pp. 333–352 (December 1986).

Ryan, Marleigh. "Japanese Fiction: Accommodated Truth." *Journal of Japanese Studies*, vol. 2, no. 2, pp. 247–266 (Summer 1976).

Ryūtanji Yū. *Apâto no onnatachi to boku to* (The Women in the Apartment and Me; 1928), in *Gendai Nihon bungaku senshū* (Collected Literature of Modern Japan), vol. 86, pp. 110–129. Chikuma Shobō, 1957.

Saeki Shōichi. "Ibuse Masuji no gyakusetsu" (The Paradox of Ibuse Masuji). *Shinchō*, vol. 72, no. 3, pp. 168–191 (March 1975).

Sakaguchi Ango. "Piero dendōsha" (The Clown Evangelist; 1931), in *Teihon Sakaguchi Ango zenshū* (Complete Works of Sakaguchi Ango, Definitive Edition), vol. 7, pp. 11–13. Tōjusha, 1967.

"Sakka ni kiku—Ibuse Masuji" (Asking the Author—Ibuse Masuji). *Bungaku*, vol. 20, no. 9, pp. 86–91 (July 1952).

Sako Jun'ichirō. "*Shinshaku shokokubanashi* o megutte." (Concerning *Shinshaku shokokubanashi*). *Kokubungaku Kaishaku to Kanshō*, vol. 32, no. 2, pp. 81–86 (February 1967).

Senda Akihiko. *Sekai wa kigeki ni keisha suru* (The World Inclines Toward Comedy). Chūsekisha, 1985.

Siegel, Lee. *Laughing Matters: Comic Tradition in India*. Chicago: University of Chicago Press, 1987.

Silverberg, Miriam. *Changing Song: The Marxist Manifestos of Nakano Shigeharu*. Princeton: Princeton University Press, 1990.

Sōma Shōichi. *Dazai Osamu to Ibuse Masuji* (Dazai Osamu and Ibuse Masuji). Hirosaki: Tsugaru Shobō, 1972.

Sōseki, *see* Natsume Sōseki.

Sypher, Wylie. "The Meanings of Comedy," in his *Comedy* (q.v.), pp. 191–255.

———, ed. *Comedy*. Garden City, N.Y.: Doubleday, Anchor Books, 1956.

Takahashi Yasunari. "Inoue Hisashi no sekai gekijō" (The World Theater of Inoue Hisashi), in *Inoue Hisashi no sekai* (q.v.), pp. 34–43.

Takami Jun. *Shōwa bungaku seisuishi* (The Rise and Fall of Shōwa Literature). Bungei Shunjū Sha, 1958.

Terada Tōru. "Ibuse Masuji ron" (On Ibuse Masuji; 1948), in Nihon Bungaku Kenkyū Shiryō Kankō Kai, ed., *Nihon bungaku kenkyū shiryō sōsho—Ibuse Masuji, Fukazawa Shichirō* (q.v.), pp. 27–41.

Teruoka Yasutaka, Matsuda Osamu, and Munemasa Isoo, eds. *Ihara Saikaku shū—2* (Ihara Saikaku Collection: Part 2). *Nihon koten bungaku zenshū*, vol. 39. Shōgakkan, 1971.

Thornbury, Barbara E. *Sukeroku's Double Identity: The Dramatic Structure of Edo Kabuki*. Ann Arbor: University of Michigan, Center for Japanese Studies, 1982.

Tōgō Katsumi. "Ibuse Masuji sobyō" (A Rough Sketch of Ibuse Masuji; 1966), in Nihon Bungaku Kenkyū Shiryō Kankō Kai, ed., *Nihon bungaku kenkyū shiryō sōsho—Ibuse Masuji, Fukazawa Shichirō* (q.v.), pp. 168–179.

———. "Sensōka no Ibuse Masuji" (Ibuse Masuji in Wartime; 1973), in Nihon Bungaku Kenkyū Shiryō Kankō Kai, ed., *Nihon bungaku kenkyū shiryō sōsho—Ibuse Masuji, Fukazawa Shichirō* (q.v.), pp. 195–211.

——— and Watabe Yoshinori, eds. *Sakuhin ron—Dazai Osamu* (Studies on the Works of Dazai Osamu). Sōbunsha, 1974.

Torrance, Robert M. "Modernism and Modernity." *Journal of the Association of Teachers of Japanese*, vol. 22, no. 2, pp. 195–223 (1988).

Tsubouchi Shōyō. *Shōsetsu shinzui* (The Essence of the Novel; 1886), in Inagaki Tatsurō, Nakamura Kan, and Umezawa Nobuo, eds., *Tsubouchi Shōyō shū* (Tsubouchi Shōyō's Works). *Nihon kindai bungaku taikei*, vol. 3. Kadokawa Shoten, 1974.

Tsuge Teruhiko. "Warai no bungakushi" (The History of Comical Literature). *Kaien*, vol. 12, no. 5. pp. 126–132 (May 1993).

Tsuji, Nobuo. *Playfulness in Japanese Art*. Joseph Seubert, tr. Lawrence, Kan.: Spencer Museum of Art, University of Kansas, 1986.

Tsurumi Shunsuke and Inoue Hisashi. "Kirikirikoku wa doko ni aru ka" (Where Is the Land of Kirikiri?). *Umi*, vol. 14, no. 3, pp. 140–166 (March 1982).

Turner, Victor. *The Ritual Process: Structure and Anti-structure*. Chicago: Aldine, 1969.

Ueda, Makoto. *Literary and Art Theories in Japan*. Cleveland: The Press of Western Reserve University, 1967.

Umehara Takeshi and Odajima Yūshi. "Kirikirikoku o aruku" (Walking through the Land of Kirikiri). *Nami*, vol. 15, no. 7, pp. 10–16 (July 1981).

Usui Yoshimi. "Dazai Osamu no warai" (The Laughter of Dazai Osamu, 1948), in Okuno Takeo, ed., *Dazai Osamu kenkyū I—Sono bungaku* (q.v.), pp. 103–107.

Usui Yoshimi, Abe Akira, and Miyoshi Yukio. "Shōwa no bungaku—Dazai Osamu" (Shōwa Literature: Dazai Osamu). *Gunzō*, vol. 30, no. 7, pp. 274–283 (July 1975).

Winston, Mathew. "Black Humor: To Weep with Laughing," in Maurice Charney, ed., *Comedy: New Perspectives*, pp. 31–43. New York: New York Literary Forum, 1978.

Yamaguchi Masao. "Inoue Hisashi no konto no sekai" (The World of Inoue Hisashi's *Contes*), in *Inoue Hisashi no sekai* (q.v.), pp. 44–51.

Yanagita Kunio. "Gesakusha no dentō" (The Tradition of the *Gesaku* Writers; 1935), in *Teihon Yanagita Kunio shū* (The Works of Yanagita Kunio, Definitive Edition), vol. 7, pp. 186–195. Chikuma Shobō, 1962.

———. "Warai no bungaku no kigen" (The Origins of the Literature of Laughter; 1928), in *Teihon Yanagita Kunio shū* (The Works of Yanagita Kunio, Definitive Edition), vol. 7, pp. 153–173. Chikuma Shobō, 1962.

Yoshida Seiichi. "Dazai Osamu to fuokuroa" (Dazai Osamu and Folklore). *Kokubungaku Kaishaku to Kanshō*, vol. 23, no. 12, pp. 130–140 (December 1958).

———. *Gendai bungaku to koten* (Contemporary Literature and the Classics). Shibundō, 1961.

Index

Note: Titles of publications are listed under the name of the author.

Harvard-Yenching Institute Monograph Series

(titles now in print)

11. *Han Shi Wai Chuan: Han Ying's Illustrations of the Didactic Application of the* Classic of Songs, translated and annotated by James Robert Hightower
21. *The Chinese Short Story: Studies in Dating, Authorship, and Composition,* by Patrick Hanan
22. *Songs of Flying Dragons: A Critical Reading,* by Peter H. Lee
23. *Early Chinese Civilization: Anthropological Perspectives,* by K. C. Chang
24. *Population, Disease, and Land in Early Japan, 645–900,* by William Wayne Farris
25. *Shikitei Sanba and the Comic Tradition in Edo Fiction,* by Robert W. Leutner
26. *Washing Silk: The Life and Selected Poetry of Wei Chuang (834?–910),* by Robin D. S. Yates
27. *National Polity and Local Power: The Transformation of Late Imperial China,* by Min Tu-ki
28. *Tang Transformation Texts: A Study of the Buddhist Contribution to the Rise of Vernacular Fiction and Drama in China,* by Victor H. Mair
29. *Mongolian Rule in China: Local Administration in the Yuan Dynasty,* by Elizabeth Endicott-West
30. *Readings in Chinese Literary Thought,* by Stephen Owen
31. *Remembering Paradise: Nativism and Nostalgia in Eighteenth-Century Japan,* by Peter Nosco
32. *Taxing Heaven's Storehouse: Horses, Bureaucrats, and the Destruction of the Sichuan Tea Industry, 1074–1224,* by Paul J. Smith

(Listing continues overfleaf)

33. *Escape from the Wasteland: Romanticism and Realism in the Fiction of Mishima Yukio and Oe Kenzaburo,* by Susan Jolliffe Napier
34. *Inside a Service Trade: Studies in Contemporary Chinese Prose,* by Rudolf G. Wagner
35. *The Willow in Autumn: Ryūtei Tanehiko, 1783–1842,* by Andrew Lawrence Markus
36. *The Confucian Transformation of Korea: A Study of Society and Ideology,* by Martina Deuchler
37. *The Korean Singer of Tales,* by Marshall R. Pihl
38. *Praying for Power: Buddhism and the Formation of Gentry Society in Late-Ming China,* by Timothy Brook
39. *Word, Image, and Deed in the Life of Su Shi,* by Ronald C. Egan
40. *The Chinese Virago: A Literary Theme,* by Yenna Wu
41. *Studies in the Comic Spirit in Modern Japanese Fiction,* by Joel R. Cohn
42. *Wind against the Mountain: The Crisis of Politics and Culture in Thirteenth-Century China,* by Richard L. Davis
43. *Powerful Relations: Kinship, Status, and the State in Sung China (960–1279),* by Beverly Bossler
44. *Limited Views: Essays on Ideas and Letters,* by Qian Zhongshu; selected and translated by Ronald Egan
45. *Sugar and Society in China: Peasants, Technology, and the World Market,* by Sucheta Mazumdar